# PINE MANOR COLLEGE

*Learning to Be Adolescent*

GERALD K. LETENDRE

# *Learning to Be Adolescent*

GROWING UP IN U.S. AND
JAPANESE MIDDLE SCHOOLS

Foreword by Thomas P. Rohlen

*Yale University Press*
*New Haven &*
*London*

Printed in the United States of America.

Library of Congress Cataloging-in-Publication Data
LeTendre, Gerald K.
Learning to be adolescent: growing up in U.S. and Japanese middle schools /Gerald K. LeTendre ; foreword by Thomas P. Rohlen.
    p.   cm.
Includes bibliographical references and index.
ISBN 0-300-08438-2 (alk. paper)
1. Adolescence — United States — Case studies.   2. Adolescence — Japan — Case studies.   3. Middle school students — United States — Conduct of life — Case studies.   4. Middle school students — Japan — Conduct of life — Case studies.   5. Adolescent psychology — Cross-cultural studies.   I. Title.
LB1135 .L47 2000
373.18 — dc21    00-036641

A catalogue record for this book is available from the British Library.

The paper in this book meets the guidelines for permanence and durability of the Committee on Production Guidelines for Book Longevity of the Council on Library Resources.

10  9  8  7  6  5  4  3  2  1

*für elise*

# Contents

# Tables and Figures

## Tables

## Figures

# Foreword

THOMAS P. ROHLEN

Neither quite one thing nor another, middle schools have received less public and scholarly attention than either elementary or secondary schools within the world of American education. Researchers and officials alike have had difficulty defining its particular essence and mission. The middle school seems to be a kind of afterthought, filling a space created by the maturational distance between sweetly smiling grade school children and fully developed high school students. Historically, too, middle schools were never a clearly conceived institution. As the need for additional schools arose, more and more school districts decided it was appropriate to separate out certain intermediate grades to form what was most commonly called junior high schools. Based on prevailing ideas of adolescent development, these schools were given the particular task of helping fledgling teenagers navigate the distance between childhood and adulthood. Which grades to separate out, however, turned out to differ somewhat across the country, further evidence that the notion of the "middle" was a relatively hazy one in terms of boundaries and essences. Nor has the creation of a middle school niche in the United States led to much consensus about the appropriate ways to teach and counsel this group's emotional and behavioral problems.

Adolescence is also a hazy transitional category, but one that holds a particular fascination for researchers, teachers, parents, and public authorities alike. As an idea, its sources are many. A great deal in U.S. society hinges on defining the state of adulthood as clearly as possible in legal and normative terms. We have structured much of this world around the idea of the independent, self-regulating adult. What is known as American individualism pivots on the explicit responsibilities and rights associated with such a category of social being. Adolescence is by definition an unstable and prior state marked by change. Because in fact achievement of independence is hardly spontaneous and never the same for any two people (and always contested between adults and kids seeking to speed up or slow down the pace), we cannot help but focus on adolescence as a particularly problematic condition. Throw into the mix two other powerful ingredients, namely, America's national preoccupation with emerging pubescent sexuality and the emergence of peer relations as central to the adolescent's emotional life, and one has a mix of expectations that easily explains why in America adolescence is generally seen as "up for grabs." The common consolation among parents that "it's just a stage that, thank God, won't last forever" only attests to people's basic alarm and disarray. Our uncertainty about middle schooling, it would seem, reflects our uncertainty about adolescence.

But is this necessarily so? Is adolescence universally the same? Are the special problems of U.S. middle schools common to school systems everywhere? Or have we Americans generated a world particular to our perceptions and assumptions? Have we, in other words, constructed a particularly American version of adolescence and its educational challenges? Serious questions, indeed, if we seek to understand and improve our schools.

Interestingly, the middle school story is not the same in Japan, and this book tells us that in fascinating and vivid detail. While no one would want to claim that Japan's middle schools or middle school students are entirely dissimilar from their American counterparts, there are indeed very real differences. Some of the differences relating to conduct and orientation can be easily observed by any foreign visitor. The students not only wear uniforms, but their grooming and general behavior reflect close supervision and considerable peer interaction in shaping one another's behavior. There is also a general orderliness to the school and its routines that no American could miss. Statistical data on delinquency and sexual behavior and academic achievement also suggest significant differences. Yet these forms of evidence tell us little about the sources and causes of such variation. This is where Gerald LeTendre's extensive research offers us exciting new insights. As we learn more and more about the actual patterns of school routines and teacher interventions we become gradually aware of a distinctly Japanese logic behind the approaches teachers use to respond to the range of challenges that middle school teachers also face in

America. We learn, for example, how Japanese thinking on the matter of student responsibility shapes their approach to such standard matters as advising, discipline, homeroom management, and student guidance. The author's field research in both Japanese and American schools allows him to carefully compare what teachers are thinking with what they are doing in both countries.

Compared to their American counterparts, furthermore, Japanese middle schools themselves are more clearly defined in terms of their mission and methodologies. The tasks of socializing and guiding the students, for example, are set forth explicitly by the national authorities. In other ways as well the seventh through ninth grade niche has a more straightforward existence and raison d'etre within the Japanese educational scheme. This too is interesting but difficult to grasp without turning to deeper matters related to how the path to adulthood is conceived. LeTendre shows us how Japanese thinking about adolescence is different, especially at the school level. How teachers interpret cause and effect in student behavior shapes many matters and the expected pace of change is centrally relevant. We are thus taken into a realm of comparison in which subtle differences of meaning and interpretation on the part of teachers in each country result in markedly different outcomes at the school level. It is precisely in this realm that many of the most interesting comparisons between Japanese and American education wait to be made. Only investigators skilled in cultural interpretation and intent on thorough and sophisticated analysis, however, can take us there.

The book proceeds from an exploration of cultural and institutional assumptions to analysis of the many challenges and circumstances shared by American and Japanese middle schools and on to the wider social context. Despite resting on an account of cultural differences, this is not a portrait of two static systems. First, the author shows us that at the school level teachers do not all agree, and he notes that in both countries they can have doubts about the approaches conventionally taken to problems. Moving from the school level where so much that is assumed is expressed in action and where there is little time to abstractly debate the merits of one idea or another, the author takes us to the level of public discourse, where he finds that in each country the meaning of adolescence is being contested, reexamined, and questioned by teachers, scholars, and education authorities alike. He shows us, for example, that there is ample awareness in Japan of the American theories of adolescence. While this perspective has influenced many official pronouncements and standard guidelines, as yet it is not part of the everyday vernacular of schools. What recommends this book, then, is not only the richness of its comparative portraits and the strength of its basic analysis, but also its finely textured treatment of the differing opinions, the uncertainty, and the conflicts in educational thinking in both countries. This additional dimension rounds things out and gives us the degree of complexity that intuitively we know to be true.

The task of international comparative research in education is a daunting one. First of all, there is the problem of obtaining culturally nuanced and accurate data from the school level in two societies. Observing student behavior and learning about how they think about what they and others are doing requires months and months of participation in classrooms and schools. The language qualifications to do this kind of ethnography alone are daunting, not to mention the empathy, cultural understanding, and great industry required to patiently record and make sense of the masses of detail that emerge. In this kind of work there is also the inevitable problem of sampling widely enough to establish that the ethnographic cases are representative of the larger picture. Careful study of the research of others and extensive examination of two sets of national statistics are thus required. There is then the effort involved in studying the larger context of popular and academic thinking, of legal constraints, and educational policy. This necessitates collecting and analyzing such publications as teacher handbooks, psychology texts, manuals of advice to parents, official policy papers, and more. Sorting out all these streams of observations and information into a coherent comparative account also entails the development of a theoretical framework that has sufficient explanatory power. There is no more challenging task in this regard than accounting for the relationship of thought and action at several levels and across two national systems. The many relevant factors to be considered must be weighed carefully and brought to bear on the topic in a manner that illuminates the essential points without so simplifying or complicating the story as to defeat understanding. This long list of tasks, each a crucial link in the research, has been accomplished admirably, as any reader of this work will come to understand.

Overly simplified comparisons of Japan and America abound in the popular literature and media in both countries. This is no such study. It is rather a sterling example of what extensive field research and assiduous thinking about two countries' middle schools can produce. In my opinion it establishes a new standard in comparative education for research design, and it will make enlightening reading for anyone interested in middle schools on either side of the Pacific for the depth of comparative insight it offers and for the elegantly structured analytic approach upon which its conclusions rest.

# Preface

This book is an analysis of how schools as institutions affect adolescent development in the United States and Japan. Based on an ethnographic study of teacher and administrator interactions with young adolescents, the book evinces the basic premise that by examining adult beliefs and attitudes in conjunction with school organization and educational policy one can isolate national sets of norms or expectations for the developing adolescent. Consequently, I provide a great deal of descriptive material that clarifies the expectations that teachers, counselors, and administrators have for adolescent development and its concomitant physical, psychological, and emotional changes. I have not been content to simply document what adults say and do in the classroom, on the playground, or in the teachers' lounge: I incorporate surveys, historical material, and an analysis of policy documents in order to identify what beliefs about adolescent development have been institutionalized within each national school system. In this way, I am able to show that at different levels (national, regional, and local) the sets of beliefs, the "story lines" of adolescence differ. I also show that conflicting sets of beliefs exist, and I argue that although certain modern or Western beliefs about adolescence are widely institutionalized in national-level documents in both countries, these beliefs are not institutionalized at the regional or local level in Japan.

The book is informed by institutional theory. I use the term *informed* because institutional theory is composed of a broad body of scholarly work by sociologists, scholars of organizational behavior, and anthropologists. Having studied with Thomas Rohlen, George Spindler, John Meyer, Dick Scott, and Jim March at Stanford, I define "institution" more broadly than does the typical literature on organizational behavior. An institution can be any one of a range of modern social phenomena from schools to one's very notion of the self. The process of institutionalization means that beliefs or expectations about these phenomena have been not only defined, rationalized, and often legally recognized, but also accepted as normal or a given in daily life. Most of this book is oriented toward the second half of this definition, as it is this aspect of institutions that most affects people's daily lives.

We assume, for example, that the normal course of human development will involve a period of adolescence in which the person will undergo puberty, attend school, and develop a somewhat adultlike sense of identity, among other things. Americans did not make these assumptions 150 years ago, before the term *adolescence* had been popularized, and many people did not go to school at all. Americans' very notions of development — physiological and psychological — are constructed within a given set of social and historical circumstances. The work of scholars like John Meyer, John Boli, and Francisco Ramirez documents that expectations or norms about the individual, self, and life course that arose in the Western nations spread throughout the world and are institutionalized in the laws and policies of various nations. They and other scholars argue that modern forms of schooling transmit a "modern self." The evidence I marshal shows that the issue is far more complex: while some expectations or norms are recognized worldwide, a variety of cultural expectations for the development of volition, self, and identity among young adolescents still exist in nations like Japan.

My interest in this topic began with my own teaching experience in Japanese public schools. The role of teacher and student as well as the institutional form of schooling in Japanese society was forged in religious and philosophic traditions that are fundamentally different from the Judeo-Christian beliefs that form the core of assumptions and expectations upon which Western educational practices and educational psychology are ultimately based. The modernization of Japan (which is associated with the Meiji Restoration of 1868) and the Allied Occupation after World War II saw the introduction of many Western pedagogical ideas and instructional practices. The integration of these ideas and practices over the decades has resulted in a system that looks modern or Western in its curriculum and organization, but that exhibits many distinctive features not found in the United States or other Western nations.

The classroom routines and teaching practices found in Japan are *not* the same as those found in American schools and classrooms. Careful analysis of these differences has yielded a significant body of knowledge that I cite at length in the notes. These studies indicate that differences in classroom routines or teaching practices do not originate simply from differences in classroom organization or school culture but are rooted in divergent conceptions of human nature and expectations for the normal life course. That is, the basic understanding of just what *learning* means to the individual has very different cultural associations in Japan. The fact that Japanese society is one in which a positive cultural value is placed on the ability of the individual to construct multiple identities (in addition to a recognition that the social participation of others is needed to bring these identities to life) has a significant impact on how Western beliefs about the individual, self, and life course are incorporated into the schools.

Cross-national and cross-cultural analysis of the most basic beliefs about adolescence shows that schools are organized around widely shared (if rarely articulated) beliefs about the nature of development. That is, to understand what a teacher or student is in the United States or Japan presupposes an understanding of what behaviors and capabilities can be reasonably expected of children, adolescents, and adults. Everyday, young adolescents in Japan and the United States encounter a range of situations and individuals that convey just what behavior is appropriate for an adolescent, and these expectations for appropriate behavior provide a good deal of information about dominant cultural beliefs about the self, life course, and the individual.

My initial investigation led me to conclude that both American and Japanese teachers share certain views about many educational practices and have a common vocabulary about the rights of individuals derived from a Western historical context; yet they share few assumptions about the nature of adolescent development. In recording what teachers said about the process of adolescent development and then comparing these data with historical studies of the social construction of childhood, I discovered what appeared to be very old beliefs about the self and life course wrapped in the language of modern institutions. Adolescence — defined simply as the stage in the life course initiated by puberty and generally ending at age twenty-one with the acquisition of full legal adult status — played a very different role in U.S. and Japanese schools.

Since my initial study, conducted in the early 1990s, I have researched a broader range of schools and furthered my investigation of how the institutional form of schooling affects adolescent life. Although I have largely approached the subject by examining what adults — teachers, counselors, and administrators — say and do with regard to young adolescents, I have paid strict attention to how such beliefs become institutionalized in policies and laws at the local, regional, and national levels. I have tried to build a theoretical bridge between the work of anthropologists like Thomas Rohlen, who analyzed the cultural form of institutions like schools and banks in modern societies, and that of such sociologists as John Meyer, who analyze how institutions organize society and give meaning to the modern world.

What goes on in organizations like schools is not a static pattern that is passed on via a set of polices or role norms; neither is the school experience simply the sum of the social interactions that occur on a daily basis. One must consider both the rules or norms that exist as well as how they are interpreted or enacted. Culture and organizations change over time and are often riven with dissent, disagreement, and even hostility generated by diverse sets of beliefs and expectations. While national patterns of beliefs and expectations for the mental and emotional development of young adolescents in the United States and Japan can be identified, I document the fact that teachers, students, and administrators within a given school can vary widely in their beliefs and expectations. The adolescent experience in each country is largely determined by institutional environments which adults organize for adolescents, but these environments are dynamic and are buffeted by events in local communities and national societies.

Through comparing the laws or polices, interviews with adults, and observations of how adults and adolescents interact in schools, it is possible to clarify the multiple layers of meaning that contextualize the adolescent school experience in the two nations. Such thick description highlights the central beliefs about the self and life course which exist in the two countries as well as discrepancies or disjunctures in how these beliefs are integrated in formal policies or school organization. The link between institutionalized expectations or norms and enacted expectations or norms is crucial for educational policy and educational reform.

The policy implications of this book are manifold. First, I show that the organization of middle grades schooling and the practices of middle school teachers in the two nations differ remarkably and that much of the variation can be linked to divergent expectations for adolescent development. Second, no matter how well researched or well documented an educational reform might be, if its findings conflict with widely held beliefs it is likely to fail to be institutionalized or it will be significantly altered in the process of institutionalization. Decades of research on adolescent development have not stopped U.S. middle school teachers from complaining about adolescent hormones or Japanese middle school teachers from worrying whether their students have a dream or not. Third, beliefs about the life course and expectations for the development of self and identity affect basic organizational choices within schools that have significant ramifications for adolescents. Teachers in Japan have more power in managing the daily life in schools than U.S. teachers because Japanese perceive a teacher's impact on students to be more diffuse. Fourth, U.S. and Japanese teachers do share beliefs about certain problems — for example, the negative impact of dysfunctional families on student behaviors — but their responses often differ. A careful study of teacher response to adolescent difficulties provides a wide range of options for potential exploration and possible adoption. Fifth, adults and adolescents are often brought into conflict in the classroom or the school office, particularly in the United States, because different expectations for development and behavior result in teachers' misunderstandings or misinterpretations of adolescent behavior.

My goal in writing this book is to open a window onto modern Japanese and American beliefs about adolescence and puberty. By gaining a clearer understanding of the way in which adults in the two countries approach the education of youth, I hope to provide a more penetrating insight into the nature of the adolescent condition and a more enlightened and compassionate disposition in the minds of adults, who are the primary architects of the organizations that adolescents must inhabit.

# A Note on Names

All of the personal and place-names in this book have been changed to conceal the identity of the respondents. Also, certain incidents and identifying characteristics (for example, how long a teacher worked in a school) have been altered to protect the anonymity of the respondents.

Japanese write their names with the family name first. On the job, Japanese teachers tend to refer to each other by family name plus the suffix for teacher (e.g., Yamamoto-sensei). Off the job, in casual situations, teachers use a variety of nicknames, although juniors tend to refer to their seniors with polite suffixes. I use the family name and honorific throughout the book as it reflects my status as a junior during my fieldwork in the schools.

In the United States teachers tend to use the polite prefix and family name only when in the presence of students (e.g., Ms. Smith). In the teachers' lounge or when students are out of hearing, teachers generally use first names. Consequently, I have used the first names of Oak Grove teachers in most places in the text.

# Acknowledgments

I would like to thank my wife, Elise Marie LeTendre. Her love and support through the hard years of fieldwork have sustained me in more than the writing of this book. My friends in Japan — Kiyomi and Seiichi Saito, Taizo Kametani, and Yoshinori Kuga — gave me both shelter and hope during the long months I spent apart from Elise. I thank my mentors in the teaching profession who gave so generously of their time: Hideo Ogawa, Yoshio Uchida, Kazuyo Yamaguchi, Chihiro Yamada, Teruyo Kitajima, Nancy Atkinson, Phil Short, Jan Grodeon, and Shelby Spain. Their work as teachers and administrators has continued to be an inspiration to me. My advisers at Stanford University, Thomas Rohlen, Francisco Ramirez, Ray McDermott, David Tyack, and Harumi Befu, provided inspiration and guidance that illuminated the dark muddles in early drafts of my dissertation. My editor, Susan Arellano, pushed me to clarify and expand the implications of my basic findings. My special thanks to Rachel Lotan, Elizabeth Cohen, and Jennifer Whitcomb, who offered their moral support and intellectual insight during the U.S. fieldwork.

Many other scholars have kindly offered advice and comments on this work: Hua Yang, Masami Kajita, Tadahiko Abiko, Yasuhiko Nakano, Hiroshi Ishida, and Jim Rosenbaum.

Finally I would like to thank the teachers and staff of the Oak Grove and

Kotani schools. By allowing me to enter their classrooms and lives, they gave me great insight into the issues discussed in this book. I have tried to describe their actions, words, and difficulties with detail and accuracy.

Any errors in fact or interpretation are mine and mine alone.

# What Is Adolescence?

What does "adolescence" mean? When does it begin? How long does it last? These are the kinds of questions that Japanese public middle school teachers asked me when I began to study how teachers counsel young adolescents in the United States and Japan. I was surprised to find that most Japanese teachers had no clear idea what adolescence was and that many failed to recognize the English loanword *adoresensu*. While developing my pilot interviews at Stanford University, I relied on Japanese professors and graduate students to read and critique my interview questions. These scholars were not only fluent in English but generally conversant with U.S. culture and educational psychology. But as more and more pilot interviews piled up in Japan, I found that with the exception of a handful of teachers, no one seemed to know what I was talking about.[1] Adolescence, for most Japanese educators, is a foreign concept requiring lengthy cultural, not psychological, explanation.

My experience in the United States was just the opposite. Every adult in my U.S. pilot study not only knew the word "adolescence," but also had very specific ideas about what it meant: the teenage years, a period of identity crisis, puberty, and hormonal fluctuation, growth spurts and at-risk behavior were among the most common themes that teachers brought up. As my work progressed, I also discovered a wide range of beliefs among American educators. Some teachers thought that young adolescents lacked a strong moral framework, which put them at risk for negative behavior in the early teen years. Others thought that pubertal changes precipitated a crisis of identity which made young adolescents prone to at-risk behaviors. Because there were so many beliefs about adolescence, teachers might focus on a handful of aspects in any single discussion.

In this book I compare U.S. and Japanese teachers' beliefs about adolescence in order to investigate general beliefs about the normal course of adolescent development, and the nature of the self and life course.[2] I am particularly interested in how the organization of schooling affects these beliefs. I argue that adolescence, as we know it in the United States, does not exist in Japan. However, Japan is not the polar opposite of the United States. U.S. and Japanese teachers actually share many concerns regarding young adolescents. In this work I will spell out how schools play a role in perpetuating these differences and similarities, and how widely held beliefs are institutionalized in the organization of the school.[3]

In both the United States and Japan, volition or will (*ishi, iyoku*) are strongly tied to beliefs about the self and the individual and are most commonly talked about in terms of self-control. The ability to control one's behavior — either physical actions or speech — is used in both nations as an indicator of maturity. An increase in self-control is seen as a normal and essential part of the maturation process for young adolescents in both nations — one that is necessary for the development of an adult sense of self. Whether or not a child or young adolescent was able to evince specific patterns of self-control (for example, completing one's homework or always greeting others in a cheerful manner) strongly affects how teachers react to a given individual and describe his or her level of maturity.

Teachers in both nations are concerned with developing the volitional capabilities of young adolescents and see the development of the will as a crucial process in maturation.[4] But, whereas most U.S. teachers believe that young adolescents need to develop an independent self that is relatively isolated from other selves, most Japanese teachers believe that young adolescents need to develop a strong consciousness of their connection to the social environment. U.S. teachers tried to provide opportunities for adolescents to display their individual powers of self-control, while Japanese teachers provided opportunities for individuals to develop group goals and display their powers of effort and persistence.

## *The Social Construction of Adolescence*

Although many classical studies of adolescence focus on physical, psychological, or emotional development, I analyze how adults construct an adolescent experience via the institution of school. Building on historical studies of the social construction of childhood and adolescence, I examine how the basic pattern of schooling — from the daily schedule to the management of extracurricular activities — reflects or transmits adult expectations for adolescent development.[5] Particular expectations for adolescence, stories about what adolescence should be, categories of adolescent problems, all come to be embedded in classroom practice, school policy, and eventually educational literature. A brief example of these illustrates how adult expectations can create substantially contrasting patterns of schooling.

For Japanese teachers, it was natural to leave a school of nearly one thousand young adolescents completely unsupervised for fifteen to twenty minutes each morning. This practice, although varying slightly from school to school, is part of the daily routine of student and teacher meetings that start the school day. No one would think that it conveyed a strong adult expectation or was an official policy. Yet for American teachers and administrators, such a course of action would be unthinkable. The American norm of close adult supervision of young adolescents, including legislation in states like California requiring an adult to be in the classroom at all times, is equally striking to Japanese educators.[6] Adult expectations for adolescent development have a tremendous impact on the schooling experience of young adolescents because they underlie the most basic decisions about the school day and school organization.

ADOLESCENCE AND THE LIFE COURSE

Schools provide an institutional structure that organizes the early life course. Studies by anthropologists like Alice Schlegel and Herbert Barry and historians like Joseph Kett suggest that modern adolescence is largely a structural phenomenon, that is, it originates in the broad social forces of mass industrialization and mass schooling.[7] Although modern adolescence bears some semblance to the liminal phases around puberty that are common in many preindustrial societies, in industrialized nations it generally lacks the puberty rituals, periods of social isolation, and extensive taboos on behavior that mark adolescence in many traditional cultures.[8] The delayed entrance of adolescents into marriage or labor market participation and their extended attendance in modern schools have created a rather long and, in terms of the range of human societies, relatively uniform experience of adolescence within developed countries.[9]

In both the United States and Japan at the close of the twentieth century, the schooling experience dominates the lives of children and early adolescents and thus represents a set of social expectations not encountered by young people in the previous century. Some theorists argue that schools are the vehicle by which a modern sense of self is transmitted in the world system at large,[10] while others hold that schools transmit a uniform concern with the individual and individual rights in the world system.[11] These sociological theories are consistent with the conclusions of Kett, who argued that the public schools were the vehicle by which a white, middle-class vision of the adolescent experience (one derived from the work of G. Stanley Hall and other psychologists) is imposed on a heterogeneous society.

### ADOLESCENCE AND THE EMERGING MODERN SELF

This middle-class adolescence emphasizes psychology and the self. In modern societies, healthy adults are expected to have a self that is an enduring and integrated whole. Western social theorists have argued that the self has as an ongoing function the task of incorporating experiences over the life course, thereby providing the continuity necessary to maintaining a sane individual in a rapidly changing and ever more fast-paced global society. The modern sense of self, these theorists argue, is a crucial element that sets apart the consciousness of humans living in modern (or postmodern) societies from those in traditional societies.

In developed nations in the twentieth century, adolescence becomes a stage in the modern life course during which youth are expected to begin displaying an adultlike sense of self. Americans and Japanese alike expect to see the first expressions of mature (i.e., adult) interests and volition — indications that the maturing individual is capable of orienting himself or herself in the complicated adult worlds of work, love, and recreation. These expectations make adolescence a critical stage in the modern life course. Adolescents must begin to display an adult self if the young person is to be allowed to participate in the general social conventions of further schooling, career, marriage, the establishment of a family, and so forth.

In the United States and Japan, the institution of school has come to play a role similar to that played by the rituals common in traditional societies — in school expectations or idealized roles are learned and demonstrated. Thus, during the middle school years adult expectations for adolescent behavior become most visible. But do schools really function to transmit a package of meanings about the modern self (as the authors of *The Homeless Mind* argue)? or are schools places where teachers and students find themselves in conflict over their views of self, identity, and development? Despite the country's wholesale adoption of Western organizations and institutions, the average Japanese teacher and student do not discuss adolescence or the development of self in ways that American teachers do. In the highly legalistic language of national curriculum guidelines or formal policy statements on education, Japan appears very Western. When one listens to conversations between teachers or between teachers and students, however, the Japanese appear very non-Western.

TRANSMISSION VIA THE SCHOOL:
ADOLESCENCE AS A CONTESTED CATEGORY

With the rise of compulsory schooling, school has become, after the family, the dominant institution in the lives of children and young adolescents.[12] With the exception of groups like the Amish and home-school advocates, Americans and Japanese in general think of school as the natural place for children and young adolescents; participation in school is accepted as part of the normal life course, even though there is profound disagreement over what education should be. Many studies show how ethnic, racial, linguistic, and economic groups contest the transmission of "school knowledge" and mainstream values.[13]

Little attention has been paid, however, to what happens when teachers regard student conceptions or expectations for development as inappropriate. Student, adolescent, and teenager are foreign concepts to certain groups in the United States.[14] Aaron Pallas demonstrated that students who are out of step with the majority of their peers in terms of the timing of major life course events (i.e., school leaving, marriage, and childbearing) suffer from reduced economic opportunities.[15] In Japan students who do not fit into the standard trajectory tend to disengage and drop out. In the United States, I argue, the expectations for adolescent development and behavior encoded in schools contradict and disrupt the life course patterns of many young people from ethnic, religious, and linguistic minority groups by emphasizing certain forms of self-display and expression. Moreover, I argue that by emphasizing deviance, vulnerability, and resistance, U.S. schools increase the likelihood that young adolescents will indeed be at risk.

The organizational structure and institutional norms of schools are not static patterns passed on from generation to generation of students. There is marked disagreement about what school should be or do in most modern societies. In Japan and the United States, I found that teachers, students, and administrators had sharply differing interpretations of or stories about what was happening in terms of the mental and emotional development of young adolescents. Rather than assuming that only one set of beliefs about adolescence is being transmitted in the schools, we must consider that there may be conflicting beliefs or at least that some adults and young adolescents contest some beliefs and expectations about adolescence. Schools, then, become the institution in which conflict over life course trajectories occurs.

Japan serves as a convenient example of how culturally different groups react to the implicit beliefs about adolescent development, life course, and self that may be transmitted via Western forms of schooling. In organizational research, several scholars have used comparisons between Japan and the United

States to show how major social institutions like banks and post offices were borrowed by the Japanese but were extensively transformed by existing organizational forms and cultural beliefs in Japan.[16] Japanese institutions appear to reflect the tension between Japan's past and its present role in the modern world economy. By comparing how beliefs about adolescence are encoded (or not encoded) in the school system of the two countries one can assess the degree to which educational policy and school organization place certain groups or individuals in conflict with the implicit norms for development.

## Rational Myths and the Story Lines of Adolescence

Documenting what expectations or beliefs are encoded in educational policy and school organization requires a two-pronged analysis. Analysis of formal policies and school organization plans reveals intended or ideal beliefs. What goes on in the day-to-day life in the schools, however, may vary significantly from the ideal plan. Fieldwork (observations and interviews) is needed to assess how the schools actually run. I have linked these two types of analysis by using them to identify what I call the story lines of adolescence.[17] Through this form of analysis we can isolate whether specific expectations or beliefs (i.e., a given story line) occur in formal policy or organizational plans and in day-to-day life. We can begin to catalog the interrelations between the basic expectations or analogies that define the ideal or normal adolescent development and identify which story lines have been codified in school policies.[18] In other words, through this analysis we can learn the degree to which specific beliefs about adolescence have become institutionalized in the middle schools of the United States and Japan.

Institutional theory proposes that social institutions provide actors with symbols, rationales, and values as well as with information and options. Institutions encode rules of rationality and causality, thereby establishing the categories and criteria that actors use to define themselves and make sense of their decisions.[19] For example, in the United States the existence of special counseling programs in middle schools encodes the belief that young adolescents have special emotional needs, that some have special problems, that these needs or problems can interfere with academic and social development, that teachers are incapable of dealing with the problems by themselves, and that teachers should refer students to counseling when they believe a problem occurs. Until the mid-1990s these programs, beliefs, and rules about who should care for adolescent emotional needs simply did not exist in Japanese middle schools. The beliefs encoded there suggest a radically alternative view of adolescent development and of the teacher's role in dealing with emotional problems.[20]

Institutional theorists further argue that although organizations and institutions in the modern world operate according to consistent sets of rules or operating procedures, the basis of these rules is a set of "rationalized myths" that have come to achieve a high degree of validity in modern society.[21] This definition of rationalized myth is very close to what I identified as the story lines of adolescence. The analysis of the story lines of adolescence is one way to analyze the rational myths found in Japanese and American schools that pertain to adolescent development. In other words, if we look at modern society in the same way that anthropologists have looked at pretechnological societies, then our most important myths, rituals or epics are to be found in the organizations that we create. The typifications or classifications of adolescent development codified in policy statements, school rules, adult work roles and duties, and in various programs such as drug abuse or teenage pregnancy prevention programs are evidence of what we believe to be true about the nature of the self, human development, and the course of human life.

I differ significantly from institutional theorists in terms of how I theorize that story lines or rational myths are transmitted and spread. Institutional theorists propose several mechanisms (coercive isomorphism, etc.) by which institutional forms are diffused.[22] My work contradicts the patterns proposed by institutional theorists.[23] The original rationalized myths of the Western organizational forms are altered, replaced, or continue over time as the social and organizational fields evolve. In cases in which rational myths of a given institution conflict with widely held social beliefs or existing organizational practices or roles, these rational myths will fail to become institutionalized or the myth will be altered to fit prevailing beliefs. Although there has been a global spread of educational practices and theories which encode a modern sense of self and individualism in laws and educational policy, my work shows that the story lines of adolescence in Japanese schools are radically different from those found in U.S. schools.

The rationalized myth that elementary and middle schools should promote democratic values and develop individuals' capacity to be responsible citizens is a good example. In the case of Japan, Western educators played a leading role in revising the educational system after World War II. Some reforms were rejected, some were accepted mechanically, and some were substantially modified.[24] The model of democratic decision-making processes of choice envisioned by many American reformers ran counter to the basic Japanese beliefs in a stratified but interdependent society. The social ideals of mutual dependence and interconnectedness conflicted deeply with Western ideals of individual autonomy. The implementation of various school and classroom activities in Japanese elementary and middle schools fosters democratic participation, but in a form in which everyone is required to participate.

Rather than emphasizing the individual, individual preferences, or individual rights, these activities highlight mutual participation, group identification, making sacrifices, and performing one's role.[25]

In both the United States and Japan, organizational features of the school (i.e., curriculum, teachers' work duties, formal channels of referral, etc.) may be affected by pervasive beliefs (myths) relating to the nature of the self, individual, and life course which derive from the specific cultural context of each society. While there is both coercive and normative pressure for modern nations to adopt schooling systems like those in other countries, there may be continued conflict between national goals, any given schools' stated aims, and the beliefs expressed by the teachers. Furthermore, when the rational myths of organizations conflict with pervasive beliefs about the self and life course in any society, the institutional rationalization for any given activity may be altered or have its emphasis changed in ways that lessen the explicit conflict.

For example, teachers and administrators may adopt procedures or theories that are originally based in research findings but that have become law or mandated policy at the regional or national level. The original findings, however, may or may not be used in the ways intended by the scientists who promulgated them or by the politicians and administrators that promoted them. In the case of ability-tracking in the California middle schools I worked in, studies which showed a link between tracking and systematic inequalities were used as evidence to support a widespread and apparently successful movement to "de-track" middle schools. Yet this mandated reform conflicted with teachers' theories of intelligence and ability: they saw ability-tracked classrooms as essential to teaching young adolescents at their correct level. Teacher and administrator beliefs about intelligence and ability reflected the impact of enduring social paradigms and there was significant, if covert, resistance to de-tracking, especially in mathematics. The result was that many California middle schools proudly claim to be de-tracked but had de facto tracking because they offered various levels of mathematics classes. This effectively changed the block scheduling of other classes. The original research and its policy mandates were not consistent with current beliefs and organizational myths.

As early as 1937, Hadley Dimeck complained, "Of books about the adolescent there is no end." His observation was prescient in that it captured the degree to which modern adolescence has been highly elaborated in social science literature. In the United States, the researcher is confronted with massive amounts of literature (often densely written) about the adolescent that have been generated in a variety of social science disciplines. This research literature is not an accurate guide to what actually goes on in schools or to what teachers, parents, and administrators believe about adolescent development. What this extensive research literature does provide is a vast repertoire of potential story lines which may (or may not) finally be incorporated into popular American beliefs about adolescence.

In this book, I present evidence that the story lines of adolescence have evolved over time. New story lines have been created as time passes, and while some older ones remain well used, others grow rare and appear to have been abandoned in favor of new theories. The story lines of adolescence appear to be affected by the accumulation of scientific research, but through accretion and synthesis whereby layers of meaning build up and do not necessarily replace the old (and scientifically refuted) ideas. Old story lines are sometimes given new rationalizations or justifications and, like a phoenix, arise from the ashes of discarded educational paradigms to be told and retold in classrooms, meeting rooms, reports, and journals.

This book is based on an ethnographic study of Japanese and American middle schools in the Oak Grove and Kotani school districts. I began the research by conducting a pilot study of how teachers in U.S. and Japanese middle schools helped counsel students with problems.[26] It rapidly became apparent that many of the things teachers had to say reflected general beliefs about the human condition. Much of the basic data I collected consisted of general descriptions of teachers' opinions or beliefs about school, childhood, adolescence, and normal development. I began to note differences in the range of meanings and associations for terms like "adolescence" and "puberty." Upon returning to the United States, I decided to change the focus of the research and look more broadly at issues of adolescent development.

The study design was significantly influenced by George and Louise Spindler's work on German and American schools, that is, Shoenhausen and Roseville. As the Spindlers have shown, a successful work of comparison must first depict for the reader the categories that the relevant parties are using. Documenting the terms adults use to discuss young adolescents and their development provided a rudimentary cultural map of the basic assumptions adults are making — a technique similar to James Spradley's "domain analysis."[27] From terminology, I moved on to try to detect themes or patterns in the stories adults told about their work. At the same time, points of conflict or differences of opinion also become more apparent, allowing the researcher to document a contested view of beliefs and practices.

During the fieldwork, research participants were incorporated into the research as collaborators and interpreters, a strategy that has been used successfully in research on teacher perspectives.[28] I used group interviews with former colleagues to discuss the issues that I was interested in and to generate questions or situations that might evoke more detailed responses. One of the major techniques used by the Spindlers was cross-cultural reflective interviewing. Using videos, pictures, or transcripts from the other country, the Spindlers invited their respondents to comment on or make sense of what they saw and heard in the depictions of their counterparts. After conducting pilot studies in each country in 1992, I was able to bring back to the field vignettes based on pilot interviews, which I used in group interviews with teachers to gain a sense of how they saw themselves in relation to teachers in the other nation. I was particularly interested in imputations of causality and tried to focus my attention (and my note taking) anytime discussions of causation emerged. For example, one teacher linked a student's poor test performance to the fact that "his mother is a drug addict who deserted the family and his grandfather died last year."

Simultaneously with the fieldwork, I began to collect local, regional, and national policy documents as well as educational literature which teachers mentioned. I analyzed the school and district plans of the four schools studied. In Japan I collected documents distributed at regional research meetings attended by the teachers I observed. These documents provided data on what basic policies and practices were common at the regional level. I also analyzed the curriculum guidelines produced by the Ministry of Education as well as articles from teacher journals that appeared to contrast with ministry views.

In the United States, I followed a similar plan up to the national level. In the United States there is no unified source for policy documents, particularly for middle schools. The lack of a distinct middle school unit or focus in the Department of Education is itself evidence of the disarray in the organizational field of middle grades schooling. In the United States, I found that national organizations (for example, the National Middle School Association) and foundations (for example, the Carnegie Foundation) produced publications that had a status similar to national policy statements. Moreover, I found that publications from these two groups tended to be widely recognized among teachers, not only in the four schools studied, but in other schools I worked with in California, Georgia, and Pennsylvania. I have used analysis of these documents, produced at the national level, to correspond with analysis of Japanese Ministry of Education documents.

SECONDARY DATA

Besides observations, interviews, and participation in local meetings and school events, I gathered data about the schools and schooling trends at the middle grade level in each country to contextualize how the schools in this sample differ from or are similar to other schools of this type. Throughout the book, I have tried to provide regional and national statistics, which will help the reader to understand the magnitude and frequency of occurrence of pertinent events. I have attempted to systematically gather and compare data on adolescent lives and middle grades schooling from both governmental and nongovernmental sources. Wherever possible I have tried to corroborate findings from multiple sources. In Japan, data from the Ministry of Education have been compared with studies conducted by independent scholars at Kyoto University and private research foundations (e.g., Benesse). In the United States, I have used a variety of materials from the Department of Education as well as studies based on National Assessment of Educational Progress, National Educational Longitudinal Study, and other data sets.

I took particular care to review and compare my findings with existing naturalistic studies of middle grades schools in the United States and Japan. I selected six studies for their academic rigor and ethnographic detail.[29] They provide salient reference points and alternative interpretations of events reported in this book and also give a textual description of middle grades schooling that shows the regional and historical variation present in each country. These works are also salient because they afford insights into what aspects of the foreign culture the researchers thought necessary to interpret for their audience. In particular, the works by Tadahiko Abiko or Hiroyoshi Shimizu and Kozo Tokuda show what Japanese researchers find noteworthy or surprising about American schools and their own. In a similar way Rebecca Fukuzawa, John Singleton, and Robert Everhart provide a mirror image of Americans looking at themselves and Japan.

Finally, my research for the Third International Math/Science Study (TIMSS) and the research on middle school organization I conducted in Georgia supplied me with qualitative and quantitative data that can be used to assess the schools I studied within a national context. The themes I identified in my initial work appeared again and again: volition was a prime consideration of teachers and parents; maturation and self-control were central concerns of teachers; beliefs about puberty were richly detailed.

### Organization of the Book

The material in this book is taken largely from an ethnographic study of four middle schools — two in the United States and two in Japan — that formed the core of my original study of counseling and teacher support. A description of the four schools and the research participants can be found in appendix 1. Chapters 3 through 8 are organized by major themes that arose during the analysis of the data and are useful for summarizing general beliefs about adolescent development: responsibility, puberty, maturity, defiance, creativity, and being at risk. Chapter 9 is dedicated to investigating how adolescence is institutionalized at various levels of schooling and educational policy. In the conclusion I discuss how this book sheds light on general beliefs about the nature of the self and will in the two cultures and what these differences mean for educational policy.

Chapter 3 analyzes the phenomenon of responsibility because it was a powerful theme shared by both American and Japanese teachers and therefore provides an interesting point from which to compare and contrast U.S. and Japanese beliefs. I show that teachers in both cultures are concerned with the development of self-control and implicitly believe that young adolescents are experiencing a change in their basic volitional capabilities. U.S. teachers, however, tend to believe that every individual follows a trajectory of development independent of his or her peers and that the best way to support this development is to reward or punish individual behavior. Japanese teachers tend to believe that young adolescents are at a crucial stage in the life course in which there is potential for expanding volitional capabilities and that this development can best be supported by organizing multiple opportunities for students to take responsibility as part of a larger group and to participate in group decision making and forming group goals.

In chapter 4, I look at how puberty is defined in each culture and analyze how basic biological events in the life course are perceived in very different ways: ways that have powerful implications for classroom practice and school rules. U.S. teachers perceive puberty as an unpredictable disruption in the life course: a trying period to be passed on the road to maturity. Japanese teachers perceive puberty as an anticipated and predictable transition in the life course: a time of growth as well as a time of uncertainty and troubled feelings. I argue that U.S. school practices tend to institutionalize a culture of disruption around adolescence whereas in Japan school practices tend to institutionalize a culture of goal setting and focus on these goals.

Chapter 5 I devote to analyzing what teachers think of maturity overall. U.S. teachers tend to emphasize increased individuation and internalization of self-control as evidence of maturity. Japanese tend to emphasize increased awareness of others and the development of individual goals as evidence of maturity. There is a stronger focus in the United States on the individual's psychological development, which is expressed in the system of rewards and punishments. This belief—that most young adolescents are going through a period of identity development—conflicts with beliefs that puberty and hormones drive adolescent behavior. In Japan, this conflict between biological and psychological forces is largely absent, but there is tension between teachers' beliefs about adolescent goals and responsibility to others. Teachers advise young adolescents to develop and cherish their individual academic goals at the same time they emphasize subjecting individual wishes or desires to the good of the group.

Chapter 6 shows how teachers respond to crises. This kind of analysis — a focus on the decidedly abnormal or extraordinary — is helpful in identifying the limits of ideal beliefs. In extraordinary circumstances there may be considerable difference between stated ideals and actions. What I found is that violence, disruption, and rebellion are linked with a prolonged adolescence in the United States. Ethnic variations in family structure, parenting styles, and life course expectations all acerbate miscommunication, and many U.S. teachers from middle-class backgrounds perceive themselves and their schools as being under siege. This was not the case in Japan, where teachers were expected to directly address student problems. Japanese teachers tended to see themselves as being in control, but they often paid a heavy price for this in the form of demanding workloads and lack of specific training in counseling techniques.

In chapter 7, I discuss defiance. This is a problem for both Japanese and U.S. teachers, but defiance — classroom disruption, juvenile delinquency, resistance, or rebellion — takes numerous forms. U.S. teachers tend to see classroom disruption as the aggressive assertion of adolescent will: a defiance of adult authority. Japanese teachers tend to see classroom disruption as immaturity and resistance to taking on the responsibility required of a maturing adolescent. The organization of school policies for dealing with various acts of defiance or disruption varies widely and tends to reinforce U.S. teachers' views that some students (particularly those from linguistic or ethnic minority groups) are defying the system. The organization of Japanese school policies places great emphasis on the teachers' ability to channel student resistance but tends to obscure the degree to which the demands of academic competition and school participation in Japan may acerbate student resistance or defiance.

Chapter 8 looks at how schools affect student creativity and self-expression. I show that both U.S. and Japanese teachers face similar dilemmas when trying to "teach" the creative process: how to balance an emphasis on discipline and mastery with an emphasis on spontaneity and expressiveness. I found that Japanese teachers actively try to stimulate and mold student creativity, but in doing so they tend to restrict self-expression and individual experimentation. U.S. teachers, on the other hand, try to create the least restrictive environment possible for self-expression and individual experimentation. Rather than teaching creativity, U.S. schools provided a range of activities and opportunities for young adolescents to engage in creative acts, although the range of opportunity appeared to be substantially affected by the socioeconomic back-ground of the student body and by school resources.

In chapter 9, I examine how adolescence is encoded or institutionalized in educational policy, law, and school policy. I show that there are many strong story lines (puberty, the identity crisis, and hormonal imbalance) around ado-lescence in the United States and that these story lines appear at the national, regional, and local levels. This suggests that adolescence plays a powerful role in how American schools are organized and how Americans think about the life course. In Japan, there are few strong story lines around adolescence, and these appear only at the national level. In place of adolescence, we find a life course organized around the school system, in which institutional roles (i.e., being a middle schooler) are associated with distinct expectations for appro-priate behavior. The analysis presented in this chapter suggests that many old, and perhaps even pathological, beliefs about adolescence have become institu-tionalized in U.S. educational policy and that more recent and accurate find-ings about adolescence do not readily affect school practice or organization.

Americans and Japanese, on balance, hold very different beliefs about the nature of the self, human development, and the will. I argue that in particular, these beliefs about the will have had strong impacts on how schooling is organized in the two cultures. The views of adolescence held in the two coun-tries flow from different conceptions of what constitutes the core of the per-son, and this affects how beliefs about adolescents and adolescent develop-ment become institutionalized. The cultural contradictions (e.g., do hormones or the psyche drive adolescent development?) in each nation are institutional-ized in the educational policies. In Japan, Western views of adolescence, of adolescent development, and of a Western self and life course are only super-ficially institutionalized. This reflects a tension between how Japanese must present themselves to the outside world and how they interact with each other on a day-to-day basis. In the United States there is considerable tension be-tween the views of human development institutionalized in educational policy, or school practice and the views held by different socioeconomic, cultural, linguistic, or religious groups.

Teachers' beliefs about adolescence reflect divergence in the conception of the self in the two nations. The different role of volition in adolescence — how teachers think about self-control and responsibility — indicates that in some key aspects Japanese teachers make basic assumptions about the nature of the human self that depart from those of American teachers. These differences suggest an alternative conceptualization of the nature of the self and the role of the individual in society. I also show, however, that proponents of a unique, modern, Western self are mistaken. Japanese beliefs convey many of the char-acteristics of a modern self yet derive from an amalgam of cultural beliefs that include very old elements. Moreover, variation in the beliefs of U.S. teachers suggests that the transmission of a modern, Western self as proposed by institutional theorists is a far more organic process than had been first hypothesized. While both Kotani and Oak Grove teachers were highly affected by the institutional rationales of schooling, there exists evidence of older beliefs about adolescence that have mutated and become institutionalized in the core rationales of modern schools in both nations.

## Implications for Educational Policy and Practice

Setting aside the more theoretical aspects of the study, what implications do these analyses have for educational policy and practice in the two nations? What practical value does this work have for teachers, counselors, and administrators who seek to improve schooling for young adolescents?

First, my work shows that Japanese and American teachers alike face significant tasks or problems that are not related to subject matter content. My work demonstrates that if educators or policymakers in either system are to make lasting changes in the way teachers teach, they will need to address a whole range of nonacademic issues. Veteran teachers on both sides of the Pacific give the same advice to novice teachers: you cannot teach a class of students until you have established a basic social relationship with the students. This means that teachers need to know how students themselves perceive their life, their future, and the biological and psychological changes that occur during adolescence.

Because Japanese generally believe in what I call a permeable sense of self — a self that has loose boundaries, where "I" exists not just in this physical body but partially in those around them — the Japanese homeroom teacher has traditionally been at the center of an extended organizational web of contacts that supported the teacher in dealing with problem behavior, emotional upset, or other problems students might have.[30] This proved to be a successful strategy for preventing and dealing with smaller problems but has proven to be largely ineffective in addressing serious problems like bullying, school violence, and school refusal. In the face of loose organization of external school support, homeroom teachers are often overwhelmed. To address these problems, the Japanese schools I visited were adopting various models for increasing student access to specialized emotional or psychological counseling. Because the fields of counseling and psychology are weakly institutionalized in Japan, school nurses, veteran teachers, and administrators are increasingly called upon to serve in the capacity of school counselor. But in the absence of training and access to more in-depth social services, these people face daunting challenges.

In the United States, powerful story lines of adolescent turmoil — deriving from both psychological and physiological sources — reinforce teachers' beliefs that many adolescent problems are outside their area of expertise and need to be referred to a specialist. In most American middle schools, teachers also tend to feel unsupported, but the organizational linkages are significantly different from those in Japan. The U.S. teacher is typically the primary referral agent — essentially acting as an "early warning" system. This system works well in many school districts to identify special needs or student problems early on and to refer the student to specialists who have specific training in working with special needs populations or counseling. The system tends to break down, however, when teachers have classrooms in which students have multiple personal and social adjustment problems. Particularly when the ethnic or linguistic backgrounds of student and teacher differ, teachers are often too overworked to learn what is going on in student lives. And, while U.S. systems work well to identify students who need special treatment, it does not work well to reintegrate such students or to help those who need some support but do not have an officially labeled special need or behavioral/emotional need.

Changing the way American or Japanese teachers think about the developing adolescent, adolescent-teacher relationships, and the role of the teachers is a crucial ingredient to successful reform efforts. I do not mean to imply, in a flippant postmodern sense, that if we recognize hegemonic ideology we can effect promising change. Rather, I point to the work of scholars from a variety of disciplines that has shown that changes in basic consciousness are necessary preliminary conditions for making substantive change in major social institutions. Joseph Kett, for example, has argued that in the United States, Hall's promotion of adolescence changed the way educators thought about the education of pubertal and postpubertal young adolescents, creating a whole new stage in the modern life course. Changing beliefs about the life course, the rise of widespread belief in adolescence, created the conditions under which the remarkable development and explosive growth of the junior high school movement were possible.

My work shows that beliefs about adolescent development in the United States are remarkably tenacious and impact the basic organizational routines and rationales upon which schooling is based. The most up-to-date studies of adolescent development and academic behavior have little impact on teacher or principal expectations for adolescent behavior in the classroom. In the United States beliefs in the inherent instability of adolescents serve to heighten the tension in classrooms and prevent teachers from seeing themselves as effective agents of change. When teachers believe that little can be done to alter the stormy course of adolescence, they are obviously unmotivated to learn new discipline techniques, investigate alternative classroom management techniques, or work with counselors. Moreover, this belief blinds teachers to the reality that many groups in the United States just don't see adolescence in the same way. Tension between middle class white teachers and students from many racial, ethnic, religious, or linguistic groups are intensified by the fact that teachers' expectations and students' expectations for the normal life course simply do not match. There is, however, no mechanism available in most schools for teachers, students, and parents to identify and discuss these differences.

Comparison offers a beginning, a way to look at ourselves more closely by looking at others. This book, then, does not advocate a simplistic learn-from-Japan model. Rather, I propose that a detailed comparison of empirical evidence about teacher beliefs, educational practice, and educational policy clarifies the cultural logic in which U.S. and Japanese school systems developed. The practices and beliefs of one nation are the catalyst which will stimulate the thinking of teachers, administrators, and scholars, providing insights into how patterns of student-teacher interaction become institutionalized in school. It is a way to begin identifying the most negative patterns and attempt to change them.

And if U.S. or Japanese educational problems are indicators of a lack of ideas about how to think problems through, then both nations appear to be lacking such ideas. Both sets of teachers in this study were perennially struggling to assess and promote appropriate behavior. They were offered limited institutional choices on how to conceptualize and deal with issues of choice, autonomy, and identity among young adolescents. There appears to be growing dissatisfaction with public schooling among many groups in the United States and Japan. Japanese and U.S. parents alike are looking for environments that allow students to exercise their volition — to express their interests, choices, and beliefs — in the ways that parents and adolescents see fit. Many seek exposure to radically more diverse patterns of the exercise of volition. This is not, however, the "de-schooled" society of Ivan Illich. Most parents and teachers in the United States and Japan want their adolescents to be more "schooled": i.e., more exposed to an environment that will positively change the young adolescent's basic ethical or moral commitments. The analysis presented in this book suggests ways in which schooling may be reformed. It also shows how beliefs about adolescent development are tenacious. If either nation wishes to make far-reaching changes in educational practice, then educators must address widely held beliefs about the nature of the individual and the development of the will.

# 2

## Oak Grove and Kotani

Over the past ten years I have conducted extensive fieldwork in four U.S. and Japanese middle schools: Wade, Pleasant Meadows, Furukawa, and Aratamachi. The schools are of roughly the same size (see table 2.1) with about eight hundred to nine hundred students each.[1] Wade and Furukawa serve low-income areas, and Wade has a sizable minority population. These two schools have the reputation as the tough schools in each district, that is, schools that teachers believe have many problems and are difficult places to work. Aratamachi and Pleasant Meadows are located in middle- to upper-middle-class neighborhoods and are considered desirable places to teach. Although the complexities of racial, ethnic, and linguistic differences were most prominent in the United States, in both countries teachers found themselves working with students' whose social backgrounds and expectations for the life course were often different from their own.

Some aspects of the comparison are less than ideal. Kotani is a small city of roughly seventy-five thousand inhabitants located in a large valley with a population of some three hundred to four hundred thousand people. The Oak Grove School district is home to only forty thousand people but is part of the metropolitan sprawl that rings San Francisco Bay. Kotani is located in a prefecture somewhat poorer and more rural than most of Japan. Oak Grove encompasses both affluent and working-class suburbs but is more affluent

*Table 2.1  Kotani and Oak Grove Schools*

| | Furukawa | Aratamachi | Pleasant Meadows | Wade |
|---|---|---|---|---|
| Kotani City, pop. 75,000 | | | Oak Grove City, pop. 38,000 | |
| Number of Middle Schools: 6 | | | Number of Middle Schools: 3 | |
| Number of High Schools: 4@ | | | High Schools — 3* | |
| Grades | 7–9 | 7–9 | 5–8 | 5–8 |
| # of Students | 838 | 700 | 850 | 980 |
| # of Teachers | 38 | 32 | 33 | 41 |
| Avg. Class Size | 40 | 38 | 29.3 | n.a. |
| % of Student Body Absent on a Given Day | 3% | 2% | 3–5% | 8–10% |
| Non-Japanese# | <1% | <1% | | |
| Ethnic Background | | | | |
| Asian-American | | | 14% | 8% |
| African-American | | | 2% | 7% |
| Hispanic | | | 13% | 26% |
| Caucasian | | | 70% | 56% |
| Other | | | 1% | 3% |

@Kotani students may also apply for admission at up to nine different public schools, and any number of private high schools.

#There are students from Korean, Chinese, and Burakumin backgrounds in the Kotani schools, as well as a growing number of Brazilian Japanese who do not read or write the language. There numbers are still quite small.

* Students may request transfers to other high schools in the surrounding area.

than most of the rest of the United States. In choosing these schools, I sacrificed typicality of setting in favor of more favorable entree to the setting and greater trust among the participants.[2]

KOTANI SCHOOLS IN NATIONAL PERSPECTIVE

Compared to other Japanese middle schools, the Kotani schools were more conservative in their regulation of student and teacher behavior. The schools were characterized by *kanri kyōiku,* a term denoting a tendency toward strict rules of deportment and the micromanagement of student behavior by teachers. Although media stories have exaggerated the range and intensity of this type of education (e.g., stories of teachers measuring a girl's skirts in millimeters), Kotani teachers engaged in monthly uniform checks and enforced a host of rules on student behavior both in and out of school. The schools in Kotani represent a more integrated and managed form of schooling than one usually finds in the environs of large cities like Nagoya or Tokyo. Young adolescents in urban areas have the opportunity to use the anonymity of the subway or large shopping centers to take them away from the watchful eyes of teachers and neighbors. Even within large cities, however, some middle schools maintain the same level of management of student behavior found in Kotani. But the difference is one of degree, not one of kind. The relationship between teachers and students at Furukawa and Aratamachi was normal in terms of the expectations of Japanese teachers.[3]

The prefecture which includes Kotani has a lower level of income than other prefectures in Japan, and students in Kotani were more likely than students in other parts of Japan to be poorer and reside in a home in which there were three generations present. Western schemas for categorizing social class do not fit well in Japan, and Japanese social scientists have tended to use models that agglomerate educational and occupational background with residential types. Thus most of Furukawa's students come from "downtown" families as opposed to Aratamachi's "new town" families.[4] Furukawa parents tended to be shopkeepers and workers that lived in the older, often dilapidated buildings near the core of the city. Aratamachi parents tended to be professionals and white-collar workers who lived in larger homes or new apartment complexes on the city periphery.[5]

There are several middle schools in the Kotani school district as well as several high schools. The high schools are administered by the prefectural board of education, but middle and elementary schools are governed by the city board of education. Teachers are hired by the city board and rotated through the six schools about once every six to seven years — standard practice in Japan. The rotation of teachers is systematic and staggered so that only a few teachers are transferred each year and overall staffing patterns are not disrupted. Principals can expect to have a full complement of teachers on staff at the start of the academic year (which begins in the spring), and every school tends to receive a similar complement of experienced teachers. There is little student turnover in Japanese middle schools. Japanese workers change jobs less than Americans do, and when job transfers do occur, many families opt to have the father move away for a year or two into temporary housing rather than disrupt the education of a young adolescent.

The educational aspirations of Kotani students appear quite similar to those of young people in the rest of Japan. My survey of student aspirations showed that 64 percent of students at Aratamachi and 73 percent of students at Furukawa hoped to go on to college. Fifteen percent of Aratamachi's students entered Kotani's most prestigious high school as compared to 20 percent of Furukawa students. The major difference between Kotani and Tokyo schools was the lack of large cram school chains in the immediate area. The lack of such chains means that Kotani students rely more on teachers for exam prep studying (*juken benkyō*) and for guidance in picking a high school.[6] Kotani teachers organize more extra classes than their counterparts in Tokyo and Kyoto. Formal ability grouping is not practiced in Japanese public elementary or middle schools during the regular school day, but teachers in many schools organize extra classes in the morning (*asagakushū*), the late afternoon, and over the holidays *(hoshū)*. In urban areas where students have easy access to national cram school chains, teachers do not need to provide such classes.

Kotani is home to Korean, Burakumin, Brazilian Japanese, and war-displaced Japanese families.[7] Students from these minority groups make up about 1 to 2 percent of the overall student population. During my fieldwork, I did not observe any ethnic or racial labeling by the teachers in either school. I did observe that the teachers were at a loss with how to deal with children of war-displaced Japanese (who spoke only Chinese) and the child of a Mormon couple from the United States. In these cases, the students were unable to participate in the full range of student activities because of their language ability, and teachers responded by trying to create special tutoring programs.

OAK GROVE SCHOOLS IN NATIONAL PERSPECTIVE

In the Bay Area, teachers considered Oak Grove a desirable district at the time of the study, although Wade was perceived as a school with many student behavior problems. "Who would want to go to Wade?" one teacher queried. "No extra pay and it's a battle zone."[8] Such differences within a single school district are not uncommon in the United States. Although many districts are far more homogenous than Oak Grove in terms of racial, ethnic, and socioeconomic characteristics, large urban districts display striking variations from school to school in student social backgrounds, quality of facilities, and teacher professional development.

Wade and Pleasant Meadows faced many of the same problems common to middle schools around the United States in the early 1990s. Both schools enrolled student populations that were more ethnically diverse than previous cohorts while the teaching staff remained largely white and middle class. At the time of the study, the teaching staff was virtually all European-American, and all the teachers quoted in this study were European-American. The combination of a nearly all-white teaching staff and a large portion of minority students was a source of tension in the Oak Grove District. The student-teacher conflicts I documented at Wade during the study are common in U.S. schools in which class, race, and language create communication problems between students and teachers.[9]

Money was another problem Oak Grove teachers faced. Both schools dealt with budget cutbacks and a lack of voter support for new funding initiatives. This led, as it did in many U.S. schools, to a general retrenching of the curriculum. Pleasant Meadows was better able to absorb these cutbacks and maintained a higher level of staff support as evidenced by an on-site counselor and librarian. Both schools were experiencing overcrowding, however, and temporary classrooms were in use at both schools.[10] Many of the Georgia and Pennsylvania schools I worked in faced similar funding problems.

Middle schools are complex organizations. The principals in Oak Grove were expected to manage many programs, such as special education or gifted and talented education, in addition to monitoring de-tracking, multidisciplinary teaming, and requests from universities for student teacher placement. These conditions are common throughout the United States where middle grades schools are called upon to provide an expanding array of social and academic programs.

The teachers and staff at Wade also faced two very common U.S. problems: instability in staffing and student turnover. Compared to more affluent districts and schools, the constant flow of staff and young adolescents in and out of schools like Wade is perhaps the most serious problem facing American middle schools. In the United States middle schools in low-income neighborhoods tend to have highly unstable organizational environments. Schools in poorer districts have high rates of teacher turnover, and administrators are frequently shifted. In addition, at one school I worked in, a teacher experienced 100 percent turnover in one class in a single academic year. U.S. teachers are often unable to contact parents because of frequent changes of address and spend a significant amount of time trying to set up meetings with parents or guardians.

THE KOTANI SCHOOLS IN LOCAL PERSPECTIVE

Both Kotani schools are three-story, ferro-concrete buildings, similar in shape and design to the other middle schools in this region. Students commute to school on foot or on bicycle. Like teachers in the rest of Kotani's middle schools, most teachers live outside the immediate neighborhood and most commute in their automobiles. In an attempt to promote contact between teachers and the neighborhood, each teacher is also assigned an area (a few *cho,* or "blocks") for which they are responsible. The extent of these responsibilities is not onerous; teachers are merely required to be familiar with their area's shops, dangerous intersections, and the like.

School reputations and character are slow to change in Japan and do not have the same range of diversity as in the United States. While teachers talk of "unsettled" and "calm" schools, my work indicates that actual rates of disruptive student behavior occupy a fairly narrow band in Japan. There were few other substantive differences between the two schools. Aratamachi is somewhat smaller than Furukawa. Teachers say that Aratamachi has a family feel. Even during the test period, when students are forbidden to enter the teacher's room (as exams are lying on the desks), a few boys and girls will sneak in to deliver things to their homeroom teacher before being shooed out. At Furukawa, the atmosphere is stricter and slightly less personal. Teachers there complained that they had to teach more classes than at Kotani's other schools. The grade chairs (*gakunenchō*) at Furukawa taught more periods per week than those at Aratamachi. The only schools in the region that differed significantly from Aratamachi and Furukawa were tiny middle schools located outside Kotani in small valleys. Such rural schools are scattered across Japan but account for a very small percentage of student enrollments.

On any given day in Kotani, one will see clumps of middle school students walking or riding their bicycles to school. The somber color of the uniforms stands in sharp contrast to the chatter and general high spirits that characterize these groups. Most of the groups are composed of either males or females, but occasionally a large group will contain members of both sexes.

Arriving at the school, students park their bikes and crowd into the student entrance to remove their shoes and put on school slippers. Most teachers will have already arrived and be busy in the teachers' room by the time students begin to arrive. In wintertime, there were always a few students and a teacher or two standing around the kerosene stove chatting and keeping warm.

The teachers at Aratamachi and Furukawa know each other well. Rotation of staff at regular intervals means that most senior teachers have worked with their present colleagues at other schools in the past. During my study, the principal at Aratamachi was a relatively hands-off administrator who left most of the decisions to his senior teachers. The principal at Furukawa was more engaged and tended to consult with a smaller group of senior teachers. The fact that all three grade chairs at Furukawa as well as the head of curriculum were experienced women teachers made the staffing patterns at Furukawa exceptional in that region of Japan.

In the intervening years, the opening of a new middle school and continued population growth have changed the student population of Furukawa somewhat, creating less difference in reputation than at the time of the study. All of the teachers have been rotated, and many of the senior teachers have moved into administrative positions, replacing the old administrators who have now retired. Uniform rules are more relaxed, but all in all the schools appear to function much as they did during my fieldwork.

### THE OAK GROVE SCHOOLS IN LOCAL PERSPECTIVE

Wade Middle School lies on the border of Sun City near a freeway artery and at the opposite end of the Oak Grove district from Pleasant Meadows. The district includes low-income areas of neighboring Sun City, and academically Wade students tended to perform below the state average. In the school "report card" mandated by law, Wade did not print its California Assessment Program scores, noting that "academics is not the only measure of success." In its report card, Pleasant Meadows proudly announced that nearly 90 percent of its students were doing better than the state average. The families at Wade range from working class to middle class, and the school was about half white, a quarter Hispanic, and with less than 10 percent of students designated as Asian or African American. About 12 percent of the students in 1991–92 were designated as limited in English speaking proficiency. Wade's population has been capped at nearly one thousand students; the overflow is being sent to Pleasant Meadows or other middle schools in the district.

Following the resignation of Wade's long-term principal, Ann Lewis, the school, in the words of one teacher, fell apart. For the next two years staff turnover was high. In one year fifteen new teachers were hired. The departure of Adrian Norris and other senior teachers seemed to further destabilize the school. This instability coincided with a heightened sensitivity to gang activity in the area. Following the recommendation of the superintendent, the principal tended to call in the police whenever there was a serious altercation between students. This was a significant departure, teachers said, from the previous school policy. As a result, several times a week a patrol car could be seen sitting outside the school office.

Wade is an urban school located near a freeway in a neighborhood of small homes. On any given day, visitors will observe students walking to school or gathering at the convenience store nearby; older students (eighth graders) stand on the sidewalk in groups while the younger children make wide detours around them. Rather than wait for the crossing light, a couple of kids may dart across the four lanes of traffic. At the school, the walkways are noisy and littered with gum wrappers, styrofoam cups, and bits of cafeteria sandwiches. All of the edible leavings are, at noon, consumed by a host of seagulls that descend like clockwork at the same time each day. During breaks, the courtyard is a sea of noise and color. Tiny fifth graders dash after one another, and a group of neatly dressed girls chat in Vietnamese and laugh. Against the lockers a couple embrace and kiss deeply.

Pleasant Meadows, as its name implies, is tucked away in a very quiet suburban neighborhood. Pleasant Meadows has the largest grounds of Oak Grove's three middle schools. The grounds are relatively clean, and students gravitate to a nearby grocery store after school. The staff at Pleasant Meadows is generally pleased with their school, although there were signs of stress in the district as a whole. While the courtyard bustled with energy during the breaks, there was noticeably less ethnic diversity at the school. Students moved about freely, and groups formed in classrooms where teachers had opened their doors for the morning.

In the years since my fieldwork, both schools have undergone many changes. Emily Saunders, Wade's principal, has weathered her first years and has worked to lift teacher morale. Wade, in the words of one teacher, has settled down. The data collected during the fieldwork, then, portrays Wade at its low phase — a time of turmoil and anxiety. During the same period, Pleasant Meadows was riding high. After my fieldwork ended, the departure of the principal, Stan Proud, and an influx of overflow students from other middle schools created an atmosphere that was, for a time, strained and disorganized. Like the broader culture itself, the character of the schools is constantly changing, but many patterns endure over long periods of time.

## The Organization of Middle Grades Education

Modern middle schools in the United States and Japan are designed specifically for the education of young adolescents. They are unlike the common elementary schools of the past in that theories about the developmental needs of young adolescents have influenced their organization, at least in the United States; further, in each country there are significant changes in curriculum, instructional style, and norms of behavior associated with the transition from elementary school to middle school.[11]

U.S. and Japanese middle schools differ in terms of governance, organizational form, and curricular objectives. Japan has a highly centralized school system that is supervised by the ministry of education (Monbusho), which creates national curriculum guidelines. There is one approved form: a school of three grades that encompasses the last years of compulsory education. In the United States, states and local districts have significant power in determining the curriculum. There are also many types of schools — middle school, intermediate school, and junior high school — that have different grade combinations.

## Middle Grades in the Japanese Educational System

The current Japanese system is largely a product of post–World War II education reform. Influenced by American reformers, the Japanese instituted a

6–3–3 system, which some older teachers still refer to as the American system. Education through ninth grade is essentially a single-track system in which all students study the same curriculum.[12]

In terms of staffing, Japanese schools are virtually teacher-run institutions. Japanese principals are called school heads (*kōchō*) and vice-principals are head teachers (*kyōtō*). These are not just empty titles. Principals and vice-principals are promoted from the ranks of teachers, and few will attain these positions without having two decades of classroom experience. Furthermore, the administrative duties of the school are diffused over a wide range of senior teachers through a system of committees that oversee all of the school functions.[13] Teachers are organized by grade level, and these grade level committees are responsible for planning and implementing the year's curriculum as well as organizing extracurricular events for the grade. In addition to overseeing the important clubs, all Japanese teachers are required to participate in several of the committees which oversee the management of the school, implementation of the curriculum, and the counseling of students (see table 2.1). Chairs of committees are appointed by the principal in consultation with senior teachers: both experience and demonstrated ability are required to take on positions of responsibility.

Japanese teachers also have numerous responsibilities outside of school. Teachers in elementary and middle schools typically visit the house of each child in their homeroom class once a year. At the middle school level, teachers and sometimes PTA representatives organize checks of traffic safety or patrol local game centers or other potential trouble spots. High schools are legally free to forbid students from taking part-time jobs and to enforce rules of dress and deportment when students are going to or leaving school. Japanese schools have a homeroom system in which a teacher is responsible for one class of students, and this class meets as a group several times a day. One of the homeroom teacher's responsibilities is to build up the sense of unity in the class, and this task of "creating a class" (*gakkyū zukuri*) is a favorite topic in practitioner journals.

In terms of academic instruction, Japanese teachers, compared to American, tend to spend fewer hours per week in class and more hours involved in committee work. Academic instruction across Japan is much more standardized than in the United States, in large part because of the presence of national curriculum standards and the impact of the high school entrance examinations. Academic competition is intense in Japanese schools, and middle school is when adolescents begin to study in earnest.[14]

Education is free and compulsory for children from ages six to fifteen, that is, those at the elementary school and middle school level. Elementary schools

*Table 2.2  The Management Structure of Japanese Schools*

---

**Committees**

    School Governing Committee
        Principal
        Vice-Principal
        Head of Curriculum
        Head of Student Guidance
        Heads of Grade Committees
    General Teachers Assembly

    9th Grade Teachers Committee
    8th Grade Teachers Committee
    7th Grade Teachers Committee

**Sections**

    Curriculum Section
    Guidance Section
    Health Section
    Physical Education Section
    Cultural Section
    Facilities Section

    General Management Section

**Academic Departments**

    Japanese
    Math
    Science
    English
    Social Studies
    Art
    Physical
    Ed./Health

---

are generally within walking distance of the child's home, and during the school year small groups of children (shepherded by older students, a parent, or teacher) can be seen walking to school. Failing students or retaining them for one year is virtually unknown at this level. As children reach the upper elementary grades, however, some do begin to fall behind the others in core academic subjects.

Differences in academic skills pose real problems for Japanese middle school teachers. Because middle school classes are not tracked, teachers must try to keep the whole class moving ahead on a single lesson. Japanese middle schools do not offer different levels of mathematics classes, but teachers do provide extra academic drills, usually starting in the second year, which are aimed at preparing the students for the high school entrance examination. At the end of three years of middle school, students must make a successful score on the high school entrance exam in order to enter the school of their choice. Although nearly all Japanese children go on to high school, none are guaranteed admission.

The transition to high school marks another disjuncture in the adolescent experience. Where students end up in this hierarchy is largely determined by their score on the practice tests given in middle school, although an increasing number of schools do admit students by recommended admissions.[15] The conditions young Japanese face in middle school are crucial for success in the entrance examination. Middle schools are still part of the compulsory education system, and as such differences in curriculum and extracurricular opportunities are not as large as those found between high schools. Which high school a student attends will largely determine his or her chances for college entrance, the kind of job he or she will obtain, and even future pay raises. As students enter their second and third year of middle school, awareness of these variations creates divisions in the harmony of the group-consciousness that teachers have tried to create.

Especially for those who are not doing well academically, the high school entrance examination looms ahead as a set of not very pleasant options. As students progress in the system, they are channeled into narrower and narrower academic concentrations. Middle school is when most of the problems associated with adolescent rebellion occur in Japan. Middle schools are a pivotal point in the educational experience of modern Japanese youth, and any understanding of the adolescent experience must begin with some understanding of life in middle schools.

## *Middle Grades in the American System*

American education is characterized by extreme diversity. In a national survey of public schools, Douglas MacIver and Joyce Epstein found that only about one quarter of the schools were middle schools, which they define as having the grade combinations 6–8, 5–8, 5–7, and 6–7, and over 30 percent of schools were some form of K–8.[16] They note that in terms of student enrollment, however, "over 80 percent of all seventh graders" were in some kind of middle or junior high school.[17] The National Middle School Association notes that the focus of the original middle school movement promoted 5–

8 or 6–8 grade combinations but now orients itself around "improving the educational experiences of 10–15 years olds."[18] Influential documents by the Carnegie Council on Adolescent Development also adopt this focus on ten to fifteen year olds, but the Superintendent's Middle Grade Task Force in California "present[s] a reform agenda for grades six, seven and eight — the middle grades."[19]

Although there has been little national consensus on the optimal grade organization for middle schools (some educators argue that the variety of forms is actually positive because it means that school districts have a variety of options to consider) there has been consensus on what should be done in middle grades schools. Middle school advocacy groups have called for educators, administrators, and support staff to be well versed in the particular characteristics of young adolescents; to provide small group settings for instruction and guidance; to teach a common academic core; to create teams of teachers; to provide varied opportunities for learning. Table 2.3 shows the basic points called for by three groups.

While there is some consensus about what a middle school is to be, it is not clear that grade organization or the use of the term "middle school," means that any given school is attempting to implement the basic points outlined in table 2.3. Studies of middle school curriculums have shown some statistically significant associations between grade organization and instructional practices. MacIver and Epstein found that 6–8 schools were more likely to use some form of group adviser or homeroom and to implement interdisciplinary teaming.[20] Henry Becker found that schools with middle or junior high school type organization were more likely to offer electives or exploratory courses. Also, seventh and eighth grade teachers in K–8 type schools were less likely to engage students in higher-order thinking and more likely to use drill.[21]

For many young adolescents, middle school or junior high school is a time of increased confusion and decreasing academic performance. Roberta Simmons and Dale Blythe found generalized decline in student grades. David Kinney notes that for many young adolescents, the entrance to high school is an opportunity to regain a sense of identity and strengthen self-esteem — especially for those children whose lack of social skills have marked them as "nerds" to their fellow students. As research indicates that the onset of puberty itself has little effect on academic performance, whereas the adolescent's developmental progress in relation to his or her peers does, the overall effects of schooling during early adolescence become even more salient.[22]

Work by Jacquelynne Eccles, Sarah Lord, and Carol Midgley suggests that the decline in adolescent motivation, so often characterized by teachers and parents alike to be the result of hormones turning on, may actually be the

*Table 2.3  Middle School Characteristics or Ideals*

| Carnegie | NMSA | California Task Force |
|---|---|---|
| Create small communities for learning | Provide curriculum that is challenging, intergrative and exploratory | Common, core curriculum; empower students with knowledge; develop capacities for critical thought; personalize ideal and make reasoned moral or ethical choices; develop a repertoire of learning strategies; sound instructional practices |
| Teach a core academic program | Provide varied teaching and learning approaches | Prepare student for range of academic secondary options; provide equal access to advanced levels of curricula; encourage underrepresented minority students; provide programs to address needs of "at-risk" students, provide physical and emotional health care programs |
| Ensure success for all students | Provide assessment and evaluation that promote learning | Student-centered philosophy; provide access to extra- and intramural programs; make students accountable for academic excellence and personal behavior; coordinate successful transitions between levels of schooling; identify middle grades as 6–8; provide access to full range of instructional and support services; use assessments that capture a broad range |
| Empower teachers and administrators to make decisions about experiences of middle grade students | Provide flexible organization structures | Teachers in middle grades should be knowledgeable of characteristics of young adolescents; teachers and administrator should engage in staff development to promote collegiality |

*Table 2.3  Continued*

| Carnegie | NMSA | California Task Force |
|---|---|---|
| Staff middle grade schools with teachers who are expert at teaching young adolescents | Provide Programs that foster health, wellness and safety | Parents, communities and school boards share accountability for reform; create partnership between school districts, colleges and Dept. of Education. |
| Improve academic performance through fostering health and fitness | Provide comprehensive guidance and support services. | |
| Reengage families in the education of young adolescents | | |
| Connect schools with communities | | |

**Source:** Carnegie Council on Adolescent Development, 1989:9; National Middle School Association, 1995: 11; Superintendent's Middle Grade Task Force, 1987.

result of a mismatch between the type of instruction and school structure and the early adolescent's learning needs.[23] Especially in large junior high schools, young adolescents tend to receive more formal, discipline-based instruction and find themselves studying with different groups of students each period. Robert Everhart's ethnography of a junior high school also documents increased rebellion and delinquency among boys who find classes uninteresting and school life confining and dull. Schools which follow the National Middle School Association guidelines attempt to create smaller learning communities and to promote homerooms and joint classes in which teachers can allow students more time to develop their own ideas and questions.

Gender is also a significant factor, and popular studies suggest that girls' academic performance and self-esteem are negatively affected by current curricular and organizational practices. While it is unclear how different the school effects are for various middle school combinations (e.g., 5–8, 6–9, 7–9), scholarly evidence suggests that the transitions involved in the middle grades are not more difficult for girls than boys. Rather, the best research shows that gender interacts with other factors like pubertal timing, family socioeconomic status, race, linguistic background, and academic ability in complex ways. Girls do have lower self-esteem, on average, than boys at this age, but to say that girls fare worse than boys socially, emotionally, or academically in the middle grades is simply not supported by existing evidence.[24]

The interaction of biology and school effects is further compounded, in the United States, by ethnic and linguistic differences. Research in the past decade shows that major ethnic groups within the United States may have very different attitudes not only toward schooling, but toward basic biological processes and the life course. African-American males show a greater tendency to adopt the "behaviors and attitudes consistent with the stereotype of adolescence."[25] Other studies have shown that there are racial differences in terms of preparedness for menarche, poor African-American girls having less accurate knowledge about the physical process of the onset of puberty.[26] And the striking differences in rates of early adolescent pregnancies indicate broad dissimilarities in attitudes toward sexual activity, parenthood, and the use of contraceptives.

There is evidence of persistent inequalities in curriculum and academic course work associated with ethnic background and socioeconomic status of student populations. Jomills Braddock found that "racially mixed or predominantly minority schools were characterized by a somewhat narrower array of curricular alternatives than other schools." He also noted that "out of all the factors that we studied in order to identify differences in the curricular and classroom experiences of students attending different types of schools, the most powerful factor was a simple measure of . . . family socioeconomic status."[27] Although the U.S. education system allows far more opportunity that the Japanese for students to change tracks and move on to better educational opportunities, the fact that schools with larger percentages of ethnic or linguistic minorities or poor students offer more limited curriculums has a significant effect when students move on to high school.

Transitions to high school are more complicated in the United States than in Japan, but evidence suggests that social class and linguistic, ethnic, or racial background affect the tracks that students are placed in. Ethnographic studies in the United States find that students often perceive little relationship between what they study in school and what will be required of them in the workplace or other adult roles. These disjunctures tend to grow, not diminish, as students grow older. In particular, middle school is crucial because it is a time when many students become disaffected with learning and begin to define themselves in terms of popularity and displays of wealth.[28]

Often by the seventh grade, students from impoverished families are already playing adult roles in their home and community. The conflict between their accelerated life course and the institutionalized life course upon which schooling is based (see Pallas 1993) creates dissonance and alienation. Linda Burton recorded the sentiments of a fifteen-year-old boy in an African-American inner-city neighborhood: "Sometimes I just don't believe how this school operates and thinks about us. Here I am a grown man. I take care of my mother and have raised my sisters. Then I come here and this know-nothing teacher treats me like I'm some dumb kid with no responsibilities. I am so frustrated. They are trying to make me something that I am not. Don't they understand I'm a man and I been a man longer than they been a woman."[29]

The frustration expressed by the young man in Burton's study appears to be widespread in young adolescents who are marginalized from middle-class culture by reason of economic circumstance, ethnicity, or language. The patterns that Burton documents have been previously demonstrated to undermine the school performance of white working-class boys and girls and working-class boys, both white and black. Studies of race, social status, and tracking find persistent differences in American schools.[30]

## U.S. and Japanese Middle Schools — Institutional Differences

The institutional form of schooling in each country produces significant differences in how teachers work with adolescents as well as in teacher expectations for adolescent development. Compared to their Japanese counterparts, the Oak Grove schools were characterized by organizational instability and almost constant change. Such instability has been noted by other scholars, both Japanese and American. The multiple forms that middle education takes in the United States — middle school, junior high school, intermediate school, K–8 schools — mean that there is no clear organizational form and no single organizational set of goals guiding middle level education in the United States[31]

The Kotani schools, on the other hand, were relatively stable environments with little student movement in or out and a well-defined process of teacher rotation that tended to maintain relative equality among schools in terms of teacher's capabilities. These schools are representative of the nation as a whole. In Japan there is only one organizational model for middle grades schools and a clear organizational set of goals: preparation for the high school entrance examination; development of basic academic skills; and promotion of social skills via participation in club and extracurricular events.

Although members of the middle school movement have tried to promote a clearer articulation of middle school ideals in the United States, there has been little movement toward a unified organizational form. The debate over what middle grades education should be reflects the elaborate but contested nature of American beliefs in adolescence. Virtually every U.S. educator I have met agrees that young adolescents need special kinds of education, but there is no consensus on what that education should be. In Japan, there is little debate about the special educational needs of adolescents, but considerable discussion about how schools can meet specific academic goals. In Japan, teachers, parents, and politicians of various parties argue about the impact of examinations on the school curriculum, the impact of the cram schools and how schools should respond to problems like school refusal.

Another major difference is the expected workload for teachers and students. Among Japanese educators, middle school teachers are believed to put in the longest hours. This stereotype has a strong basis in reality. Elementary school teachers in Japan have a lighter schedule because children go home earlier and there is no examination preparation study. Japanese middle school teachers are required to provide intense academic instruction as well as many activities aimed at social development. In the United States, middle school teachers are often thought to have a more difficult job, but not because of the academic demands of the curriculum. American middle school teachers are perceived to have more discipline problems and more difficulty getting students to concentrate on schoolwork. Most U.S. educators perceive the academic standards in middle grades schools to be rather low.[32]

Much of the variation in the two countries' academic achievement at the middle grade–level has been attributed to the presence of high-stakes testing in Japan. As compulsory education ends after middle school, middle school students and teachers in Japan share a clear academic goal: getting into high school. The fact that failure to enter high school is widely believed to have extreme negative effects on future life chances means that teachers, students, and parents are all highly motivated to support academic achievement. The high school entrance examinations test only five subjects, which reduces the range of topics in the curriculum. This system appears effective in producing high average national test scores, but it limits a student's course of study.

Finally, local conditions have a much greater impact on determining the quality of education in U.S. middle schools than in Japanese. Schools in affluent, stable neighborhoods like Pleasant Meadows are often protected from the kind of organizational instability that so heavily impacted a school like Wade. Even within the same district, then, there is unequal distribution of resources, particularly in terms of the experience of the teaching staff. Individual districts are given great latitude in deciding the basic organizational form of the school, not just for middle schools, but for all levels. Staffing patterns, allocation of resources, textbook selection, and many other important features of running the schools are made on the local level. Japanese school districts and prefectures appear to do a much better job of assuring that the quality of education is the same throughout a district and that district-to-district variation is slight. Further, the Japanese districts' policy of teacher rotation means that experienced teachers are distributed throughout the district and not concentrated in a single school.

## Implications

Differences in policy and organization have pronounced effects on the education of young adolescents. The lack of a unified organizational form for the middle grades in the United States means that there can be no consistent American educational policy for young adolescents. A junior high school (grades 7 and 8) with an enrollment of one thousand students cannot operate in the same way that a middle school (grades 5 to 8) with an enrollment of six hundred students can. The multiple organizational forms, local control of curriculum, state-to-state variations in teacher certification as well as the highly mobile American citizenry all combine to create a system that is best characterized by extreme variability and instability.[33]

Advocates of the middle school movement in the United States have argued that large junior high schools that pool students from many elementary schools and offer a largely academic course with multiple levels of classes (e.g., remedial mathematics, mathematics, algebra) create impersonal learning environments that adversely affect the young adolescent. Critics of the middle school movement argue that the middle school's focus on social development fosters poor academic performance in core subjects.[34] Much of the disagreement in this area arises from confusion over grade-level organization versus actual practices. The best data currently available show that when schools truly implement the basic structural elements of middle school reform — interdisciplinary teams, student-teacher advisory relationships, and small learning communities — the middle school model has a significant positive effect on academic achievement.[35]

Other data suggest that a single middle grades school with multiple grade levels would be better suited for the education of young adolescents. Work by sociologists and psychologists in the United States shows that, in broad terms, transitions (whether they be from one school to another, from one grade to another, or simply from one class to another) can have negative effects on adolescent social adjustment and academic performance. The ideal organizational form for young adolescents would be a school with multiple grades (e.g. 5–8 or 6–8) in which students progress from one grade to another with a cohort of students they know; in which there is a strong homeroom system that allows the teacher to develop significant relationships with each student;

in which the school day is divided into relatively few periods, allowing students to study a single subject or a multidisciplinary subject in great detail.

With one well-defined set of schools, the Japanese have been able to institute a set of organizational norms or goals which are similar in many respects to those advocated by the middle school movement advocates in the United States: teachers form interdisciplinary teams, there is a strong homeroom system that allows a teacher to become a true adviser to students, and transitions during the day are kept to a minimum (students remain in their homeroom for most of the day). This unified organization form also means that when families move (which happens much more in the United States than Japan) young adolescents will transfer to a school with similar features to the one they left.

Overall, the organizational form of Japanese middle grades schools is better suited to the educational needs of young adolescents than that found in the United States, but this does not mean that Japanese education is somehow better. Many other factors need to be considered, including the quality of instruction, range of extracurricular activities offered, emphasis on moral, psychological, or social development as well as opportunities to develop creativity, to learn the basic principles of democracy, and to learn to accept responsibility. In particular, it would be a rare American parent who would want to give up local control of the school to the state or federal government. The price of local control need not be as great as it is in the United States. More uniform practices in middle grades education would not necessarily mean a reduction in parent input into the school. American policymakers need to think about ways to homogenize the quality of instruction (e.g., by adopting a policy of teacher rotation) without removing all decision-making powers from local school boards. Policymakers must also realize that from the teacher's viewpoint, the most pressing problems have little to do with academic instruction per se and much to do with inculcating such basic character traits as responsibility.

3

# The Common Problem of Responsibility

Dear Mrs. Lee,

You may not know this, but while you are not here, our class loses control. They talk out of turn, and yell across the classroom. Miss Boyd, our substitute, receives no respect, but she does receive much back talk and defiance. Not only are the kids in our class disrespectful to the substitute, they are also disrespectful to each other. Insults and profanity are common. Unless action is taken immediately, Miss Boyd may quit!

There are many ways to improve the behavior of the class. The most direct way to impose stricter punishment, such as double detention and janitorial help. You could also suspend repeated offenders from this class. Rewarding "good" kids would put personal pressure on troublemakers to behave. Exclusion from special activities might also work. Whichever you use, use it soon before its too late.

Unanimously (sic) yours,

Mrs. X.

(Letter from student posted on Lynn Jing's classroom wall along with student short stories.)

This student's letter eloquently, although perhaps sarcastically, summarizes the major problem facing U.S. middle school teachers on a daily basis:

how to manage a classroom full of young adolescents. The assumption of students and teachers alike is that young adolescents need to be supervised at all times. Indeed, even substitute teachers or other adults not known to the adolescents may not be able to maintain order. While I suspect the young writer of being overly dramatic, there is nothing unusual about young adolescents favoring strict punishment of individuals who fail to follow the rules: young adolescents as well as teachers feel the disrespect of their peers. In Oak Grove, most young adolescents believe that adults need to mete out punishments to troublemakers to keep order. In the United States people believe that young adolescents, left to themselves, are not capable of being responsible for conducting class in an orderly manner.

This is simply not the case in Japan, where groups of young adolescents are left for long periods without adult supervision. Japanese teachers rely heavily on students to be self-monitoring and self-correcting in their behavior. Teachers believed that almost all young adolescents are capable of working well together without adult supervision given the proper socialization. The differences between Japanese and U.S. teachers' attitudes are reflected in the way in which the school day is organized and highlights the kinds of assumptions that adults have about how young adolescents learn to become responsible. The beginning of each school day provides clear examples of adult expectations.

### *Arriving at School*
#### WHERE ARE THE TEACHERS?

On a chilly October morning, Mrs. Kawaguchi was carrying out the role of *shūban*[1] and stood at the top of the steps in front of the student entrance at Furukawa. Despite the cold and fog, she did not wear a coat or hat. She vigorously greeted each student, alternating between shouts of "Good morning" and "Hurry up!" As soon as the fifteen-minute bell rang the students surged into the school. Mrs. Kawaguchi then walked the halls checking for late students. About five minutes after the first warning bell, a second bell chimes at Furukawa to announce the start of the morning teachers' meeting. During this period all adults in the school assemble in the teachers' room to hear the daily instructions. On the days when I chose to survey the students rather than participate in the teachers' meeting, I routinely saw the entire student body in their classes, all holding meetings much like the one going on in the teachers' room. Many classes were struggling to hold meetings — several students would play or talk — but that did not stop the *tōban* (student in charge) from trying to conduct the meetings.

There were also subtle differences in how the students carried out these meetings. First-year students generally started out the year trying to cover all the business to which they were assigned but were generally too unorganized to finish in the allotted time, forcing the homeroom teacher to cover class business when he or she arrived in class for the homeroom period. Second-year students fared about the same as the first-years, but the student *tōban* and kakari appeared more efficient in collecting homework assignments, recording absences, and surveying the class for students who felt ill.[2] The third-year students tended to conclude their business with great rapidity. While the *tōban* directed the meeting, most students were studying or putting the final touches on assignments.

The teachers' morning meeting lasted ten to fifteen minutes on most days but occasionally went as long as thirty minutes, as when when teachers discussed an accident that had happened during a school trip. During these periods, Kotani students were unsupervised in the classroom wings of the building, which are out of sight and hearing from the teachers' room. Although noise levels in some classes were often high, there was a general attempt to hold meetings. Students knew what tasks they had to do and generally tried to do them. Despite the lack of immediate adult supervision, students did not attempt to vandalize school property or attack one another. Windows were not broken, walls were not defaced with graffiti, equipment was not destroyed, and fights did not break out. Of the ten incidents of equipment breakage recorded in the fall of 1992 at Furukawa, eight occurred after school or during break periods between classes.

THE WATCHFUL EYE OF THE TEACHER

On my first day of fieldwork at Wade Middle School my attention was drawn to the vice-principal, Dave Forest,. who stood by the bike racks and in a loud voice kept telling students to walk their bikes. Around the corner from Dave's post, the din of student conversation was punctuated with the slamming of locker doors. In Japan, students have a hook on the wall outside the classroom and a desk, whereas each American student had a small locker. As Oak Grove is located in California, there were no internal hallways in the school: breezeways and overhanging eaves connected classrooms. Students moved in and out of the office, but only a few headed for their classrooms because most of the rooms were locked. Until the first-period teacher came to open the door, students at both Wade and Pleasant Meadows had to wait outside under the eaves.

About five to ten minutes before class all the teachers were in their rooms. By the two-minute warning bell, the courtyard had not even half-emptied of students, but as thirty seconds approached a tremendous surge took place.

After the start-of-class bell about ten students were still in the yard, sauntering to class under Dave's verbal harangue.

There was no morning teachers' meeting in the middle schools of the Oak Grove school district. Teachers arrived, made their photocopies, prepared their lessons, grabbed a cup of coffee, and headed to their classrooms. Every teacher, along with the vice-principal and principal, rotated through a set of supervisory positions during the morning and afternoon when students arrived and left school. Some teachers arrived early and opened their doors to students who wanted to study or get extra help on schoolwork. On occasion, the teacher I was shadowing locked himself or herself into the classroom in order to finish last-minute preparations or merely sit and have a cup of coffee. Many Oak Grove teachers used the classroom door as a mechanism to regulate contact with students or to make sure that students were not left unsupervised.[3]

After entering their classrooms, teachers in Oak Grove usually admonished students to be quiet (with varying rates of success) so that all could listen to the morning announcements. At both Wade and Pleasant Meadows, the principal or vice-principal would use the loudspeaker system to announce the day's events, describe the lunch menu, give words of encouragement or warning, and then turn the microphone over to student helpers, who would read the birthdays and announce the winners of any student events. The students were generally noisier during the principal's announcements than when their peers were speaking. After the announcements, the class almost always broke out into a myriad of conversations until the teacher would quiet them down and begin the lesson of the day.

DAILY ROUTINES AND THE DISTRIBUTION OF RESPONSIBILITY

The way the day starts in Oak Grove and Kotani provides a good illustration of how responsibility is determined and assigned in American and Japanese schools. Superficial comparisons of American and Japanese schools tend to depict U.S. schools as open and free and those in Japan as suffering under onerous regimentation. American students have no uniforms and appear to wander freely about the campus before and after school, whereas Japanese students are subject to uniform inspections and teachers organize patrols of neighborhood streets. But a closer examination of American schools shows that administrators and teachers rotate through the school grounds, making sure that some adult is supervising students at all times. At key points in the day, there may be several supervising adults on Oak Grove campuses, particularly at key transition times like bus duty time. Kotani teachers had similar duties, but in Kotani supervision is highly delimited. At the very start of the day, at homeroom time, and during class, young adolescents are with adults. During the teachers' meeting, after school, and in the ten-minute break between classes, there may be no adult near the students.

I have worked with middle schools in Georgia and Pennsylvania in which a police officer is present on campus during the entire school day. In such schools teachers are highly unlikely to leave students unattended even for a few minutes. Teachers and administrators in these schools also used various forms of technology — walkie-talkies, phones in each classroom, and video cameras — to monitor student behavior. Even in the Oak Grove district, police officers would do a walk through of the campus several times a week. Such activities would be simply unimaginable in Japan.

Japanese teachers believe that young adolescents can manage their own behavior given the proper supporting social structure. Japanese teachers closely monitor major transitions: arriving and leaving school, moving to the auditorium for special events, beginning and ending the daily cleaning. In this regard, Japanese and U.S. teachers do not vary. They both perceive transition times to carry a greater risk of disruption: times when students will act irresponsibly. Once Japanese students are engaged in a specific set of routines, however — morning meeting, class work, and cleaning or club activities — teachers believe they will be self-monitoring and that peers will censor disruptive or irresponsible behavior. Individual responsibility is contingent upon group routines and peer monitoring.

The Japanese teachers I interviewed in my own study and for the TIMSS research noted that there were cases in which individual students were not capable of following these routines, and I will discuss some of the incidents I witnessed later in this chapter. Nonetheless, teachers saw the inability to act responsibly as stemming from unusual home conditions. The teachers did not see peer influence as being negative in and of itself. Peer influence, if organized properly, helped young adolescents to learn how to become more responsible, teachers believed.

I found these beliefs to be quite widespread in Japan, even in large urban middle schools in working-class neighborhoods. Conversely, the attitudes of American teachers appeared to be highly affected by the student population. In middle schools in affluent neighborhoods that I have worked with, teachers were more likely to leave students alone. In Oak Grove, teachers were more likely to step out of class for a moment at Pleasant Meadows than at Wade.

Part of the difference in the United States, one might argue, lies in the fact that American society has greater socioeconomic, racial, and linguistic diversity than Japan. My work suggests that this is part of the explanation why U.S. and Japanese teachers tend to expect different things from their students. Japanese teachers in poor schools with large minority populations follow the same basic pattern as the teachers in Kotani.[4] In the United States, even in middle schools that employed full-time police officers, certain students or groups of students were selected to perform tasks (for example, working in the office or on the grounds or taking messages) during which they were not under direct adult supervision. This suggests that U.S. and Japanese teachers differ substantially in the degree to which they see peers as a source of negative influence; in how much they believe teacher-initiated routines can affect student behavior; how much individual variation in student capacity for responsibility they see.

### THE ROLE OF ROUTINES IN THE SCHOOL

Japanese teachers believed in the power of routine. The start of each school day is important in both countries because both groups of teachers believe that disruptions early in the day will snowball toward afternoon, but it was considered crucial in Japan. Kotani teachers were especially concerned with the transition from community to school in the morning. Students arriving by foot and bicycle in the morning were expected to make a transition from home or community norms of behavior to school norms. This transition was marked by a number of daily routines or rituals: teachers and students greeting arrivals, students removing their street shoes and putting on school slippers, teachers and peers offering standard morning greetings in the halls. Once students were ensconced in the classroom and the routine of the morning meeting had been activated, teachers appeared to relax a bit and let down their guard.

This emphasis on group routine is consistent with general Japanese expectations that a function of elementary and middle school education is to teach children and young adolescents to learn how to work in large groups (*shūdan seikatsu*). In fact, almost every aspect of life in a Japanese middle school is arranged so that some group is responsible for the conduct of its members. Student greeters stood alongside Mrs. Kawaguchi on her morning duty, and in each class various students have specific duties to perform within the context of the functioning of the larger class. Individual responsibility is thus never really individual: it is always linked to others in some form.[5]

This was not the case in Oak Grove, where responsibility for or supervising of student behavior is largely in the hands of the teachers and administrators, and each student is expected to be responsible for himself or herself only. There is little overall expectation that a class would be responsible for the conduct of its members.[6] Student positions in Oak Grove were very limited — students with honors grades were selected to help in the office and act as runners to carry messages to classes but had no specific assignments. There was no systematic curriculum designed to incorporate students into the run-ning of the day-to-day life of the schools, as in Japan.

## Extracurricular Events and Teacher Supervision

The evidence so far shows that Kotani teachers place a great deal of responsibility for the daily operation of the school on the student groups and routines, while Oak Grove teachers place responsibility on adults to manage situations and may give individual students extra responsibility or privilege. Individual students, deemed responsible to monitor their own behavior, may be assigned to specific tasks in Oak Grove, but leaving large groups of students unattended by an adult was strictly avoided. Delegation of responsibility to large groups of students was part of the standard routines in Japan.

Studying extracurricular events can help to clarify these patterns of expecta-tions even further. In both school districts, students are engaged in a number of after-school activities, and teachers are generally responsible for supervising their activities. Teachers assigned more responsibility to students for manag-ing their own affairs after school was over than they did during the school period. In both nations, students involved in extracurricular activities were perceived as being both more socially mature and more academically compe-tent.[7] By making a commitment to put in time and effort in clubs or sports, students signaled to teachers that they were capable of a higher level of respon-sibility. In both nations, teachers believe that students who have exhibited appropriate behavior in such extracurriculars are more responsible (i.e., more adultlike).

This fact is highly salient. Teachers in both countries use capacity for re-sponsibility to distinguish between student levels of maturity. But in Oak Grove, teachers assigned far more responsibility to individual students for planning and carrying out extracurricular activities than the Kotani teachers did. With regard to extracurricular activities, Japanese teachers tried to im-pose the same kinds of routines that they used during the school day. They sought to organize students into consistent sets of group routines. Again, once these group routines were put in place, teachers tended to reduce their moni-toring of student behavior.

For example, at Aratamachi, teachers in charge of the seventh grade field trip spent meeting after meeting going over the details of the route, what to do about bathrooms, how much money students could bring, and what kinds of snacks students would be allowed to bring. These planning sessions were typical of the preparation that occurred before any event in Japanese middle schools. At the event itself, teachers often were detached from direct supervision of the event, just as they were often detached from the day-to-day running of affairs. The use of routines and detailed planning mean that at the time of the event, teachers do not have to take direct control of events.

In sharp contrast, U.S. teachers tend to let students make many significant decisions for extracurricular events and to bear the responsibility for any problems or deficits in performance or preparation. I do not mean that Oak Grove teachers let students carry out dangerous activities or let them fail. On the contrary, they monitor extracurriculars carefully but do not intervene unless there is risk involved in some proposed activity. The Oak Grove teachers encourage students and provide guidance but do not micromanage students as do the Kotani teachers.

Preparation for a talent show at Pleasant Meadows, for example, proceeded with minimal planning or direction from the teachers. Students were largely responsible for determining the form and content of the event. They planned ticket sales and went shopping (with parents) for materials. Not only was teacher involvement more limited than would have been characteristic in Kotani, but teachers did not worry about the success or failure of an event the way Kotani teachers did. Kotani teachers spent a great deal of time organizing, planning, and directing to assure that the events would go smoothly and that each student would feel that he or she had successfully participated. Pleasant Meadow teachers let the students decide how much they needed to prepare or rehearse in order to assure a quality performance.

The result of these two styles is that performances in Kotani schools (for example, choral competitions) tended to be relatively uniform across groups, without any exceptional performances. The performances at Oak Grove's talent show ranged from out-of-tune solos to remarkably innovative dance numbers with live music. Moreover, the kinds of performances included traditional singing and instrumental pieces, dances, and drama skits as well as performances that choreographed music and dance.[8] Students received the level of applause that the audience deemed fit.

Again, there was little variation in how extracurriculars were conducted across schools in Japan. Teachers in a wide range of middle schools, like their Kotani counterparts, assumed responsibility for providing a detailed frame for each event students participated in, spending a great deal of time planning and organizing, then pulling back and allowing students to interact during the event with reduced supervision. In the United States, however, schools varied in terms of the responsibility they assigned to students.

At Wade, teachers organized the festival more than at Pleasant Meadow; students were involved in the planning only to a limited degree. Teachers decided the events and conducted the performances in each room. The teachers also determined the order of the events. On the day of the festival, students were given a schedule that instructed them as to when and what rooms they were supposed to see; each room was dedicated to a specific activity, like storytelling. The only input that students appeared to have was in the kind of costumes they chose to wear. In subsequent years, it appears that students have become more involved in the planning of this event.[9]

Students as a group were assigned high degrees of responsibility in Kotani schools to carry out specific tasks or routines. On a day-to-day basis, both students and teachers were involved to a high degree in managing the daily operations of the school. When coordinating special events, however, Kotani teachers literally orchestrated the entire event, planning each stage in minute detail. This suggests that Kotani teachers did not expect young adolescents to be able to act responsibly when teacher-organized (i.e., school-based) routines were not in place. Moreover, Kotani teachers tried to make sure that all groups performed much alike, which tended to remove responsibility from groups and individuals for the quality of their performance.

In Oak Grove, students were generally not given any responsibility for carrying out day-to-day school routines. Throughout the day, the mass of students was highly supervised by adults, who acted as the source of order or authority. Individual students or small groups of students were sometimes given remarkable leeway to organize and carry out events at the school.[10] Indeed, teachers tended to emphasize student participation more in these extracurricular events. The U.S. middle schools displayed two separate and distinct modes of distributing responsibility to students. The teachers also emphasized that each group or individual was responsible for his or her performance, thus making extracurriculars significant learning experiences in taking on responsibility. Teachers in Oak Grove expected and believed there were wide differences in how much responsibility students could take. In Oak Grove schools, responsibility was assigned according to individual characteristics, whereas in Kotani it was diffused over groups via established routines.

Extracurricular events play very different roles in U.S. and Japanese schools. In Japan, clubs and special events appear to be extensions of the social curriculum of the school and are characterized by the same planning and routines as daily activities.[11] In the United States, extracurricular events are distinct from the daily set of routines and expectations. Students are given more autonomy and are given opportunities to learn how to plan, manage, and otherwise take on responsibility for a task. My work suggests that extracurricular activities (clubs, sports, excursions, and special events) play a crucial role in U.S. middle grades education precisely because they allow students to develop responsibility in ways in which class work does not.

## Exceptional Incidents

Daily routines and common activities provide data on the basic patterns of expectations and norms in any given society or organization. Critical incidents — events that surprise participants or otherwise disrupt the expected order — offer another way to assess implicit norms or beliefs. In analyzing my field notes, I found that in both nations I had detailed accounts of how administrators dealt with incidents involving bribes and theft among students. How teachers and administrators worked to deal with theft further illustrates the implicit assumptions about adolescent capacity for responsibility that are in play in each nation. The two incidents also demonstrate how basic beliefs (e.g., individual versus group responsibility) result in organizational routines that then have specific, if often unintended, consequences for teachers.

### GUILTY PARTIES

Murata is small even for a seventh grader, and standing before his seniors in the Furukawa fencing club, Miuchi and Yabushita, he appears a slingless David facing two Goliaths.[12] But as Mr. Yamagata (Murata's homeroom teacher and coach of the fencing club) and Mrs. Kawaguchi (the chair of the ninth grade teachers) look on, a tear forms and runs down *Yabushita's* face. With great effort he apologizes for taking Murata's money. After Yabushita finishes, Miuchi, the captain of the fencing club, acknowledges that *he* should have returned the three hundred dollars that older boys in the club had taken from Murata over the past six months. Miuchi declares, "It was my fault entirely. I did not fulfill my responsibilities as captain of the fencing club. I let the club down."

Although the teachers know that Murata offered most of the money to the older boys — and that he stole the cash from his parents' cafe — at this point they completely ignore the issue of theft and treat the incident as the sole responsibility of the senior boys in the club.[13] In one-on-one interviews with Yabushita and Miuchi, Mrs. Kawaguchi has relentlessly pounded home the point that because they are seniors it was their duty to set a positive example and assure that other members of the club did not break club rules. This formal apology, then, has been orchestrated more for their benefit and the fencing club's than for Murata's. In Mrs. Kawaguchi's opinion, it is crucial to the educational success of the two older boys that they reflect on how they failed in their role as seniors and be prepared to make amends.

Murata had joined the fencing club because he felt it was something he might be good at. In elementary school, Murata had not been successful at sports because of his smallness, and upon entering middle school he joined a club in order to pursue an activity he had not tried. Club attendance is mandatory in Kotani, and teachers strongly believe that the club experience is a significant part of a student's education. The fact that Murata's seniors were lax enough to accept money from him was a source of great concern to the teachers. As Mrs. Kawaguchi remarked, juniors are expected to learn to obey their seniors' orders without complaining. Thus, the senior members' power can easily be used to pressure or extort junior members, and this kind of problem is not uncommon in middle schools. So it was imperative for the teachers to regain the trust of the fencing club members in the senior-junior relationships by calling on Miuchi and Yabushita to take public responsibility for what they had done.

Because clubs are so important in the life of the school, Mrs. Kawaguchi and Mr. Yamagata wanted to make sure that the fencing club hierarchy managed and disciplined the situation in a way teachers thought appropriate. As seniors, Miuchi and Yabushita were held responsible. Mrs. Kawaguchi accented their responsibility while downplaying Murata's. They were ordered to collect money from all the other fencing club students who had taken Murata's money and return it to him, which they did at the time of the formal apology. Mrs. Kawaguchi consciously orchestrated a series of events that illustrated to Miuchi and Yabushita the mistakes they had made and the moral lessons they should learn. She specifically described to Yabushita the shame he should feel and the resolve to correct his mistakes that such shame should bring.

As the ninth grade committee chair Mrs. Kawaguchi felt it was her responsibility to make sure that ninth graders Yabushita and Miuchi received appropriate counseling. Both boys were entering a crucial time in their life preparing for the upcoming high school entrance examination. Coordinating her efforts with other teachers, Mrs. Kawaguchi repeatedly met with the two boys and had them write reflective papers on the matter, sometimes scolding them for up to half an hour.[14] She called an after-school meeting with Yabushita's parents. The next day I asked her how it went. She said, "Oh, it was a great success. His mother cried and his father got angry and shouted. When we see that [kind of parental reaction] we know the student will change for the better. Yabushita-kun was very moved and he also cried."

Mrs. Kawaguchi and Mr. Yamagata apparently thought the breakdown in the club hierarchy was a far more pressing problem than Murata's troubles. They did not ignore Murata (Mr. Yamagata spent hours talking with him after school), yet their immediate concern was reestablishing order in the fencing club. Only in subsequent sessions with Murata and his mother was the issue of theft raised. Moreover, Murata's individual responsibility in the breakdown of the fencing club's function of inculcating certain values was downplayed. The club, as a group, was held accountable and therefore the leaders of the group were held responsible.

WHO DONE IT?

The following account of an incident involving theft and peer conflict was recorded at Pleasant Meadows Middle School. The first two hours of the morning, Dave Jarvis has been responding to various calls from teachers about classroom disturbances. He has just returned to his office after quieting students in a class with a substitute teacher. There are two boys waiting for him outside his office.[15]

Ben is a tall, slightly overweight African-American boy. His Bengal tiger sweatshirt has streaks of yellow dirt, and he slumps back in his chair. Oliver is a slender, angular Euro-American boy dressed in a clean white shirt and jeans. This is the first time I have met Ben. Oliver, on the other hand, is well known to me from classes and from teacher gossip. His older brother, Jesse, has been the subject of much rumor around the school for his disruptive behavior and defiant attitude.

Oliver accuses Ben of stealing his holographic video game cards: the video-age equivalent of baseball cards, video game cards depict figures from cartoons, comics, or video games in a three-dimensional layout. The problem surfaced in third period English class when the boys got into an argument. Oliver discovered his binder of cards was missing. Both boys have been here for about twenty minutes. Dave calls Pierre (a third boy from the class) from class to be a witness for Oliver. Dave expresses his exasperation: "Should I even waste my time on this? Oliver, you know you are not supposed to bring cards in. Should I just let your Mom call the police?"

Dave called Ben's house to confirm Ben's story that he had just bought some cards. The father was out (he works nearly forty miles away in another city), but the father's girlfriend confirmed that Ben was given ten dollars to buy new cards. At this point, Dave departs to attend a previously arranged meeting with Stan (the principal) and leaves the boys alone in the office with me, with the door open, telling them to come to some settlement among themselves.

Oliver and Pierre accuse Ben of stealing the cards. Ben adamantly maintains that the cards are his. Pierre describes how he saw Ben "messing around" with Oliver's bag. He says that he saw Ben take something out of the bag. However, Oliver kept his cards in a type of green folder which many of the students have, so there is no way to be sure Ben took Oliver's folder. Pierre further accuses Ben of trying to sell some of Oliver's cards to him. Oliver and Pierre now get excited as they talk about the Spiderman card they believe that Ben tried to sell. This card, they say, is very rare (worth fifty dollars) and can't be found readily in the local card shops. Having this card in his possession would prove Ben did it.

The case is full of twists and turns. Ben admits he had a Spiderman card but says he has already sold the card to someone else. Just as this revelation comes to light, Dave brings in Michael, Roy, and Nick, who have been accused of throwing an eraser at a substitute — an offense punishable by suspension. Michael describes the scene: "The whole room was up and moving. One kid threw an eraser at the sub. Somebody yelled, 'Michael you did it.'"

Dave sends Oliver and Pierre back to class. Ben is made to wait in the office. Dave meanwhile questions Michael, Roy, and Nick, trying to find out who threw a small lemon-colored, heart-shaped pencil eraser at the substitute teacher. The offending bit of rubber sits on Dave's desk, and he toys with it occasionally. Rachel, a chubby girl in a stripped shirt, is called in. She says that she saw Mike pick up the eraser. Dave, however, seems inclined to think that Nick did it and tells him, "If you are in here again, I'll have to suspend you." The office secretary pokes her head in and says in a strained voice that the teacher in 112, yet another classroom, needs an administrator.

Dave ignores this, and we proceed to walk to Nick, Roy, and Michael's classroom. Dave takes over from the substitute, a rotund man in jeans and a jeans-shirt with round eyeglasses, and berates the class for not listening to the substitute. Nick and many of the other kids giggle when Dave holds up the offending eraser.

We leave this class and go back to the office. Besides Ben, six other young adolescents are waiting to see Dave, and we still have not visited 112. We quickly go out to yet another classroom so that Dave can check on a new substitute, and then proceed back to the office, where Dave takes two fifth graders (a boy and girl) and brings them into the office. The boy called the girl dumb and the girl hit the boy. Dave brings up the young adolescents' telephone numbers on his computer screen and calls the parents. Both are given detention; the little girl is sobbing though the boy seems nonchalant.

It is now lunchtime. Ben is still waiting, but Dave has to supervise the lunch line and also hand out balls for students to play with on the basketball courts. Returning near the end of lunch period, Dave finds the office is now clear of students except for Ben. Ben has been there since the beginning of third period (more than three hours). Dave gives him some pretzels since the boy did not get a chance to eat any lunch. Dave tries again to call the father and gets through, confirming that Ben did have money for cards. The father agrees to round up any cards Ben has at home and bring them into the school. Finally, late in the fifth period, Ben is given a pass to go back to class at the start of sixth period.

Ben and the card incident quickly dropped out of sight. Each day brought similar loads of student problems to the vice-principal's office. When I asked Dave about the incident two days later, I found out that Ben's father had come in after school the next day bringing Ben and all of *his* cards. Oliver was not able to positively identify any of the stolen cards. The Spiderman card had somehow been returned. I asked Dave if it might be possible that Oliver was lying and that Ben was in the clear all along. He answered, "No, I think he took them, but he's smart enough to get away with it."

WHO'S RESPONSIBLE?

Both Murata and Ben were involved in incidents in which theft, lying, and conflict among students were central issues: Murata stole money from his mother's coffeeshop to offer to seniors in order to buy their friendship, and Ben was accused of stealing cards. Murata's theft came to light in the context of the fencing club, Ben's in class. Despite these and other divergences in details, the way that teachers and administrators dealt with the boys demonstrate striking differences in how responsibility was distributed and the concomitant organizational roles and delegation of responsibility among adults.

Oak Grove teachers were not responsible for students in the way that Kotani teachers were. Any kind of disruption in a Kotani middle school, whether in the homeroom teacher's class or not, is the homeroom teacher's primary responsibility. In the Murata case, the homeroom teacher had a number of people that he could call on for assistance or even to temporarily take over the matter. This form of discipline referral is found throughout Japan, and the homeroom teacher is never left out of the process.[16] In Oak Grove, once the adolescent was referred to the vice-principal the teacher was rarely involved in what happened. Oak Grove teachers even said to their students, "Look I don't want to send you out. If you get sent down to the principal's office, it's an automatic detention."

Responsibility was highly individualized and contextualized. Each person, teacher or adolescent, is responsible for his or her behavior in U.S. schools, and administrators must take this into account in dealing with any incident. Dave could not ask Ben and Oliver's homeroom teacher to solve the issue, and he certainly could not hold the class responsible. He attempted to put responsibility on the boys to find a solution, but when that failed, he became responsible for resolving the incident. And when Dave tried to make the disruptive classrooms he visited take responsibility as a group, he met with limited success and numerous individual complaints: "It wasn't me," "I didn't do it."

Consequently, the vice-principal's office in every middle school I have worked with is virtually awash in students on some mornings. At Wade 187 students passed through the office for one reason or another during one *morning* that the secretaries described as medium.[17] Each of these young adolescents expected that the office staff would deal with him or her as an individual. So even if only a fraction of students are discipline referrals, vice-principals are unable to spend adequate time on each case. Dave did want to counsel the students he dealt with, and I watched his frustration on most days when he had to play cop or administer "fast-food discipline" as he described it. Dave frequently expressed his dislike of the vice-principal job and resigned after one year.[18] The organization of both Oak Grove schools appeared to set up a process in which the vice-principal is essentially made to be judge and jury in cases like that of Ben and Oliver.

In the exceptional incidents that had taken place in Furukawa and Aratamachi in the past, the entire class was questioned, and everyone was held somewhat responsible — sometimes an entire grade may be asked to write papers in which they reflect on an incident.[19] At all points in Kotani, responsibility was expanded to include as many actors as possible. In Oak Grove, it was limited to as few individuals as possible. Consequently, there were far fewer incidents requiring the attention of senior teachers or administrators. The grade-level chairs or the head of student guidance had time to concentrate on cases like Murata's, playing detective to a degree that both Oak Grove vice-principals would have admired. Indeed, my impression was that both of the Oak Grove vice-principals were highly aware of the constraints that the organization of discipline referral placed on their effectiveness as administrators.

Both Dave and Mrs. Kawaguchi had a problem they felt compelled to address, but the overwhelming demands of time and other students pushed Dave toward the most immediate solution: get the cards back to Oliver and, if evidence warranted it, punish the thief. Mrs. Kawaguchi had both the time and the support to frame the problem broadly and work on getting Miuchi and Yabushita to recognize and understand why they had acted wrongly and to restore confidence in the hierarchy of the fencing club. The returning of the money was of little consequence as restitution but of significant consequence as a symbolic enactment of responsibilities and duties within a group.

Responsibility is directed at the individual at every turn in American schools. If the individual breaks the rules (and steals) the individual is to be punished. If an individual breaks the rules in a Japanese school, the act warrants an investigation into the actions of everyone connected with that individual to see how they might or might not have prevented it. Fundamental assumptions about what individual responsibility is differ: Americans emphasize an individual failing when rules are broken (e.g., "I wasn't told it was against the rules" or "He threw the eraser, I just watched"), and Japanese emphasize the damage to the group ("I let the fencing club down.")

Moreover, the system in Oak Grove and in many American middle schools denies the main actor (the vice-principal) access to the information he or she needs. Classroom teachers are far closer to the squabbles of the students than an administrator. If the students in Ben and Oliver's class had been asked to write papers and the papers had been compared by the teacher for inconsistencies in the way Mrs. Kawaguchi had done, there would undoubtedly have been more detailed information available to Dave. Under the system then in place, Dave was never able to resolve the incident to his satisfaction. For Ben, forced to wait and miss three hours of class time, the event must have seemed a terrible injustice. Because of his prior contact with the office, he was assumed guilty until proven innocent.

The emphasis on individual responsibility works in such a way that action becomes uncoordinated within the organization. Discipline problems are referred to the office, special counseling is referred out to certified counselors, and fights are referred to the police.[20] In U.S. schools the teacher's responsibility or connection to the young adolescent is weak compared to the Japanese teacher's. At no point did the teacher of Oliver and Ben's English class know what the decision was, nor do I think that she tried to find out. It was not her responsibility.

## Japanese Perceptions of American Responsibility

This structuring of responsibility in the United States may explain why Abiko (1989) was so puzzled by American adolescents' inability to take responsibility for their actions. The first section of Abiko's ethnography of a Florida middle school is entitled "Your responsibility." At many points in the day, he argues, the school is organized to focus responsibility on adolescents, who in turn work hard to avoid responsibility. Having spent nearly a year observing in a Florida middle school (his daughter attended a neighboring middle school), Abiko noted how responsibility was handled differently from Japan. He argued that each adolescent is required to bear the entire brunt of his or her actions, even if others may have played a role by instigating that behavior. Abiko thought that such responsibility was too much for most young adolescents to accept — hence they tried to avoid it.

Like the teachers at Furukawa and Aratamachi, Abiko had an innate expectation that at puberty and for some time thereafter (essentially through middle school) students are *kodomo*. That is, they are essentially *junsui*—pure, innocent, untainted. His shock at seeing students lie to teachers, evade responsibility, and dodge the truth is evident throughout his book. His astonishment at the sophistication of adolescent prevarication and at the way they dodged responsibility shows that he, like the teachers at Furukawa and Aratamachi, expects most young adolescents to be obedient (*sunao*) and compliant (*otonashii*).

For example, the Kotani teachers I talked with told me about offenses they had counseled (ranging from gum chewing to substance abuse) without indicating to me that they thought the student might be deliberately deceiving or manipulating them. The middle school student, even one as troubled as Murata, is still considered to have a pure core. Over and over I was struck by this faith. In the Murata case, I asked Mrs. Kawaguchi if she didn't worry about the boys lying. She readily acknowledged that they would at first try to hide the facts, but that as soon as she began to cross-question them rigorously they would tell everything.

In fact, both Miuchi and Yabushita did try to hide how much money they had received from Murata. When I pointed this out to Mrs. Kawaguchi, she said that they were scared of being punished and so tried to hide (not lie about) the amount. She also said that she would have scolded them less severely if they had told the whole truth immediately. And in scolding Yabushita, Mrs. Kawaguchi vigorously pressed him for more details: "Did you really tell us all the money you got? You haven't been truthful with us up to now. How much money did you take?"

Mrs. Kawaguchi, then, exhibited inconsistencies between what she said she believed and how she acted. She was aware that Yabushita was lying (or not telling the whole truth) because she had read Miuchi's reflection sheet (*hanseisho*), and the amounts and times didn't tally. (Miuchi and Yabushita were repeatedly asked to rewrite their reflection sheets until Mrs. Kawaguchi was satisfied with the content.) After the meeting with Yabushita's parents, however, Mrs. Kawaguchi appeared to have her trust in Yabushita restored. It seemed as if his emotional outburst convinced her that he had indeed realized his mistakes.

It appears, then, that except in extreme circumstances Kotani teachers do not see the child as *willfully* bad. Teachers obviously were aware that a middle school student can obfuscate but often made a distinction between this and willful deception. It was expected that Japanese students would readily admit most mistakes and apologize for them. Admitting a mistake, in Japanese schools, immediately opens inquiries into who else was involved, and responsibility for the offense is usually diffused. What Abiko saw that so shocked him was willful deception: young adolescents "coolly evading" the truth. Yet, at the same time, Abiko was struck by the sense of self, the confidence these American adolescents possessed.

Viewed from the Japanese cultural perspective, there is an underlying belief in American society that human beings are autonomous, almost isolated, individuals solely responsible for their actions, and that Americans learn at a very early age to guide their actions by their own internal moral compass. School-teachers, like most Americans, are not likely to accept the excuse "everyone else was doing it." Nor are they likely to hold everyone responsible if only one or two individuals were caught in some infraction. For the Japanese, who possess an underlying sense of self that is more diffuse, who hold people responsible for their own and others' actions, and who regard group consensus as a powerful moral compass, it would be unnatural to impute such strict individual responsibility to young American adolescents. Although Japanese tend to be impressed by the overall maturity of young adolescents, many would wonder if American schools assign responsibility in ways that hinder young adolescents' learning how to accept responsibility as part of a group.

## Implications

The topic of responsibility elicits several key differences in Japanese and American teachers' conceptions of the individual. Is responsibility assigned to individuals or to groups? Japanese teachers prefer to assign responsibility to groups and Americans to individuals. When is a student responsible, when is a teacher responsible? Japanese tend to create minute rules and routines to clarify responsibility, while Americans are comfortable with distributing responsibility to individuals and letting individuals gauge the situation. What things are students expected to be responsible for? Americans expect children to be responsible and mature as they grow up, but they also expect that the effects of adolescence will make them somewhat irresponsible. In Japan, teachers expect young adolescents to responsibly carry out most of the activities of the school if they are given clear structure and orientation.

Teachers in Japan expect young adolescents to be responsible for a number of orderly transitions throughout the day and do not assume that constant teacher presence is needed. On the other hand, Japanese teachers also assume that it is the teacher's responsibility to notice warning signs — uniforms in disarray or illegal hair styles — and to maintain a highly ordered atmosphere in which each group of students knows its duties and how to carry them out. Japanese teachers monitor certain aspects of student life in minute detail while simultaneously allowing students to go unsupervised for long periods of time.

This means a heavy workload for teachers, at least at the elementary and middle grade levels.

Japanese schools demand tremendous conformity in external presentation. In addition to school uniforms, schools require students to behave with certain decorum coming and going from school. Any irregularities in the basic routine — whether an incorrect uniform, use of nail polish, or too much talking at student assembly — were interpreted as signaling potential problems in either individual or group routine. Thus Japanese schooling does not give students much chance to develop a sense of individual responsibility or to practice making decisions independent of others. Rather, school reinforces adolescents' sense of belonging (and responsibility for) overlapping groups.

American teachers assign individuals the responsibility for their deportment and tend to allow students as much latitude as possible in dress, mannerisms, and other forms of external appearance. In the United States, rules are also essential to order, but every individual is responsible for knowing and following the rules. Teachers and administrators clearly explain the rules and then expect students to follow them. The school provides adolescents with instruction in proper behavior, but it is the responsibility of the adolescent, the parent, or, in some cities, the police to enforce these behaviors.[21] When young adolescents break the rules, teachers (and students) believe they should reap the consequences. This means that many young adolescents will try to dodge responsibility because they have not reached a level of maturity required to accept it. And students may develop a resentment against school or a belief in the injustice of the school as teachers and administrators can never perfectly catch all the students whose behavior bothers others. On the other hand, students who excel academically and who manage responsibility well are allowed special privileges or given special assignments.

The Oak Grove schools that I observed used a form of discipline referral commonly used across the United States. This organization of discipline so overloads the vice-principal (or other assigned disciplinarian) that students had a good chance of evading punishment altogether by denying their actions. The flip side of "It's your responsibility" is "It's not my fault." In a system like Kotani's, students are better off quickly admitting their involvement and displaying a willingness to take responsibility, acts which often result in a reduced sentence. U.S. vice-principals rarely have time to read and compare reflection papers, as Mrs. Kawaguchi did. If, as in the case of the thrown eraser at Pleasant Meadows, no one can be clearly isolated, no punishment is usually given. Young adolescents thus get lessons in taking and evading individual responsibility. The focus on individual responsibility in U.S. schools gives young adolescents ample opportunity to exercise their own will, but creates situations in which neither teacher nor administrators have the time to adequately deal with individual students when problems arise.

On the other hand, responsibility in Japanese schools is diffuse and encompassing in the sense that many people are responsible for any given incident. This results in a very limited sense of the individual's realm of action and responsibility. The organization (school or, later, work) may place broad claims on members' actions, even to the point of dictating how they should dress and behave when not present at the physical location and during what Americans would call private time. Adolescents have little opportunity to experiment with (and reap the consequences of) making decisions on their own. Japanese teachers, then, must work very hard to get students to think about their individual goals and make decisions about their future life.[22]

## Summary

Teachers in both nations basically believe that young adolescents are capable of learning to take on responsibility in an adult manner and organize the school day in ways that encourage young adolescents to take responsibility as it is defined in that culture. The fact that Oak Grove and Kotani teachers had such divergent beliefs about and expectations for responsibility clearly demonstrates that there are powerful differences between Japanese and Americans in terms of their beliefs in the nature of the individual, the self, and the development of the will.

Specifically, Japanese school organization and practices indicate a belief in a fluid or loosely define sense of self. Furthermore, one's ability to take responsibility for one's individual actions is something that young adolescents are not expected to be readily able to do outside of a highly organized social environment. U.S. school organization and practices indicate that young adolescents are ready to take on some responsibility and should already have developed a concrete or highly defined sense of self. Teachers expect the school to provide only a loosely organized environment in which there are clear boundaries to appropriate behavior, but in which individuals can make many choices and bear the responsibility of having made those choices.

The American tendency to isolate responsibility and thereby increase the consequences for individuals of personal success and failure appears to have the effect of making many young adolescents seek to avoid taking responsibility while others learn to excel at being responsible. The Japanese tendency to diffuse responsibility, increasing the consequences for individuals of group success or failure, appears to have the effect of making young adolescents overall very vulnerable to peer pressure and group attitudes. The Japanese belief that external appearance affects one's internal state of affairs acerbates this tendency, making it difficult for Japanese teachers to stimulate young adolescents to speak out for themselves.

Abiko's reaction to young adolescents in Florida perfectly captures the Japanese cultural attitude. Given his Japanese background, to Abiko American middle school students seemed adultlike, ready to express their preferences and opinions. On the other hand, he thought that they lied shamefully and would not own up to their actions. In the same way, Americans who go to Japan are highly impressed by the good behavior of Japanese young adolescents but shocked by the degree to which teachers manage student lives. Over the years I have participated in various educator exchange programs and watched these reactions time and time again. Each group sees something positive in the other side but does not seem willing to accept the costs associated with the positive feature.[23]

Having demonstrated how the common concern with responsibility is expressed in ways consonant with different cultural beliefs about the individual and will, in the next chapter I pursue an analysis of how teachers think about the process of maturation, especially physical and mental maturation. Both U.S. and Japanese teachers believe that young adolescents are approaching adulthood yet have differing ideas about what kind of responsibility the young adolescent was ready for. I use puberty as a means to understand what changes teachers expect to see (i.e., what they believe is the normal course of human development), how they react to these changes, and how they think these changes affect adolescent behavior.

# 4

## *Puberty and Sexuality — Hormones, Energy, and Rebellion*

It's ridiculous to put all those eighth graders, with their hormones raging, all together.                                  — Lynn Jing, Pleasant Meadows

The kids that are growing really start to take off. In terms of grades and also in a mental way, we say the kids are being fulfilled (becoming complete). I'd guess they have come into the most intense period of life.
                                        — Yashiko Chino, Furukawa

In chapter 3 I analyzed how Japanese and American teachers dealt with the common problem of responsibility, a dominant theme on both sides of the Pacific. The topic of this chapter, puberty, was not. Puberty was a major topic for U.S. teachers but was rarely mentioned by Japanese teachers. This does not mean that Japanese teachers did not see or believe in puberty. Rather, they thought puberty was an important but limited phase in the natural development of youth. For Americans, puberty was an extended, difficult phase that gave rise to problems for young adolescents and educators.

In studying how teachers determined an adolescent's level of maturity — for example, just how much responsibility he or she could take on — I found that teachers used many factors to make their assessment. They used past behavior to gauge mental and emotional ability, but they also often mentioned physical development. In the early days of my pilot study it was difficult to find a point to begin talking about adolescence with Japanese teachers. In struggling to translate terms like "adolescence," "developmentally appropriate," or "at risk," I discovered that puberty was recognized in both cultures. The physical events of puberty (e.g., menarche, growth spurt, changes in body fat ratio, appearance of facial hair, etc.) are universal in normal human development and provide a starting point from which to begin mapping teachers' beliefs about adolescent development.

Teachers at Aratamachi and Furukawa use the word "puberty" (*shishunki*) spontaneously and connect it with menarche, a growth spurt, and an increased awareness of sexuality and the opposite sex. In both Oak Grove and Kotani schools, puberty was linked by adults to a set of changes in the bodies and minds of young adolescents. Teachers perceived that physical and emotional changes were related and had a significant impact on the behavior of young adolescents. But, as the two epigraphs above show, American and Japanese teachers emphasize different aspects of the change, and Americans and Japanese draw varying conclusions about the effects of puberty and how schools should respond. Oak Grove teachers tend to focus on issues of biological change that entail emotional turmoil and potential mental and behavior problems. Kotani teachers tend to focus on the physical and mental energy of the pubescent, especially their bright (*akarui*) disposition.[1] As I will show, U.S. teachers also think puberty starts earlier and lasts longer than do teachers in Japan. And, most significantly, American teachers attribute many negative behavioral traits specifically to pubertal changes (raging hormones), something that none of the Japanese teachers did.

Superficially, one could say that in the United States puberty had largely negative connotations and in Japan it had positive ones. Few, if any, American teachers would respond in the way a middle-aged male Japanese teacher did when I asked him what associations he had with the term "puberty." He replied, "Blue skies and fun!" However, teacher beliefs are more complicated than can be contained in a simple dichotomy. The data in this chapter show that U.S. and Japanese teachers worry about the impact of pubertal changes on adolescent development at different times and in different ways.

I begin by discussing differences in teacher beliefs about the onset and duration of puberty and show how these beliefs are linked to middle grade school organization in both nations. I will then analyze the ways in which teachers believe that puberty affects behavior: the causal links between pubertal change and mental, emotional behavior or academic outcomes. Using the theme of disruption as a focal point, I show that Japanese teachers see the impact of puberty as limited in scope and intensity whereas Americans see puberty as strongly affecting almost every aspect of the young adolescent's life. In particular I note that the American story line — that hormones cause many of the problems of puberty — is not present in Japan. I also show that American teachers tend to link adolescent defiance with rebellion or disruption, whereas Japanese teachers tend to link defiance with resistance (*hankō*).

Teacher beliefs and middle school practices have a powerful impact on young adolescents. The emphasis on the disruptive nature of puberty and the supposed biological imperative of "raging hormones" becomes a self-fulfilling prophecy in the United States.[2] Disruptive behavior is essentially normalized in U.S. middle schools. Older story lines about the promise of youth, which were part of American beliefs about adolescence in G. Stanley Hall's day, have largely disappeared, whereas in Japan such beliefs remain relatively powerful. This difference, I argue, leads Japanese teachers to be active in trying to alter or guide young adolescent behavior because they believe they can substantially change behavior in positive ways. For most U.S. teachers, puberty is an immutable constant in the course of human development, and they are simply unable to change its effects.

## Cultural Expectations for Puberty

A wide variety of cultures have a stage in the life course between childhood and adulthood equivalent to adolescence. The onset of this stage is generally heralded by the arrival of puberty. Other than menarche, however, finding reliable indicators of puberty has proven difficult.[3] From a strictly physiological standpoint, the appearance of genital hair, growth of the genitalia, and girls' breast development are processes that occur over a period of months or years.[4] Some research indicates that traits associated with puberty — breast development and menarche — may occur up to two years apart.[5] Thus societies and cultures throughout the world have used different physiological benchmarks associated with puberty as markers of the pubertal process itself.[6]

Consequently, research on puberty must be framed in models that reflect this complex interaction of biology and culture.[7] That is, neither a strictly social constructivist nor a biological determinist argument adequately describes how humans make sense of pubertal changes.[8] Although puberty is a universal in terms of human development, the exact timing and duration of puberty may vary greatly from individual to individual. This means that a young adolescent may indeed experience biological puberty long before he or she experiences a change in social expectations associated with puberty.

Using the timing of physical development at puberty as a measure of pubertal change, scholars have shown that puberty has effects on self-esteem and school achievement in the United States.[9] Hormonal changes associated with puberty have been linked to general changes in mental health.[10] The onset of puberty, particularly when one is a late or early developer, can have significant ramifications for young adolescents. But what do teachers see as late or early? Are there sets of expectations or norms for pubertal change that are held across a wide range of teachers?

TEACHERS' PERCEPTIONS OF THE TIMING OF PUBERTY

To paraphrase an Oak Grove teacher, "A lot is going on at puberty." Perhaps because puberty is such a complex process — one in which biological and cultural factors interact — there are likely to be major divergences in the way an individual teacher or young adolescent thinks about puberty. While individual teachers in either country might have positive or negative associations regarding puberty, there were clearly identifiable patterns of beliefs in the United States and Japan about the nature of puberty and its relation to social and mental development.

After analyzing my pilot study interviews, I created a survey of teacher beliefs about puberty and administered it to all of the teachers in the four schools in which the fieldwork was conducted, as well as to a group of urban Japanese teachers in Nagoya and teachers or student teachers in Georgia.[11] This was not a random sample, and therefore I have not subjected the data to elaborate statistical tests; nonetheless the differences are intriguing. There are substantial and consistent differences in when and how long Japanese and American teachers believe puberty begins and lasts (see table 4.1). Overall, American teachers saw puberty as lasting far longer than their Japanese counterparts did.

In particular, Americans gave a strikingly early average age of onset of puberty for girls: about ten years of age, more than a full year earlier than Japanese teachers suggested.[12] This would put the average girl experiencing menarche in the fifth grade! Yet researchers in Hawaii found that the average onset of menarche for both Asian and Caucasian populations occurred after age twelve.[13] Japanese teachers saw puberty lasting for about three and a half years for boys to nearly four years for girls while the teachers in Oak Grove thought puberty lasted over five years for both boys and girls.

From a life course perspective, it is significant that the ages given by Japanese teachers for the onset of puberty are consonant with the ages that students start middle school and that the average age of cessation of puberty in Japanese teachers' eyes corresponds with the typical age of a first-year student in high school. The duration of puberty, in the minds of these Japanese teachers, coincided with the middle school years. In contrast, the American teachers

*Table 4.1  Differences Between U.S. and Japanese Teachers In Gauging Onset and Duration of Puberty*

|  | FEMALES | | | | MALES | | | |
|---|---|---|---|---|---|---|---|---|
|  | JAPAN | USA | F | Sig. | JAPAN | USA | F | Sig. |
| Start of Puberty | | | | | | | | |
| Mean | 11.7* | 10.3 | 72.9 | .000 | 13.0 | 11.7 | 56.0 | .000 |
| SD | 1.3 | 1.0 | | | 1.2 | 1.0 | | |
| N | 77 | 97 | | | 77 | 97 | | |
| End of Puberty | 15.5 | 15.3 | .326 | .569 | 16.4 | 16.8 | 1.84 | .176 |
|  | 2.6 | 1.8 | | | 2.4 | 2.2 | | |
|  | 77 | 93 | | | 77 | 93 | | |
| Duration of | 3.7 | 5.1 | 16.4 | .000 | 3.4 | 5.2 | 26.5 | .000 |
| Puberty | 2.4 | 1.9 | | | 2.2 | 2.3 | | |
|  | 77 | 93 | | | 77 | 93 | | |

*The numbers for the start and the end are age, and the numbers for the duration are years.

recorded ages of onset that could include fifth graders in the earliest and seniors in high school in the latest extreme.[14] This suggests that puberty, like adolescent or teenager, is viewed as a more diffuse stage of development in the United States. In the United States, puberty as it is socially or culturally defined is something that can happen from elementary school to high school and that spans at least two levels of schooling.

These survey data would support the interpretation that Japanese teachers do not have the same expectations for pubertal development as U.S. teachers and that certain characteristics associated with puberty in particular and adolescence in general in the United States are more narrowly linked by Japanese adults to middle school students. In the cultural logic of American schools, the behavior of a pimply-faced seventeen year old in a high school might well be linked to puberty by his or her teachers. Teachers in Japan are unlikely to make such a causal link.

The nature of middle grades organization appears to reinforce these separate views. Middle schools in the United States often include sixth and even fifth grades; hence U.S. teachers are probably prone to seeing an earlier puberty. And in the United States some junior high schools include the ninth grade, an organizational feature that would also prompt U.S. teachers to view puberty as rather extended. The irregular organization of middle grades education enhances American views of puberty as a diffuse time. In contrast,

Japanese middle grades education begins with the seventh year of compulsory schooling and ends with the ninth year throughout the nation. Moreover, the end of middle school marks the end of compulsory schooling altogether. Students must pass a high school entrance examination to further their studies. The uniform organization of middle grades schools and the clear transition to high school in Japan tends to limit Japanese teachers' views of the duration of puberty.

The relationship between cultural beliefs and school structure is one of mutual influence. The diffuse nature of American adolescence has been historically documented, as has the tendency of U.S. schools to transmit certain age-graded norms.[15] The organization of U.S. middle grades suggests that Americans believe adolescence is a special time in the life course and requires special attention. The Japanese also believe this, but there appears to be general agreement in Japan that puberty and adolescence are not long-term, disruptive processes. Where the two cultures differ most clearly is in how they view the duration and impact of puberty. While U.S. educators have been seeking the correct form of school to deal with the problem of young adolescents for more than a century, the Japanese appear quite content with the model evolved in the wake of World War II.

### THE HORMONAL STORY LINE

For the Oak Grove teachers, puberty had unsettling implications for education; the onset of puberty was associated with educational problems. The Oak Grove teachers believed that there was a strong association between puberty and the onset of sexual interest or activity, and they had clearly articulated reasons supporting this association. In the minds of Oak Grove's teachers, puberty signaled the fact that hormones had begun to produce changes in the body of the early adolescent. Teachers linked the subsequent behavioral and emotional disruptions that occurred directly to hormonal "imbalance" or "fluctuation."

Hormones are the reason, as one teacher colorfully put it, that adolescents are "so squirrelly." Oak Grove teachers explicitly linked the biophysical processes of puberty with the unique characteristics of the young adolescent and the need for special educational interventions. The condition of puberty alone was enough to destabilize the mental and emotional balance of the young adolescent. Changes in the body of the young adolescent put them out of control, and young adolescents in general were believed to require some kind of counseling or guidance to regain control. Middle school students were, a priori, in need of special treatment. One teacher at a Wade staff meeting said, "Here are kids who are showing middle school needs, middle school characteristics. We need student-counseling groups. They're seeking a place for acceptance. They don't understand what's happening to their body. We need to bring them into student counseling groups."

Oak Grove teachers gave more detailed accounts of the link between student behavior and puberty than that contained in the national and regional literature in the United States. That is, on the local level the story lines of puberty, hormones, and physical, mental, or emotional imbalance were even more embellished than the ones represented in the national literature (see chapter 9). Oak Grove teachers explicitly referred to hormones as the source of a child's inattention, misbehavior, inability to concentrate, poor grades, obsession with the opposite sex, and aggressive behavior.

My observations indicate that the presence of this powerful story line of hormonal disruption affects the ways in which teachers view their students and may even acerbate the very behavior teachers find disturbing. For example, Hattie Sonval at Wade said that a hormonal attraction caused Karenna and Zachariah (seventh grade girl and boy) in her sixth-period class to keep talking to each other. Because of their attraction, Hattie reasoned, they simply *could not* stop talking to each other. Thus it made no sense, in the cultural logic of American middle schools, for Hattie as a teacher to try to counsel or guide these students. Hormones, when they appeared, were seen as simply overpowering. In a similar way, Sandy Briotte at Wade also talked about the sudden changes in one of her students: "The last two weeks he's really been acting up. Must be his hormones acting up. He's a really sweet kid. You don't want to suppress that personality coming out, but. . . ."

In U.S. schools, the adolescent's personality is seen as constituted apart from the effects of the hormones. That is, the young adolescent is perceived to be at the mercy of biophysical processes he or she cannot control. The Oak Grove *Middle School Guide* stated that "chemical and hormonal imbalance during transescence trigger emotions that are little understood by the transescent."[16] Although teachers did not think every adolescent experienced a dramatic puberty, they expressed a belief that all students were affected by puberty and that undergoing a traumatic adolescence was normal. The description of hormonal effects given by teachers resembled a description of some foreign chemical ingested into the body that produced strange, ungovernable behavior. For teachers at Wade and Pleasant Meadows, once hormones turned on, adolescents couldn't control themselves. Self and identity among Oak Grove adolescents were perceived by teachers to be significantly impacted by hormones. The hormonal change, which marked the onset of puberty, was something that stood as a challenge for the adolescent self to overcome: a test of self-control, a test of will.

Teachers' beliefs about hormones were also linked to their ideas about school organization and instruction. Many Oak Grove teachers preferred teaching in the lower grades, shunning the disruptive (hormone-induced) behavior of the seventh and eighth graders. However, while Oak Grove teachers believed that hormonal effects were stronger in the upper grades, hormones were commonly blamed for disruptive behavior among very young students. John Beyer, in a discussion of year-long teaching strategies for the fifth grade, told me, "You have to get a structure in place early. Even if they seem like a good class, halfway through the year they get disordered. The hormones kick in and they are all rambunctious." Discipline and classroom management for all teachers in Oak Grove was impacted by their beliefs in the hormonal story line.

The hormonal story line was simply missing in the Kotani schools.[17] Kotani teachers believed that early adolescents developed a sexual consciousness (*ishiki*) and were interested in members of the opposite sex. Mrs. Chino remarked that about half of the students got boy or girl crazy at sometime in middle school and that this might temporarily impair their ability to study. But Mrs. Chino did not believe that puberty automatically impeded a nascent adolescent's concentration or motivation. Most Kotani teachers did not believe that a heightened awareness of sex or sexuality dictated that all students would go boy crazy or girl crazy. And when young adolescents were crazy about the opposite sex, Kotani teachers saw this phase as decidedly limited: a temporary interruption in the normal adolescent regime of long hours of study and intense club activity.

U.S. teachers express a strong belief in the biological aspect of puberty and adolescence. To use a metaphor from the computer industry, they believe that behaviors are hardwired to hormones. The fact that the most detailed research on the effects of hormones has shown only limited impact on adolescent behavior has not had any observable effect on the teachers I have worked with in California, Pennsylvania, and Georgia. The belief in hormones is an active part of the current culture of American middle grades education, yet in Japan teachers never talk about hormones

### Puberty and Sexuality

Oak Grove teachers also connected the presence of hormones with heightened, even dangerous, sexual drives. In talking about student sexual activity, Nick Brisbane at Wade angrily noted that a fourteen-year-old former student of his was now pregnant even though sometime earlier Nick had asked the mother to put the girl "on the pill." With a strong touch of bitterness in his voice Nick concluded, "We're gonna have an AIDS epidemic around here."

The movie "Nightmare on Puberty Street," shown to all seventh and eighth grades at Pleasant Meadows, portrayed the links between bodily changes at puberty and sexual abuse, sexual relations, and suicide. The sexuality or sexual activity engendered by the hormones was discussed by teachers in ways that emphasized volatility and danger, particularly when groups of students were brought together. Hormonal change, sex, and social disruption were often linked in the stories teachers told.

Walking the halls, teachers at Wade expressed no visible reaction to eighth grade students who were kissing and body pressing each other against the lockers.[18] Puberty, adolescence, and sexuality seemed of one cloth. The teachers appeared to assume that students' lack of sexual control was prima facie evidence of the effect of hormones.[19] Some young adolescents were perceived to lack the self-control or willpower needed to countermand the effects of the hormones.

Kotani teachers did make links between student sexual behavior and school failure, but this link occurred only in extreme cases. Powerful expression of sexual feelings by young adolescents (such as kissing and body pressing) would be highly disturbing to Kotani teachers. Interviews with Aratamachi and Furukawa teachers showed that the teachers linked attraction to erotic pictures with severe mental (*seishin*) and family problems.[20] In only one case (an Aratamachi boy considered to have severe emotional problems) did teachers attribute disruptive behavior to sexual attraction or sexual problems. Kotani teachers reported that normal middle school students would still be innocent (*junsui*) in sexual matters.

In September 1992 the third-year teachers at Furukawa (whose students ranged in age from fourteen to fifteen) met to discuss the worries that the students were having and to design ways to counsel the students. Teachers focused on the upcoming examination season. This was, I learned, a time when students' worries multiply. Throughout the hour-long discussion, the topics of dating, sex, gang activity, pregnancy, and sexually transmitted disease were never mentioned, although they were common topics of discussion in Oak Grove schools.[21] There was a qualitative difference in the way that U.S. teachers and Japanese teachers discussed pregnancy in early (twelve to fourteen year olds) adolescents. In Kotani, such a pregnancy was typically talked about in the abstract and characterized as a rare and tragic occurrence since few teachers had worked with pregnant middle school students. In the United States, many teachers I have worked with have actually had experience with a pregnant young teen in their class.

When sexual contact between young adolescents in Japan was discussed, it was inevitably linked with exceptional circumstances. Mr. Shimoda told me, in a remark made in the hallway and far from the tape recorder, that he thought a couple of girls in the third-year class might be sexually active. But there was no sense that most students would be seriously tempted to engage in sexual intercourse. At Furukawa, which included Kotani's most economically depressed population, both pregnancy and sexual activity among middle school students were considered to be serious but extremely rare problems.[22] Teenage pregnancy was virtually absent in Kotani. The wider acceptance of abortion, its widespread availability, and continued extreme social stigma attached with teenage pregnancy must account for this absence to a large extent. Nonetheless, there was widespread sentiment among parents and teachers that middle school students would not be having sex or be likely to have sex, except in unusual circumstances.

The fact of the matter was that in the day-to-day life of the Kotani schools, teachers and students did not talk about sex very much at all. When the Furukawa teachers believed a girl was sexually active they did not discuss the matter publicly or gossip about it in the teachers' room. The only references I heard to sexually active students were made during guidance meetings and in private interviews I had with teachers. In America, sometimes several times in a week, I overheard snippets of teacher conversation about student sexual activity.

Kotani teachers were aware of what they termed problems in adolescent sexual awareness. Many teachers expressed a concern that high school *and* middle school males who became discouraged in school might become attracted to various types of cartoon pornography available in Japan.[23] The Youth Counseling Center in Kotani in 1992 issued a warning to the schools about certain pornographic books that were being sold in local bookstores under covers that made them appear to be novels. While the Youth Counseling Center's warning was of concern to Kotani teachers, no student at either Furukawa or Aratamachi was actually found to be reading pornographic material during my study.

In the United States, on the other hand, sometimes an adolescent's supposed inability to suppress natural urges occasionally bought students some leniency in discipline. When boys in her class found an advertisement for *Playboy* in a magazine and subsequently disrupted the class by shouting about the pictures, Janice Leitskov quietly took the magazine away but did not scold or reprimand the boys as she usually did when their noise disrupted the class.[24]

In general, teachers in Oak Grove thought that there was a strong connection between puberty and the sexual awakening of the young adolescent, the maturation of secondary sexual characteristics, and a sexual interest in the opposite gender. This strong association between puberty and sex appears common in the United States and is significant because the psychological and physiological changes that generally accompany puberty affect far more than the development of the reproductive organs.

Kotani teachers associated puberty with both an increased awareness of sexuality and curiosity about the opposite sex, but at Aratamachi and Furukawa teachers viewed uncontrollable sexual attraction as distinctly abnormal. Teachers failed to link not only puberty and hormones, but also disruptive behavior and disruptive sexual energy. These differences may be due in part to the fact that Japanese schools have strong rules against dating. Holding hands, let alone kissing, was forbidden in Kotani schools and in all Japanese middle and high schools I visited. Overall, school rules in Japan appear to govern a wider range of behaviors and be more strictly enforced than in the United States, a fact that may account for part of the reason teachers failed to report any connection between puberty and disruptive behavior. In high school, teachers do worry about students dating and not studying, and the high school students I taught often wrote love letters in class, passing them along in the shoeboxes, which served as an underground mailbox system.[25] In the minds of most Japanese, however, middle school students are not believed to be developmentally prone to an overpowering attraction to the opposite sex.

## Puberty and Disruption

Puberty was not all "blue skies and fun" in the minds of Kotani teachers. Teachers made a strong connection between the middle school years and a period of resistance known in Japan as *hankōki*. Such resistance is viewed as a natural phenomenon. Teachers and parents alike noted that students in middle school tended to resist school rules and parental control over their behavior. Only in specific situations was this resistance seen as potentially harmful for the adolescent.

The exact associations around *hankōki* differed somewhat from teacher to teacher. Some saw it as a passing phase on the way to adulthood. In fact, several older teachers expressed the opinion that students in present-day Japan did not resist enough! They thought that today's students did not have the "gumption" to oppose parents and teachers. For most Kotani teachers, adolescent resistance was not directly linked with behaviors like smoking, skipping school, or hanging out with students who had dropped out of school. Kotani teachers were concerned that resistance could evolve into school refusal (*tōkō kyohi*) or dropping out (*ochikobore*) if the student became too discouraged in his or her studies or too isolated from peers, but they believed that all young adolescents would exhibit some resistance as part of the process of maturation.[26] This difference in views reflects different patterns of associations that Kotani teachers had about adolescent development. Teachers generally believed that at puberty the early adolescent experienced an upwelling of energy and experienced the development of the mental faculties. Some teachers thought that students exhibited resistance because they did not wish to grow up and assume the more adultlike responsibilities demanded of middle school students. Other teachers saw resistance as a testing of the limits of parental or school rules. This kind of resistance was generally considered to be positive because the early adolescent would eventually learn that rules are created to ensure that all members of a group (family or school) can coexist given limited space and resources. Some teachers even argued that resistance was an essential characteristic of leaders. To be a leader, one must be able to challenge rules and stand up for one's convictions.

However, when students become disconnected from the positive life of the school and club activities, Kotani teachers reasoned, they were prone to divert their energies into negative behaviors. Kotani teachers strongly linked students' emotional or mental states to the overall spirit or climate of the school. The teachers thought that problems in student behavior were common during times when the ordinary regimen was absent. Disruptive behavior and a resistant attitude were not linked to a physical, hormonal reaction caused by the onset of puberty but to the weak points in the chain or cycle of school involvement: the festival, the summer vacation, the second year—times when students are least connected to school activities. As Setsuko Ritsukawa wrote in a Furukawa Health-Section handout, "Just before and after the cultural festival the connection [relationship—*tsunagari*] to the opposite sex is stronger. Right now, among the girls, there is a change of atmosphere—they're more flashy, more rebellious, and as some would say, apathetic [*mukiryoku*].

In these dangerous transition times students must find some goal, teachers warned. If they did not have a goal, then a resistant attitude could lead to involvement in high-risk behavior. Failure to find goal was often seen as the cause of too strong an interest in the opposite sex, *not vice versa*. The appearance of "flashy" clothes or sloppiness in uniform signaled a troubled or rebellious attitude that could be remedied by strictness in dress, intensive pep talks, and urging of adolescents to set their hopes on high school. Kotani teachers placed great emphasis on routines and motivational exercises as ways to improve the mental and emotional character of the student. The Japanese teachers place heavy emphasis on keeping a tight ship as both prevention and treatment for problems.[27]

In Oak Grove, teachers frequently used words like "rebellious" to describe adolescent behavior. But Oak Grove teachers did not tightly connect puberty with rebellion. Teachers tended to see puberty as a time when hormones were released and the body started growing, leading the young adolescent into difficult conflicts between bodily urges and social restrictions. Defiance of parental authority and rebellion were believed to start even before puberty. Many of the students at Wade who were experiencing difficulties in schools were described as having problems with authority that started in the early years of elementary school. While puberty was seen to accelerate young adolescent desires for autonomy and independence, Oak Grove teachers saw an increase in rebelliousness as part of the more diffuse characteristics of adolescence. Rebellion was partly a function of maturation, partly a function of family influence (see chapter 7). Puberty created an unstable condition that put the young adolescent at risk for rebellious behaviors and attitudes.

## The Role of Teachers in Learning About Sexual Maturation

For both Oak Grove and Kotani teachers, puberty was associated with a changed sexual consciousness. Yet the expression of sexuality and its relation to basic issues of adolescent identity or self-control continued to diverge along the lines described above. In Oak Grove, teachers perceived adolescents to be in a struggle to control their behavior and actions in the face of the effects of hormones. In Kotani, teachers saw themselves as struggling to provide proper channels for adolescent energy and guarding adolescents from situations that might lead to early sexual experimentation. These basic differences in views seemed to give Kotani teachers a greater sense of efficacy and motivated them to work to guide young adolescents.

The role of the teacher in U.S. and Japanese middle schools is cast in very different ways. While teachers in both nations felt that parents expect them to have an impact on young adolescent sexuality, school organization and cultural expectations for the role of the teacher supported Kotani teachers in guiding young adolescents and organizing school activities to maximize teachers' effect on students. In Oak Grove, teachers were supported by neither school organization nor cultural expectation, which meant that any teacher who attempted to become significantly involved in guiding students might place themselves at risk of professional censure or legal action. The effect of these different levels of support can be made clear by examining how teachers dealt with sex education.

### SEX EDUCATION AND VIEWS OF SEXUALITY

Teachers in both nations stated that sex education was a difficult topic to deal with. In Kotani, teachers noted that their main problem was in conveying messages about safe sex and abstinence in middle school. Teachers said that in their elementary school science classes, young adolescents learn that reproduction is good and that curiosity is good. Mrs. Banba said, "We tell them this [sex] is good, this is good in elementary school, and then in middle school we tell them not to do it." These reactions suggest that Japanese teachers may be more concerned about adolescent sexual activity than their reactions toward puberty or teenage pregnancy would indicate. When talking about the topic of sex education, I discovered that many Kotani teachers were worried that young adolescents could become sexually active too early if the school did not provide the proper social atmosphere and guidance.

If anything, Oak Grove teachers viewed sex education as even more difficult, and the topic tended to generate emotionally charged responses about early sexual activity, declining moral standards, parental pressure, and the constraints teachers faced when teaching this class.

In the United States there are significant limits as to what can and can't be taught during sex education classes in public schools. In Oak Grove, the schools circulate a letter informing parents that their child is going to be in a class that includes material on "bodily changes that occur during puberty" and "pregnancy and the birth process." Parents are then asked to sign and return a form either allowing their child to attend the class or not. In sharp contrast, no fliers were distributed and no parents complained about the sex education lessons offered in Kotani, even though classes covered such topics as human sexuality, AIDS, pregnancy, and contraception.

So although Japanese teachers may have some concerns about early sexual activity, they clearly believe that they can provide instruction and guidance that will help prevent sexual activity in young adolescents, and they are generally supported in this work by the community. The situation in Oak Grove was one in which teachers faced not only a difficult topic, but one that appeared politically charged as well. In Charles Johnson's class the tensions around sexuality and reproductive rights in Oak Grove sex education classes surfaced when one student asked him if a fetus is alive. Mrs. Cummings, a middle-aged volunteer who typically was silent for the entire period, interrupted Charles's explanation to state emphatically that the fetus was alive. She later said to me in a whispered aside, "I just didn't want to let that one pass." Teachers in Oak Grove and in many parts of the United States view sex education as difficult not because the topic is embarrassing, but because it can generate potentially divisive conflict with parents.

The idea that sex education is more politically divisive in the United States than in Japan is supported by the content of sex education lessons in Kotani and Oak Grove schools. The most striking difference was the American focus on the biological mechanisms of reproduction and the reproductive organs. Oak Grove teachers tended to focus on terminology (urethra, glans penis, follicle) and biological function rather than on emotional reactions to developmental changes. This focus seemed to resonate with American teachers' perceptions that young adolescents are preoccupied by the biological changes they are going through, the "mechanics" of change in breast size and genital development. The focus on mechanics appeared to be useful to teachers because it allowed them to discuss sexual development without bringing up the potentially divisive issues of birth control, sexually transmitted disease, and abortion.

Much of the sex education instruction that I saw in Kotani focused on disease and pregnancy prevention, the complex nature of sexual relations, and sexual feelings or consciousness. This is due in part to the fact that young adolescents in Kotani elementary schools have been introduced to the mechanics of reproduction in plants and animals in science classes. At Furukawa, Mrs. Banba coordinated sex education classes by year with emphasis on bodily changes for the seventh graders and discussions of puberty, sexual arousal, and "positive sexuality" in the eighth grade. These topics were supplemented by material on AIDS produced by the prefectural office.

Kotani teachers also thought that sex education had a prophylactic effect on later sexual activity. Teachers also saw it as their job to provide students with correct information about sexual diseases, and much of the material on AIDs that Mrs. Banba distributed focused on reassuring students that transmission did not occur from sneezing or using the same toilet. Furthermore, Kotani teachers, in their role as homeroom teachers, frequently dealt with students' questions about physical changes, sexual consciousness, and worries about the opposite sex. Mrs. Kawamura noted that girls in her homeroom class sometimes wrote questions about menstruation and other women's issues in the daily diaries that students keep.

In private, Oak Grove teachers often remarked that they would like to see more detailed information in sex education but pointed to the risk that teachers could incur for raising topics like sexual consciousness, abortion, or even sexually transmitted disease. Oak Grove teachers had no formal mechanism, like the Kotani teachers, through which teachers and students could engage in private discussions pertaining to young adolescents' curiosity or concerns about bodily changes and sexual awareness. This meant that open dialogue about sexuality between young adolescents and adults in Oak Grove was virtually nonexistent, although many teachers saw a greater need for such communication.

The fact that Kotani teachers saw a need for sex education and expressed concerns about early adolescent sexuality when discussing this issue suggests that there may be some conflict within current Japanese society over sex and adolescent sexuality. The concern expressed, however, was far more infrequent and never as charged with emotion as it was in Oak Grove. For Oak Grove teachers, sex education was not just a potentially difficult subject, but a potentially disastrous subject — a fact that suggests deep conflicts in American society about the role of sexual maturation and sexual awareness in adolescent development. While Kotani teachers expected students to be basically pure in terms of sexual activity, they thought that sexual curiosity was a natural part of development and that sex education was a necessary, even effective, part of their repertoire in helping young adolescents understand the bodily and emotional changes they were experiencing. Oak Grove teachers also thought they could do more to help students if they had the freedom to teach sex education courses as they saw fit but were very much afraid of parental pressure. Although several teachers in Oak Grove also believed that sexual curiosity was natural, they did not have the freedom to teach this topic.

## Summary: The Role of Puberty in Middle Grade Schools

Puberty *as it is culturally defined in the United States* is interpreted by Oak Grove teachers to be a universal, biological fact. Teachers at Wade and Pleasant Meadows see puberty as a signal of the onset of a natural period when young adolescents will be difficult to control and prone to dangerous behavior. Teachers see puberty as a major event because it marks the onset of adult sexuality and the identification of the young adolescent with adult heterosexual roles. Teachers do not want to suppress the individual personality that is coming out and hope the adolescent will soon be able to master his or her urges. At the same because of political conflict over the role of sex education in schools, policy "ties teachers' hands," to use Adrian Norris's words. The religious or moral convictions of families take precedence over teachers' beliefs and appear to prevent teachers from dealing with adolescent sexuality as they would like. The institutional role of teacher in the United States is more limited than in Japan, and there are more areas of adolescent development that teachers in Japan can and do address.

Despite similar concerns, U.S. and Japanese teachers have very different understandings about the role of puberty in adolescent development. In the United States, puberty is seen as tightly linked with the hormones. Teachers in U.S. schools can attribute behavior in young adolescents or even in children to hormonal processes even when there are no visible signs of puberty: a seventh grade boy with no facial hair and a decidedly childlike voice can be described by teachers to "have entered puberty" and be subject to "raging hormones" if his behavior is highly disruptive and he evinces an interest in girls.[28]

The hormonal story line does not have much congruence with either historically powerful symbols of youth in Japanese culture or with common beliefs about physical and sexual maturation. U.S. teachers do not often talk about puberty or pubertal changes in a positive way. Teachers in Japan are much more likely to do so, but this may be in part derived from the fact that teachers feel confident that they can discuss and inform students about sexual issues, not just the mechanics of change. Japanese teachers do exhibit some conflicting views: they believe that young adolescents are innocent (*mujyaki),* but yet most believe that middle school is an intense (*hageshii*) time of life in which young adolescents may experience worries (*nayami*). Perhaps the crucial difference is that teachers in Japan do not believe in a strong causal link between puberty and the problems adolescents face.

That all normal young adolescents undergo puberty is a common and accepted fact in Japan but is not seen to inherently affect the adolescent mental state or, in Japanese terms, the sense of innocence and genuineness adults attribute to young adolescents. Puberty is part of a natural burst of growth and energy in the life course that signals the time has come for strict discipline and training. The concern over giving students correct guidance can be seen in the amount of effort that teachers put into student guidance or lifestyle guidance. Tremendous amounts of teacher time and energy went into organizing every aspect of the students' lives. The adolescent's life, his or her dreams, worries, and hopes, are open to the teacher's inspection through a variety of interventions such as diaries, reflective essays, or home visits.

For American teachers, the biological imperative of puberty and its attendant changes irrevocably put young adolescents on a road to further development and in some sense beyond the teacher's ability to influence. Some teachers who worked on collaborative projects on curriculum or discipline (among them, Gretchen Jondervag, Adrian Norris, Tom Brabeck) believed that revising basic classroom routines could lead to substantially different life experiences for and behaviors among students. These teachers tended to have more of a socially constructed view of puberty, and this view was associated with a greater sense of teacher efficacy. Like the Kotani teachers, Gretchen, Adrian, and Tom thought of puberty as a biological fact, but not one that totally dominated the development of young adolescents.

Puberty and sexual energy were seen as making Oak Grove adolescents more prone to a range of physical and emotional ills. In particular, hormonal "imbalance" was linked in the minds of Oak Grove teachers with emotional imbalance. The core of the students might be unchanged, but the behavior of the adolescent became erratic and at risk. Such at-riskness was emphasized more for girls than for boys and also appeared to be associated with students from poor, Hispanic, and African-American homes.

Teachers reacted to issues of sex among students in ways that suggested highly mixed emotions. On the one hand, Oak Grove teachers seemed inured to student displays of physical affection or (for boys in particular) attraction to erotic pictures in magazines or books. Yet they frequently expressed concern about adolescent sexual activity and fear about the consequences of these activities. And although all teachers talked about sexual development as a normal part of life, formal classes on sex education appeared stressful for teachers. There was no official teacher discourse on adolescent sexual desire, although in informal settings teachers readily discussed student sexuality and hormonal urges.

While American teachers make strong connections between puberty, the sexual desires of young adolescents, and the problem of sexual activity in young adolescents,[29] most Japanese teachers emphasize the connection between puberty and physical or emotional energy. Puberty to Mrs. Chino, as the above epigraph indicates, is associated with increased energy and activity in young adolescents. Like the other teachers at Furukawa and Aratamachi, her first reaction to the topic of puberty was to describe an upwelling of energy. In one interview she said, "The energy turns on, the energy turns on. You know, it's like, in the cases when they try positively, the students who persevere . . . they really are fulfilled." Japanese teachers associated pubertal energy with a brightness (*akarui*), fun (*tanoshii*), and a potential for growth in many areas. Mrs. Chino once said that pubertal energy can actually increase a child's ability to succeed academically.

The teachers at Furukawa and Aratamachi believed that when children enter puberty they can start studying with a new intensity. American teachers (without exception in this study) expressed the opinion that pubertal energy leads to restlessness or emotional instability. Although some American teachers connected the pubertal energy with greater artistic creativity or athletic achievement, they did not link it with better concentration, memorization, or study habits. Sports and other physical outlets were mentioned by some Americans as a way to let off the steam or burn up excess energy.

There is a fundamental divergence in how teachers believe that the energy of puberty can be harnessed. For teachers in Japan, puberty was a signal of emotional maturation as well as emotional energy. In Japanese schools, young adolescents' growing awareness of their own and others' sexuality is linked by teachers to an increased understanding of appropriate gender roles and the ability to take a more mature view of the sexes. The teachers saw that puberty was seen as part of the overall development of the adolescent, including an increased capability for volition. Americans saw puberty as indicative of a young adolescent's growing sexual interests but tended to see these interests as further unbalancing the adolescent. The Oak Grove teachers did not appear to see that pubertal development included increased capability for autonomous volition. Rather, their words and actions suggest a view that opposed the will and the body. Students had to learn to deal with the hormonal imbalance — if they were successful, then they would strengthen their volitional capacity; if not, they would continue to be at the mercy of a variety of negative influences, both internal and external.

Above and beyond variations produced by very different social patterns of early sexuality, when and how teachers worried about their students' sex lives was markedly different. The American context is heavily imbued not only with concerns about unwanted pregnancy, but with worries over sexually transmitted disease, sexual harassment, sexual assault, and the molestation of children. The dissimilarity in rates of pregnancy and sexual activity between the two societies demonstrates that there is a strong link in American culture between puberty, adultlike sexuality, and social problems. Puberty is tightly linked to adolescence in the United States by a belief that hormones, which turn on at puberty, produce a strong sex drive and emotional instability. This link appears to be missing in Japan, and as a result Japanese teachers describe varying ideal assumptions about sexual maturity and sexual consciousness. The belief in the effect of hormones or lack there of is a significant factor in overall beliefs in the nature of the life course. The presence of hormones, American teachers say, accounts for many of the behaviors characteristic to adolescence.

## Implications

The major educational implication of the differences in how puberty is viewed in the two countries' schools appears to be on teachers' roles and assumptions of efficacy. Japanese teachers work very hard to guide and mold adolescent social behavior because they think they can do it, and such work is generally supported by the society as a whole. American teachers are far less sure of the impact they will have, and in some communities teachers fear that attempts to introduce topics like safe sex and abstinence will result in hostile attacks from parents, who assume the teacher is promoting one or another moral view of sex. In Kotani, the teachers believed that they were responsible for changing behavior and took a proactive stance with significant emphasis on prevention. The school's role in prevention was considerably less in Oak Grove and typically involved the dissemination of information (about sexually transmitted disease, drugs, and other dangers) produced by social service organizations.[30]

A more subtle implication, but one with potentially far-reaching academic effects, is the degree to which school or teacher emphasis on puberty as disruptive may create a self-fulfilling prophecy in American schools. Across Japan, the teachers that I have interviewed and worked with adamantly believe that if a positive school atmosphere is maintained—that is, if the general school spirit is bright (*akarui*) and serious (*majime*)—the vast majority of young adolescents will thrive academically and socially. The problems of disruption and resistance are viewed less as outgrowths of the disruption engendered by maturation than as symptoms of ineffective school organization and teacher preparation.[31] As teacher self-efficacy has been shown to be a persistently strong factor in quality of instruction in the United States, we should question the degree to which middle grade schools and cultural beliefs undermine this sense of efficacy.

I do not suggest that changing teachers' attitudes will suddenly alleviate all the problems of adolescence in the United States, but the impact of widespread, consistent reforms at the middle grade level could have a substantial impact on many of the problems facing young adolescents. At the time of writing this book, newspapers are reporting dramatic reductions in teenage pregnancy in the United States. The data have yet to be effectively analyzed, but some analysts suggest that prevention and abstinence programs may have played an important role. What this study shows is the difficulty that teachers in Oak Grove and other American middle schools would have if they were to try to implement the same kinds of prevention activities or take the same role in guidance that Japanese teachers did. The belief that puberty is a time of hormonal imbalance that systematically disrupts learning and behavior needs to be confronted on a wider social level if U.S. middle school teachers are to gain the kind of broad support for intensive prevention and guidance that Japanese teachers have.

# 5

## Toward Maturity: Self-Control and Academic Goals

In a culture that emphasizes the autonomy and self-reliance of the individual, the primary problems of childhood are what some psychoanalysts call separation and individuation — indeed, childhood is chiefly preparation for the all-important event of leaving home. Though the issues of separation, individuation, and leaving home come to a head in late adolescence, they are recurrent themes in the lives of Americans, and few if any of us ever leave them entirely behind.[1]

While considering such matters [youth and rebellion], I was reminded of the story of Momotarō, so beloved of Japanese children. For all his closeness to his parents, Momotarō could not identify with them; he found something unsatisfactory about the parents who had found and raised him. When he grew up, however, he discovered a goal in life — the conquest of Demon Island — toward which he could direct the feelings he could not direct toward his parents, and thanks to which he was transformed into an adult, full of adult self-confidence. For him, the conquest of the demons was a kind of initiation into adulthood. . . . The more I reflect on this Momotarō story, the more strongly I feel the resemblance to modern youth . . . They too, like Momotarō, require some Demon Island on which to expend their energies.[2]

In most cultures, the major social task facing adolescents is to establish themselves in adult roles. Adolescents must demonstrate that they are mature. In the United States maturation is strongly linked with autonomy (and even separation) from the parents. The child becomes an adult when he or she becomes autonomous and self-reliant. Erik Erikson believed that the task of the adolescent was to establish a separate identity. The young adolescent must display the capacity to identify, articulate, and organize his or her individual preferences and beliefs.[3] Robert Bellah argues that adolescents are preparing for the crucial social (and symbolic) act of leaving home in the United States — the final separation.

In Japan, where three-generation households are still looked upon as ideal, the emphasis on physical and psychological separation is muted.[4] Rather, the task for Japanese adolescents is to find a goal or activity through which they can assert their individuality and create a set of individual goals that are distinct (though not divorced) from family goals. Takeo Doi, a Freudian psychoanalyst, believed that having such a distinct goal was necessary for adolescents' development because it allowed them a way to express (and hence work out) feelings of aggression or resentment they could not express toward their parents.[5]

In both Japan and the United States, then, the adolescent is expected to develop the skills needed to deal with challenging, adultlike situations. But according to the definitions present in national literature on U.S. middle schools and in the words of teachers in Oak Grove themselves, American middle school students are at risk. They are susceptible or vulnerable to crises that may arise in their lives, particularly because they are making important transitions to adulthood. Japanese middle school students, in contrast, are variously described as both prone to rebellion as well as energetic and earnest: the middle school years are considered an intense period of significant growth and the opportunity for growth. Teachers in Kotani did not see their students as being at risk unless they lacked a dream or a goal.

In the United States and Japan, young adolescents are expected to learn how to manage their social worlds and to maintain an academic record that will allow them to progress to high school. The bulk of teachers' work, in either country, comes down to seeing that students achieve some form of social and academic competence during middle school. The venues for developing academic and social competence include the classroom and the hallway, afterschool extracurricular activities, and weekend detention. Within each school, teachers organize a variety of activities that are designed to help students study better and learn how to manage their lives in the adult world. And in both cultures, academic success is a key factor in future social success.

In this chapter I analyze the ways in which U.S. and Japanese teachers organize classroom instruction and academic guidance to help young adolescents set academic goals and work to meet them and to increase the self-control necessary for future academic success and social maturity. The Oak Grove teachers, like most American middle school teachers, emphasize individual responsibility in academic achievement, encourage students to increase their self-control (discipline or willpower), and otherwise use a rewards and punishment strategy to motivate students. The Oak Grove teachers strongly emphasize instruction in academic subjects as the key to future academic success and downplay the role of extracurriculars. The Kotani teachers, like their counterparts across Japan, emphasize individual responsibility in academic achievement but connect individual student academic success to both the students' and their family's future. Kotani teachers first seek to develop student goals in order to provide them with the motivation to increase their self-control and to exert themselves in studying. The Kotani teachers organize an elaborate system of guidance and motivation and put far more emphasis on the role of extracurriculars as a way to support academic achievement and help students attain social maturity.

## In the Classroom

The organization of academic life in Oak Grove differs profoundly from that in Kotani. Beginning with the most elementary matters, such as the placement of classrooms, the Oak Grove schools are laid out in a way that weakens student identification with a specific homeroom or grade and maximizes individual ability to move from class to class. Although students are assigned to a homeroom, each grade of homerooms is assigned classrooms on a certain wing. At Wade and Pleasant Meadows, there are periodic flows as students move from one subject to another between periods. Common areas between the wings maximize student chances to interact with students from other grades.

In the Kotani schools all homeroom classes for a given grade occupy one floor on the same hallway. There is a strict hierarchy of grades, the third-year students occupying the top floor and first-year students the bottom floor. Students remain in their homerooms for core classes like mathematics, Japanese, social studies, science, and English — usually for the entire morning. For classes like home economics and physical education, for which special facilities are used, students move with their homeroom to special rooms. In the same way, entire homerooms move to science or language laboratories for special classes in science or English. In Kotani there are no school cafeterias, so students eat in their classroom. This practice serves to strengthen students' sense of identification with the homeroom class and limit contact with students from other grades.[6]

The interior space of U.S. classrooms varies enormously. At Wade and Pleasant Meadows alone I saw classrooms with rectangular tables and chairs, round tables and chairs, chair-desks, workbenches, and combinations of all of the above. Depending on the individual teacher, the classroom seating arrangements may be organized to accommodate learning centers, group work, and individual seat work or pair work. In most classes the teacher assigned individual seating. For example, students in Adrian Norris's language arts/social studies class, the chair-desks were arranged in single lines with teacher-assigned seats so that students could simply turn their desks to form pairs or four-person small groups — an organization style that supported her use of individual seat work, pair work, and group work activities. In Nick Brisbane's history class, the chair-desks were arranged in a similar way, but students worked in groups much less frequently. In Sandy Briotte's home economics classroom, students sat where ever they chose around large worktables. In going from one class to another, students would not only change subjects, but might enter a totally new physical environment with distinct instructional routines.

With the exception of the science, home economics, and language laboratories, Japanese classrooms in Kotani (and all other Japanese classrooms I have observed) have chairs and desks arranged in rows. Each desk is marked with an individual's name and is used to store belongings. A student will rarely, if ever, use a desk that is not his. Teachers for the academic subjects rotate to the different homerooms, and there is much less variation in the range of instructional strategies teachers use.[7]

Finally, the decoration of the classroom reflects key differences in how teachers think the classroom should function. In Oak Grove schools, the room is the teacher's room and he or she is responsible for the care and decoration of the room; compared to Japanese classrooms, every room at Wade and Pleasant Meadows was highly decorated. Individual teachers varied greatly in the degree to which they incorporated student work into the decoration. In some classes, student projects were suspended from the ceilings and student drawings hung on the walls. In others, only a few examples of student work were posted and the rest of the classroom wall space was devoted to materials that the teacher deemed appropriate.[8]

In Japan as a nation, middle school classrooms are monotonously similar. Classroom walls are sparsely decorated. Wall space is limited as classrooms tend to have windows on the exterior and hallway walls, allowing as much natural light as possible to flow into the classroom. Bulletin boards are used to post announcements and daily homework lessons. Sometimes a class at Aratamachi or Furukawa would maintain a vase of cut flowers in one corner.[9] The feel of the classroom is sparse and utilitarian, yet all materials and information in the classroom have been selected by or are directly related to the homeroom class that uses that room.

The basic layout of the classrooms, arrangement of chairs and desks, and decoration suggest that Oak Grove teachers emphasize individual variation and choice for both teacher and adolescent in the learning environment. The Kotani classrooms, on the other hand, emphasize uniformity in groups and established routines. These patterns set the stage for two distinct types of academic school days. In Oak Grove, the academic parts of the school day are loosely organized and filled with individual choices and opportunities for individuals to make decisions and take initiative in terms of their studying. In Kotani, the academic parts of the school day are highly organized and restrict individual choice and opportunities for individuals to make decisions.

### POLISHED ROUTINES

Like other researchers of Japanese classroom practices, I found that the Kotani teachers used an elaborate set of routines to manage the class and that they spent little time on discipline or management.[10] Classes in most of the core academic courses tended to be teacher-directed but involved high levels of student activity at specific points (videotapes of Japanese classrooms distributed by the National Center for Education Statistics clearly show these tendencies). Despite large class size (sometimes more than forty students in a class), teachers actively engaged students through pair work, group work, or classes held in special rooms equipped for experiments or language study.

Kotani teachers placed great emphasis on having students explain their answers and focused their classes more on student reasoning than on obtaining the correct answer.[11] When teachers dealt with disruptions or misbehaviors in class they most often did so by redirecting student behavior to an academic task. Kotani teachers did not use charts of rewards or punishments common in the classrooms of Wade and Pleasant Meadows. They did not send students to the principal or threaten that bad classroom behavior would lower a student's grade. Again and again, I witnessed a consistent pattern of redirection. My notebooks contain many passages like the following:

> Mrs. Egami is already in class passing out papers by the time the bell rings. After the initial bow she briefly outlines the lesson for the day: using algebraic equations to solve the problem of dividing X numbers of bean paste cake between different numbers of people so that each person gets three pieces.
>
> Mrs. Egami asks students to give possible solutions to the problem. One girl

stands and gives the answer: $X = 3Y + 2$. Mrs. E. than asks the class if they agree or not with the answer. Continuing with this process, Mrs. E. goes around the room asking students to give answers and explain. This process continues for nearly thirty minutes when Mrs. E. hands out a print.

While she is going around helping students with the print one girl tries to empty her eraser pieces into a boy's hair. He turns and slaps her hand away, complaining: "She put erasings in my hair."

Mrs. E. tries to brush the pieces from his head. Smiling, she takes him by the shoulder and turns him around in his seat saying, "Look at this. Please try to get this." She then spends over a minute working with the boy on the problem.

In Kotani's schools, student time on task was consistently high, and students rarely seemed bored and rarely disrupted the class. During the first month of fieldwork, when I was trying to see what behaviors teachers considered a problem, I found myself becoming fatigued and bored. Day after day, period after period, Aratamachi and Furukawa students would come to class with their lessons prepared, follow the directions in class, and leave the classroom without any verbal admonishment from the teachers. There was little if any talking among students in class and virtually no note passing or verbal harassment — actions which I recorded on an hourly basis in every Oak Grove class that I observed. There was a range of variation within both the Oak Grove and Kotani classrooms in terms of disruptiveness, but the only Kotani classes which approached the level of disruption I found in Oak Grove were the music and calligraphy classes at Furukawa. In all other academic and nonacademic classes, Kotani students appeared highly engaged, motivated, and quick to respond to their teachers.

When students did exhibit behavior that U.S. teachers might label disruptive — for example, like that described above in Mr. Egami's class — many Kotani teachers did not seem to take this behavior to indicate a lack of maturity or lack of academic success. Instead, the most common response was to ignore the behavior and redirect students to the task and routines laid out. The second most common response was to admonish students for their lack of attention, disruption, and so on and redirect them to the task and routines. Occasionally teachers would give the entire class a prolonged scolding, mentioning a lack of appropriate behavior and admonishing all students to take responsibility.

REWARDS AND CONSEQUENCES

"You can't talk in the library. That shows me you're not mature enough to handle it."
— Janice Leitskov

While Kotani teachers relied largely on routines to guide academic work, teachers in Oak Grove relied on rewards and punishments for individuals.

Furthermore, Kotani teachers tended to emphasize proper group behavior and sharing responsibility as signs of maturity, whereas teachers at Wade and Pleasant Meadows made it clear to students that they saw a direct link between individual classroom performance, academic success, and social maturity. Teachers tried a variety of ways to provide incentives for students to study and allowed students chance after chance to make up work, get extra credit, or turn in alternative assignments. Teachers at Wade and Pleasant Meadows ascribed maturity to those students who came to class promptly and followed the teacher's instructions without prompting. Moreover, Oak Grove teachers did not consider time spent on reprimanding students or getting students organized to be "real teaching."

For example, Sandy Briotte linked classroom behavior with maturity and rewarded or punished individuals accordingly. The day after a substitute had been in her nutrition class, Sandy confronted her class:

> SANDY: "What happened yesterday?"
> ROBERT: "A lot of folks like me were taking advantage of her."
> SANDY: "Why do you take advantage of a sub? Why don't you control your behavior?"
> TIM: "People think the sub won't get mad."
> LAURA: "The sub doesn't give a grade."
> MITCH: "She won't come back and yell at us."
> SANDY: "When there is a sub here [in the future], we will not cook. There won't be fruit out. The pantry is locked. I have the only key."
>
> Sandy reads out the sub's note. She then notes: "We'll redo yesterday's lesson. You'll write a response. You can leave when you finish and you won't get credit."

Like most teachers in Oak Grove, Sandy assumed that students who misbehaved in class were choosing, individually, to act in an inappropriate or immature manner. But in reacting to the students' misbehavior the day before, Sandy demonstrated that there are times when teachers do hold groups responsible for their actions. When groups of students participate in a coordinated or persistent set of defiant or disruptive behaviors, teachers will mete out punishment to groups. Teachers also believed that by making academic performance contingent upon classroom behavior, they could effectively motivate students to display appropriate behavior. Part of the reason that substitute teachers faced higher levels of disruption was their inability to mete out similar sanctions, and while substitute teachers try the same strategies as regular teachers, the results are usually quite different because students do not see themselves as being responsible to a substitute teacher.

After the third period bell rings, Lynn Jing begins class by asking questions about the book the class is reading—*Maniac Magee*. Students raise their hands and answer the question, and after each answer, Lynn rephrases the student's answer. Most of the questions are about definitions, and Lynn seems to feel the answers need to be clarified for the class.

About 15 minutes into class, a woman that I do not know enters the class, an aide perhaps? Lynn continues with questions for another 10 minutes then asks class to read quietly. While the students are reading the noise from next door grows louder. A teacher's voice can be heard shouting "Arthur, you have another mark." Lynn walks by me and says:

"Can you tell there is a sub next door?"

After 10 minutes Lynn goes back to questioning. She makes each student keep answering until she is satisfied with the answer. "If you haven't answered a question this morning, be ready to answer one."

Performance in class was taken as a direct measure of both students' academic ability and social maturity. Teachers rewarded or punished misbehavior with consequences that had both academic and social outcomes. Students could lose points for behavior or be excluded the next time treats were passed out. Students were often assigned extra work for misbehaving. Clearly, Oak Grove teachers believed that maturity, in the form of control over behavior in class, was something that they could influence with a variety of academic or behavioral sanctions. Despite their efforts, Oak Grove classrooms were repeatedly disrupted by students.[12] The actions and accounts of the Oak Grove teachers stand in contradiction to each other. Indeed, I found Oak Grove teachers to be inconsistent in their explanations of student behavior, in terms of both social maturity and academic success. Teachers thought that hormones might significantly affect a student's ability to concentrate, yet they still expected individual students to maintain self-control. While often blaming basic physiological processes for inattentiveness, irritability, or defiance in young adolescents, the Oak Grove teachers held them accountable for their individual behavior. As I will discuss at length in the summary, Oak Grove teachers expected students to demonstrate self-control over their impulses, but the teachers did not see it as their job to teach students how to achieve self-control.

GENERALIST OR SPECIALIST?

Kotani teachers prided themselves on their ability to teach a subject, manage a class, and supervise a homeroom. Being a homeroom teacher in a Japanese middle school is a significant responsibility as well as a sign of professional status. New teachers and interns are not allowed to be homeroom teachers. The homeroom teachers at Kotani spent a great deal of time outlining routines and having students practice patterns of organizing and carrying out duties. Occasionally the Kotani teachers did express resentment that they were doing so much child rearing. Nonetheless they believed that working to promote positive social interactions that would provide opportunities for students to learn how to control their behavior was a central part of their job.[13]

Teachers in Oak Grove used the term "baby-sitting" to refer to those classes in which they spent most of their time on management and little on instruction. The term "baby-sitting" highlighted the fact that the teachers saw a strong link between inappropriate classroom behavior and immaturity. At the same time, they did not see this kind of work as a fulfilling or important part of their role as teacher and even expressed resentment at having to carry it out.

Stan Proud asked a committee of teachers at Pleasant Meadows to fill in the following statement: "If there was one thing that could be changed at this school . . ." The top response was "For teachers to be specialists." "Development of social skills" was number five out of eight. While the literature at the state and district level calls for significant attention to the social development of young adolescents, most teachers in Oak Grove did not place a high priority on this area and most expressed the desire to do less work on social skills and more on academic material.

At the same time, senior teachers at Pleasant Meadows were keenly aware of the limitations of their current discipline policies. At a spring meeting the school's team leaders tried to think of alternative discipline policies. The teachers noted that the school did not appear to meet the emotional and social needs of many of the students, and that students seemed to be increasingly involved in such negative behavior as name calling and fighting. The group suggested creating an advisement program and instituting a curriculum on sexual harassment and discussed some of the innovative programs around the district.

Oak Grove teachers used some routines—such as where students kept papers, when they were allowed to go to the bathroom and so on—but these varied from teacher to teacher. While teachers judged students who were well organized and academically successful as more mature, they did not view working on these organizational skills to be central to their work as teachers. Most Oak Grove teachers operated their classrooms on the assumption that students were capable of controlling their behavior if they chose to do so and that engaging in inappropriate behavior or immature behavior was a volitional act on the part of young adolescents. Many teachers preferred not to deal with in-class disruptions at all and tried to send all students who broke the rules to the vice-principal's office. Thus, it has proven difficult for the administrators and senior teachers at Oak Grove schools to shed traditional discipline policies and implement advisement, counseling, or conflict resolution programs.

The expectation of schooling among most Oak Grove teachers was that the school would provide classes that were enriching, but that it was the students' responsibility not only to motivate themselves academically and to exercise self-control of behavior in the classroom, but also to control their emotions (or hormones) during class time (this topic will be developed more in the next chapter). In a sense teachers judged adolescent maturity by how well students independently learned to modify and control their behavior in class.[14] Those students who quickly learned to adjust to an individual teacher's routines and learning expectations each time they entered a new classroom were often described as mature, bright, and self-confident. Teachers appeared to believe that student maturation — that is, adolescent mental development of self-control — went on independently of the academic process.

For Kotani teachers, character (*seikaku*) development was a crucial component in building academic competence. Students who lack social maturity will not be likely to succeed on the entrance examinations. Clubs and activities are as integral to the curriculum as reading and writing. The school is organized to foster the development of certain values in all children by means of identical measures. There is little emphasis on individual differences — though there is much emphasis placed on promoting the individual's welfare. Teachers saw the training of students in appropriate social behavior as a worthwhile and even central part of their work. Maturity, then, was a prerequisite for developing goals and the self-control necessary to succeed in the academic process. No where was this difference between U.S. and Japanese expectations more clear than in how teachers worked with students to plan their academic future.

## *Individual Responsibility and Future Plans*

Young adolescents face very important educational decisions toward the end of their time in middle school. They must choose a high school and a course of study. In Japan, teachers actively organize this process and offer a great deal of guidance to students. In the United States, teachers are less engaged in guiding students into high school but can have a powerful effect on students' high school experience by the kinds of grades they give. Many U.S. middle schools remain tracked in core subjects like mathematics — a practice that effectively segregates students into future high school tracks.[15] While Japanese middle schools do not have such tracking, teachers engage in specialized placement counseling, using practice test results, to virtually assign students to future schools in the most extreme cases.[16]

Previous ethnographies of Japanese schooling suggest that teachers in the two countries have very different ideas about responsibility in terms of students' future success. To simply let students fumble along without motivation or guidance would seem gross negligence to most Japanese teachers. A middle school student failing to enter high school (and thus being forced to spend a year in limbo waiting for next year's examination) is a sign that teachers and the school have failed. As both Kaori Okano and I have shown, teachers act to raise students' aspirations, provide students with information their family would never have obtained, and shield students of non-Japanese background from discrimination when facing the transition to high school or work.[17]

In Kotani City, the teachers organize events designed to motivate students. Most second-year students engage in some ceremony of this sort. Mrs. Chino recounted her son's experience at Furukawa some four years before. The Furukawa teachers secretly asked parents to write a letter to their children explaining all the work the parents had done in raising the child. The teachers took the letter with them on an overnight trip to a local camping facility. After dark, the teachers gave the students the letter and told them to go off by themselves and read the letter alone by flashlight. Soon the facility was filled with the sounds of weeping as students read how their parents had sacrificed so much for them.

Another example that exemplifies how teachers promote the idea that the adolescent's future plans include the whole family, and thus make the adolescent responsible for his or her family, comes from a speech given at a motivation event at Furukawa. Seiichi Ogihara, the son of a local middle school teacher and the grandson of a principal, simultaneously focused his speech on the debt he owed his parents and on his own personal responsibility. Seiichi connected his parents' sacrifice over the years directly with his own efforts to enter a good high school. The various activities that teachers organize for students emphasize the connections between family and individual sacrifice again and again. Actively stimulating students' reflection on their relations and duties to others (*omoiyari*) is a central part of the events organized at Furukawa and Aratamachi. The self-awareness promoted by teachers is not limited to guidance about future choices. Middle schools throughout Japan conduct various events in which a major goal is to develop the adolescent's sense of self and responsibility in relation to his family and school.

The quintessential question of adolescence, Who am I? in Japanese middle schools is overshadowed by What school can I get into? High school, some form of training or perhaps college, work, and finally marriage will be needed to complete the cycle. As many scholars have pointed out, high school graduate or college graduate (*kōsotsu* or *daisotsu*) is often the relevant distinction individuals carry throughout the life course.[18] Thus virtually every activity in Japanese middle schools, including extracurricular events and activities, is connected to the goal of getting students into high school.

As I have already described in an article, current Japanese middle schools spend tremendous amounts of time organizing a regimen of study and examination taking to prepare students for the high school entrance exam.[19] A large percentage of students spend their evenings in cram schools preparing for these tests. In Kotani and in most of the middle schools I studied in Japan, students were required to resign (*intai*) from clubs during their final year of middle school. The imposition of such high-stakes testing at the end of the middle school years means that if teachers can succeed in getting students to set a goal for themselves, in the form of a certain high school they wish to enter, then students will be powerfully motivated to study to attain this goal.

In sharp contrast, teachers at Wade and Pleasant Meadows offered no organized set of events or activities related to future school placement. Middle schools were visited each year by the representatives of local high schools, but several Oak Grove teachers and secretaries described the event as burdensome and felt that the high school staff were condescending toward them. Information about high schools is provided to students, but whereas at Furukawa a student might receive twenty two- to three- page handouts in his or her last year alone, the American materials consisted largely of passing on the registration forms provided by the high school.

In individual cases, however, teachers did take an active role, particularly when a student showed academic promise or approached the teacher for information. Teachers' attitudes seemed to reflect the ideal written in the Pleasant Meadows School Level Plan: "The school must assist the student to meet his/her potential." But the school was in no way responsible for the student's ultimate success or failure in future educational endeavors, as in Japan.

Rather, the emphasis at Wade and Pleasant Meadows was on providing instruction appropriate to the current level of the student. Students who did well in classes were encouraged to take more advanced mathematics classes. Many middle schools in the United States have now implemented Gifted and Talented classes that further promote individual academic excellence. On the other hand, states require schools to write an Individual Educational Plan that addresses a "student's individual needs, strengths, weaknesses and learning styles" when students have a diagnosed physical, learning, behavioral, or emotional disability.

The degree of attention given to individual learning styles, learning disabilities, and other disabilities in the Oak Grove schools was truly remarkable. Both Oak Grove schools implemented an aggressive mainstreaming model that meant that only students with the most severe behavioral or developmental disabilities were placed in separate classrooms. The district also supported a special program for students with severe emotional disabilities at the third middle school in the district. The majority of the students with diagnosed physical, learning, behavioral, or emotional disabilities were either main-streamed for all or part of the day in the regular classrooms.

For example, both Wade and Pleasant Meadows were largely wheelchair accessible with special ramps built for the newest classrooms. At both schools, students with limitations on their physical mobility (including one girl in a wheel chair) had access to the entire range of school facilities. These students spent their entire day in the regular classroom. This kind of mainstreaming was simply out of the question in Kotani, where the schools did not have even an elevator. In Japan, students with moderate to severe disabilities do not have access to mainstream academic instruction.

Both Oak Grove schools also had "resource rooms" where students with diagnosed learning disabilities could receive special tutoring. The student-teacher ratio in this room over the course of the day was about six to one, not including the aides who read to the students or helped them with their class work. Several computers were available for the students to use. The atmosphere in these classrooms tended to be very relaxed — similar to a library or learning center where students could talk about their work with an adult.

More impressive, in my experience, was the practice of teaming special education and regular teachers. In several classrooms, the special education teacher came in to the regular class to work with students who had learning disabilities. In some cases, the classroom teacher and special education teacher effectively taught a team lesson. This teaming meant that students with special learning needs were exposed to the same curriculum as other students but received a good deal of one-on-one instruction from adults. Since both aides and student teachers were common in Oak Grove, there were sometimes three adults (excluding myself) working with students in these class rooms.

Individual students and families are responsible for their academic future in the United States. The teachers at Wade and Pleasant Meadows were very concerned with teaching the students to the best of their ability but did not see themselves as being responsible for guiding students in selecting high schools or high school courses. The schools provided a wide range of services for individuals, but not much guidance in terms of future academic planning. As every student is guaranteed entrance to high school in the United States, most middle schools make no attempt to orchestrate an elaborate system of placement guidance.[20] In the United States, young adolescents are, compared to Japan, on their own with regard to future academic choice.[21]

Much of the intense preparation in Japan, of course, is made necessary by the imposition of high stakes testing at the end of compulsory education. This has the effect, however, of virtually eliminating the kind of individualized education that Oak Grove students received. Students in Kotani all receive the same basic curriculum, and there is no room for teachers to substantially deviate from this curriculum. To provide the kind of specialized instruction provided by Oak Grove special education teachers would, in Japan, be seen as giving some students an unequal chance.[22] The prevailing attitude in Japan is that it would be inappropriate to let young adolescents face such choices without significant guidance (both academic and emotional) from teachers. Oak Grove teachers saw their responsibility as to individuals: promoting individual academic development as much as possible.

## *Supporting Academic Achievement through Extracurricular Activities*

Japanese and U.S. teachers also differed in their attitudes toward and use of extracurricular activities. In Oak Grove, extracurricular activities were seen as just what the name implies: something special done outside the curriculum. For Kotani teachers, these activities were an integral part of the overall middle grades' curriculum, and they used these activities to modify adolescent behavior far more than their counterparts in Oak Grove. The teachers at Furukawa and Aratamachi used extracurricular events and activities both to stimulate adolescent motivation and a sense of responsibility and to teach adolescents self-control (*enryo*). Teachers saw the development of an ability to work in clearly hierarchical social situations (junior/senior divisions — *kōhai/senpai*) while maintaining individual goals as an essential step on the road to adulthood. And the Kotani teachers relied heavily on extracurricular clubs and athletic teams as the means to promote these abilities. Mr. Mizuno, a former elementary school teacher and head of the guidance department (*shidō-buchō*) at Aratamachi, said, "There are some who equate club activity with student guidance." Club activities are essential in training students to behave in a group life (*shūdan seikatsu*).

> Mr. Mizuno: "A major difference between middle schools and elementary schools is the student's sense of senior-junior relations (*senpai-kōhai*). You really don't find that sense of senior and junior in elementary school.
> Author: "What causes this?"
> Mr. Mizuno: "It is the clubs. . . . I guess that it is a tradition. There is this idea that seniors should teach juniors. Elementary school children do not have this sense of responsibility for teaching others, but that sense is strong in the clubs."

This sense of responsibility requires self-control in expressing one's opinions and desires, but also a capacity to care for other's desires.[23] Self-restraint (*enryo*) and the ability to indulge others in their desires or need for love (*amayakasu*) are considered active characteristics by Japanese teachers: characteristics that show a maturity of the spirit (*kokoro*).

The ability to consider other's wants, to determine what they need without them saying so openly, to allow them to be dependent is a crucial ability for mature Japanese. Given this attitude, it is easier to understand what Mrs. Kawaguchi was trying to accomplish with Miuchi and Yabushita. As leaders of the fencing club, they had displayed neither the restraint nor the consideration of others that seniors *must* display. Individual responsibility is responsibility not only for group actions but for group feelings or emotions.

In Oak Grove, administrators at both schools were working to save funding for their after-school and special event programs. Although many teachers thought that clubs and events had a positive effect on students, the staff often had a hard time defending these trips as necessary to academic success. In discussing the trip to New York, the Pleasant Meadows' staff said, "We can't defend the trip educationally." Many of these field trips, while rooted in an idea of broadening students' horizons, were no longer seen as core academics in the mid-1990s.

There was no systematic organization of extracurricular activities and class time on a daily basis as in the Kotani schools. Classes were sometimes organized before special events (like Wade's School Festival), but this also varied from teacher to teacher. Just as Oak Grove teachers had no systematic plan for academic advising and guidance, neither did they have a systematic plan for using extracurricular and class time to achieve distinct educational goals.

Moreover, supervising an extracurricular club in Kotani was part of the normal duties of a teacher. In Oak Grove it was not. Some teachers received a small amount of money to coach or provide certain sports programs, but most worked with various clubs and activities as a form of service to the school and community. Many individual teachers spent long hours after school working on plays, arts, music, and other activities with groups of students who wanted to participate in these activities. The commitment of these teachers was remarkable, but the system itself reinforced the basic idea that such activities were, indeed, extra, and individual student (or teacher) motivation and initiative determined that participation.

Oak Grove teachers saw their primary duty as one of providing a stable classroom environment in which young adolescents could learn a given subject. Unlike the Kotani teachers, who were expected to perform a great many nonteaching activities, Oak Grove teachers focused on academic instruction.[24] In Oak Grove schools teachers did not wish to act as counselors and saw counseling as a secondary function of middle schools.[25] Social skills were seen as something that the young adolescent should already have acquired, at least as far as the ability to correctly follow instruction in class was concerned. They did not see extracurricular activities as a means to develop social skills or promote emotional development that teachers could effectively employ.

Yet teachers' success in engaging students in academics, at least as measured in the amount of time spent on discipline, was comparatively low in Oak Grove. Even when staffed by thirty-year veterans of enormous talent and energy like Gretchen Jondervag, Oak Grove classrooms, compared to those in Kotani, were beset by instability. For Kotani teachers, middle school students were at an age they perceived to be uniquely receptive to learning about self-discipline and self-control. They viewed young adolescents as having both tremendous energy and increased mental capacities. In teachers' minds, even the most severely troubled students will respond to the treatment of teachers. Oak Grove teachers saw students as beset with fluctuating hormones and unreceptive to lessons in self-discipline or self-control. They believed that individual differences in maturation made for significant variations in student self-control, motivation, and academic success.

Rather than trying to change students' basic capacities for self-control or group awareness through extracurricular activities, Oak Grove teachers offered a range of opportunities throughout the day for students to take part in learning. They made tremendous efforts to speak with individuals and to modify lessons to meet individual levels of reading, mathematics, or other academic level of comprehension but rarely worked on managing emotions or conflict resolution. And despite the fact that they often blamed hormones in their discussions of adolescent instability, they expected young adolescents to be in control of themselves during class time and assumed that each individual should be mature enough to maintain self-control.

The teachers in Kotani maintained a rich program of social development through great effort. They used outside classroom activities as their primary means to achieve these ends: an option that was simply not available to Oak Grove teachers. Even for those teachers such as Winnie Rawler, who enthusiastically supported school activities associated with learning German, it was difficult to integrate the activities into the daily routine of the school, as they were not core academic courses. Such activities, as I will discuss in the next chapter, were viewed not as part of the general educational experience all students should have, but as part of a set of academic electives that motivated students could chose from.

## Summary

In terms of academics, Oak Grove teachers, like their counterparts across America, worked to develop each student's ability to the level to which he or she was developmentally capable. The concept of developmentally appropriate curriculum appeared to be widely accepted in Oak Grove but was interpreted to mean that individual students had developmental limits on what he or she could learn. Teachers were not able to influence the basic process of maturation. If teachers thought a student was too immature to handle the workload, they did not see themselves as able to significantly adjust this process. Students might not be making academic progress either because they chose not to (were defiant) or could not (were immature). Teachers did not, however, believe that they could affect these tendencies much beyond offering rewards for positive behavior and sanctions for negative behavior.

In Kotani, teachers put comparatively little emphasis on developing each student's ability to the level he or she was capable of. The concept of developmentally appropriate curriculum is also strong in Japan, but the emphasis is on the group level. In other words, is this problem (or unit) appropriate for seventh graders? Furthermore, Japanese teachers tended to place more emphasis on prior knowledge than on developmental constraints. While Oak Grove teachers often discussed whether the conceptual level of a lesson was appropriate, Kotani teachers usually evaluated a lesson based on whether the students had studied the topic in the past. Both sets of teachers were aware of the concept of developmentally appropriate curriculum, but the Oak Grove teachers applied this concept along highly individual lines while he Kotani teachers applied it to groups or cohorts of students.

In his work on the self, Doi makes much of the centrality of dependency in human relations within Japanese culture. Young adolescents exhibiting selfish behavior or unacceptable social behavior are generally deemed in need not of discipline, but of love, attention, and guidance. Japanese teachers often rush in to correct these perceived deficiencies, and that results in a social life in schools in which almost every detail is planned and guided by teachers. Given the powerful influence of the high school entrance examination system on top of these general beliefs, virtually every aspect of Japanese middle schools is organized to achieve this academic success.

The system has many drawbacks, and many Japanese scholars fault the Japanese school system for stunting the individuality and sense of self of its students.[26] Abiko, in particular, was impressed by the way in which American teachers allowed students to decide the details of life for themselves, even though he felt that American students sometimes lacked the ability to discern their errors.[27] Many parents I interviewed in Japan thought that young adolescents in modern society had only narrow goals, such as passing the entrance examination. They did not believe that modern Japanese middle schools inculcated the broader ideals they recalled from their own school days. These same parents noted that increased competition on entrance examinations forced both teachers and students to curtail issues related to social maturity in favor of concentrating on academic advancement. While Japanese extracurriculars are currently quite popular, there is widespread concern that competition for high school entrance has negatively affected the educational condition of Japanese middle schools, undermining the very values of self-control and responsibility for others that teachers have worked hard to maintain.[28]

To Americans, Japanese teachers often appear overly controlling, and students in Japanese middle schools appear quite socially immature. On the opposite end, American teachers to many Japanese can appear callous or cold toward their students. This difference appears to be linked to just how teachers are expected to interact with their students. Americans do not believe it is the teacher's job to teach students how to be socially mature except by setting the example of being mature, independent professionals. The underlying belief about human development is similar to that found in the quotation from Bellah in the epigraph to this chapter: separation and individuation are emphasized; self-control over behavior is the quintessential marker of maturity. What is unstated but crucial for middle schools is that the development of self-control, separation, and individuation among young adolescents is not perceived as a process that teachers can easily influence.

For Japanese teachers such views would be unthinkable. The basic task of maturation involves creating strong individual goals, but even these are generated within an elaborately organized social context. The task Japanese teachers see as paramount is getting students to find a goal, hopefully one that is related to academic success. Adolescent development requires finding some goal or dream that will provide organization in one's life. In a sense, Japanese give young adolescents very few opportunities to be completely responsible for their own actions, to display self-control on their own, but organize many group routines or "scripts" for adolescents to follow. Maturity becomes defined by how well one follows the scripts.

As early as the fifth grade, the child in an American school is seen as having an autonomous self with a core of internal will. The child is expected to hear the rules (once!), understand them, and follow them. Infractions result in individual punishments. Individuals are compared on academic performance as well as behavioral performance in most classrooms. It is common to enter a fifth grade classroom and see a chart with stars showing how many books each child has read and at the same time glance at the chalkboard and see whose name has been put up as punishment for talking in class. Teachers like Urma Baxter and Bill Joiner regularly assigned detention for academic and behavioral offenses to their fifth grade students and expected students to be able to justify their actions when questioned. The teacher sits in judgment assessing individual performance and arbitrating disputes.

Both sets of teachers, then, believe that they are promoting social maturity by the actions they take, but they see maturity in different ways and have differing beliefs about how to nurture or promote it. The Japanese emphasize practice in group routines, constant peer and adult support, and a generally intense regimen of guided activities. The Americans emphasize setting clear expectations and holding each student accountable for his or her actions. In academics as well as in social interactions American teachers set out a system of rewards for positive behavior and sanctions for negative behavior that is expected to stimulate the young adolescent to behave in a mature way because it would be in his or her self-interest to do so. The Japanese teachers set out to make academic achievement as much like social interaction as they can: an activity in which young adolescents feel that many people are counting on them to play their role and get good grades or scores.

The American belief in a highly autonomous self is, however, in conflict with equally American beliefs about the essentially biological nature of human maturation. Thus Oak Grove teachers displayed an inconsistency or contradiction in their attitudes toward young adolescent development. Sometimes they expressed a belief that physiological factors were overriding or overpowering in young adolescents, at others they emphasized the ability to control these factors and take individual responsibility. I argue in chapter 4 that when student behavior was viewed as a gap or break in attention (perhaps an impulsive spit ball) or was interpreted to be a distraction (looking out the window or talking to the boy in the next seat) teachers often explained it as a biological imperative. When the behavior was viewed as resistance or defiance, the teachers regarded it as caused by mental or family conditions.

## Implications

There is not perfect agreement in either nation about the best way to help young adolescents achieve social maturity or even to promote social competence and academic achievement. My work in Oak Grove and Kotani showed considerable dissatisfaction among a significant percentage of teachers in both nations. In both, teachers are facing what they perceive to be increasing problems among young adolescents. The process of maturation is perceived to be more difficult and more fraught with peril for current than for previous generations.

In both cultures young adolescents are perceived by teachers to be in the middle of crucial changes in social maturity and academic competence. There was a strong emphasis on self-control in both Oak Grove and Kotani. Becoming an adult meant having (or gaining) the appropriate self-control to deal with social and academic issues. In Japanese middle schools one often hears terms like "human nature" (*jinkaku*), "human life" (*jinsei*), or "character" (*seikaku*) when teachers are talking about the maturation of students. During the middle school years, young adolescents are expected to make crucial decisions about their future. In order to make these decisions, students need to become aware of who they are. They must know their nature if they are to make adequate decisions.[29] For Japanese teachers, guiding students in attaining such self-knowledge is just as crucial as educating such qualities as endurance (*gambare*) or thoughtfulness (*omoiyari*) or as instructing students in the basic academic competencies.

The fact that Oak Grove teachers had such difficulties in maintaining classroom order and getting students to study is related to several factors. First, although Oak Grove teachers told their students that studying was important, there was little immediate connection between student grades, tests, and future options. Oak Grove students simply did not see a strong link between classroom performance and their future lives, whereas Kotani students did. Second, classroom time in Oak Grove schools was frequently disrupted by students' late arrival by announcements, and by calls to send students to the office. These distractions and disruptions constantly broke up the flow of the lesson. In Kotani these disruptions were extremely rare. Announcements were made at break time, and late students were held in the teachers' room until the next class period. Kotani teachers had a full, uninterrupted period to work with students.

But Kotani teachers also worked to create a set of classroom routines that shifted much of the basic paperwork and management of the classroom tasks to the students. This third factor is highly salient because it not only made less work for teachers, but also gave young adolescents experience in how to organize and manage their educational affairs. Some Oak Grove teachers like Gretchen created similar routines in their classes, but in the absence of a schoolwide commitment, these teachers had to be constantly reminding students of the routines. Kotani teachers also went to great lengths to motivate students by organizing events that gave students a larger goal or dream. Use of point tallies, writing names on the board, and denying rewards were not used in the classrooms I observed. Rather than expecting students to have come to school with goals, Kotani teachers saw it as their responsibility to instill goals and dreams in students.

Many U.S. middle schools already support extracurriculars that are integrated with core academics. Experiments with peer mediation, group counseling, and other techniques for teaching students how to control their emotions and work out problems were tried, with considerable success, in Oak Grove.[30] Indeed, teachers like Tom Brabeck were active in implementing alternative classroom management strategies. Without widespread social support, however, such programs and even extracurriculars themselves are doomed to remain extras. The emphasis on individuals as responsible for their own academic achievement or failure is strong in both systems, but in the United States there is little teachers can draw on to work toward this goal. The Japanese must work against the opposite tendency. The Ministry of Education has instituted programs to try to break the cycle of increasing emphasis on testing and tests.

The problems produced by academic competition and entrance examinations in Japan are not the dramatic examples of suicide that the media love to describe.[31] Rather, the biggest problem Japanese teachers face is the constant pressure to narrow the curriculum to a few areas covered by the tests. Proponents of national testing in the United States might pause to consider the unintended impact of such testing in U.S. schools. While middle grades education in the United States could benefit from improved curriculum and more consistent teaching practices, such progress can be achieved without a rigid national curriculum or sacrificing the current U.S. focus on meeting individual learning needs. The state of Georgia's middle grades' certification program is one way of increasing teaching standards without implementing rigid tests. The ideal school system would be one that could provide the individual instruction and variety of classes offered in Oak Grove schools with the integrated extracurriculars and high-level core academic courses of Kotani.

# 6

## Managing Crises

American middle school students are often perceived to be at risk.[1] They are susceptible or vulnerable to crises that may arise in their lives, particularly because they are making important transitions to adulthood. Japanese middle school students are variously described as prone to rebellion but energetic and earnest; the middle school years are considered an intense period which places significant stress on young adolescents but offers the opportunity for growth. In both Japan and the U.S., the mature adult is expected to be able to deal with challenging situations, and teachers in each nation organize events that support students in dealing with crisis and help them obtain counseling or guidance in order to begin preparing them for adult life. Both nations have recently seen dramatic incidents of violence in the middle grades and a heightened concern for the emotional well-being of young adolescents.

In this chapter I first outline the basic procedures and organizational patterns that occur in the schools when student problems arise. The most common patterns in the United States work to disconnect teachers from students, while common Japanese patterns work to overburden teachers. Specific examples show how the systems worked with regard to individual crises (cases of suicide), schoolwide crisis (student death and grief), and violence. These differences are linked to divergent beliefs in the nature of the self. U.S. teachers evince a strong belief in theories of Western personality development that necessitate the use of professionals when problems arise. Japanese teachers evince a belief in a more fluid sense of self that calls on the teacher to play a role in counseling.

## *Japan: The Homeroom Teacher System*

Japanese schools are organized around the homeroom system, in which the homeroom teacher is responsible for discipline and guidance in his or her class. Homeroom teachers are supported in this work by a variety of committees that oversee the running of the school (see table 2.2). When there is a discipline problem, such as the theft of material, the problem or incident is always referred to the students' homeroom teacher. From then on, the homeroom teacher will play a significant role in dealing with the students' problems, although he or she may call upon other staff members for assistance.

The most important school committees for matters of counseling, guidance, and discipline are the grade committees, the student guidance committee, and the school governing committee. When teachers discover that a student has a problem or if they find that students have not performed certain routines, they can discuss the matter with the student (the most common option) or bring it up with the grade committee. The grade committee functions as the workhorse committee of the school, handling classroom management, curriculum implementation, and school activity planning in addition to addressing student problems. If the problem is more than a minor one, the grade committee chair will take up the matter with the school governing committee or refer the homeroom teacher directly to the student guidance committee chair.

At Furukawa, the committee meetings are arranged so that the grade committee meets early in the week, followed by the student guidance committee and the school governance committee. In this way pressing problems can be referred to the next level and addressed by senior members of the teaching staff in rapid order. Among the most serious issues that teachers at Furukawa dealt with during my fieldwork were several runaways, three children abandoned by their parents, students drinking off campus, and plans to curtail gang activity.[2]

The student guidance committee chair at Furukawa, Mr. Shimada, regularly communicated with the guidance committees at the other schools and with the Municipal Youth Counseling Center. Mr. Shimada and other guidance chairs from around Kotani also met monthly with the municipal police. In any given week, Mr. Shimada spent a considerable amount of time talking on the telephone with his counterparts at other middle schools. Problems of misconduct within the school were usually referred directly back to the home-

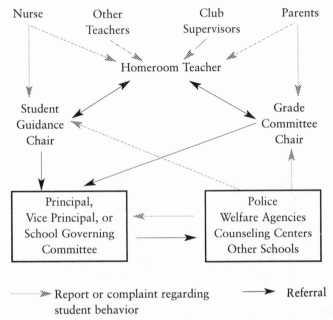

Nurse   Other   Club   Parents
Teachers   Supervisors

Homeroom Teacher

Student
Guidance
Chair

Grade
Committee
Chair

Principal,
Vice Principal, or
School Governing
Committee

Police
Welfare Agencies
Counseling Centers
Other Schools

⤜⤜⤜ Report or complaint regarding   ⟶ Referral
student behavior

Figure 6.1. Discipline Referrals in Kotani Schools

room teacher, but incidents that occurred outside school were usually filtered through Mr. Shimada.

The student guidance committee generally deals with only the most severe problems. In more routine cases, homeroom teachers call on other groups and individuals for support. Clubs play a major role in the treatment of student problems. Because most Japanese educators equate problem behavior with a disruption in routine or a disconnection from peers, teachers often try to use club participation as a way to reintegrate children with their peers and establish a daily regimen, as in the Murata case. Once students have a sense of belonging in a club, teachers reasoned, they can more easily be brought back into the classroom. Consequently, teachers who act as club advisers play a key role in the overall guidance system of the school. Because teachers have multiple roles in the school, any club adviser will supervise a wide range of students, some of whom may be in his or her own homeroom class. This built-in overlap makes it possible for several teachers to address the needs of a specific child.

Consequently, in Kotani homerooms are the basic unit of discipline in Japanese middle schools. Problems of behavior are referred back to the homeroom teacher, who then decides whether or not to ask members of the grade committee or the student guidance committee to intervene, as in the case of Murata described in chapter 3 (see fig. 6.1).

## COUNSELING AND GUIDANCE POSITIONS

The school nurse also has a key role in supporting homeroom teachers. School nurses routinely record the names and complaints of each student who comes to the nurse's office and transmits this information to the homeroom teacher and the student guidance committee. Furukawa's nurse, Mrs. Banba, conducted periodic examinations of students, paying particular attention to any signs that students might be undergoing stress. Mrs. Banba had links directly to parents, as she coordinated a nutrition program for parents, thereby adding to the total pool of information that homeroom teachers receive.

At the time of this study a small but growing number of Japanese middle schools have formal counselor positions, such as the one held by Mr. Deguchi at nearby Sakuragawa Middle School and by Mrs. Ritsukawa at Furukawa.[3] Mr. Deguchi and the other counselors, despite their extra duty, are required to teach a normal load of classes for a senior teacher (about eighteen per week) and were not exempted from participating in the various teacher committees that run the school. These counselors often deal with the most serious problems in the school. In particular, both school counselors and school nurses are dealing with greater numbers of students with school refusal syndrome in recent years. At Furukawa, Mrs. Ritsukawa has converted an unused classroom to be used by students whom she is slowly helping make the transition back into the classroom. The emphasis in every school I visited was on reintegrating these students into their original homeroom class. In no case did Mrs. Ritsukawa or any other counselor I worked with use a pull out program for students who were having trouble in class.

The close links between the nurse's office, clubs, the committees, and the homeroom teacher provide teachers with manifold sources of information and support. Although teachers are called upon to be the primary counselors and sources of discipline for their class, they can enlist a wide range of help within the school on short notice. The committees themselves have access to a wide range of external sources of support and are often the primary actors involved in negotiating external counseling or care for students. Some teachers may directly seek to advise parents on counseling options, but the school governing committee reviews most of the referrals.

## RULES, UNIFORMS AND ROUTINES

Uniforms and strict rules of deportment are also used as treatment for minor problems and constitute another organizational strategy that helps teachers maintain discipline and counsel students. Teachers at both Furukawa and Aratamachi paid close attention to student uniforms. Several times teachers expressed to me the concern that sloppy dress indicated a lassitude of spirit. Many teachers also felt that if students put an effort into their dress and deportment (i.e., loudly greeting each other in the morning, bowing with military precision) these actions would have a positive effect on their emotional state. One of the greatest fears among teachers at Furukawa and Aratamachi was that during lapses in the overall school spirit, misbehaving students (*furyō/ warui nakama*) would pull (*hipparu*) other students into problematic or illegal behavior.[4]

Teachers also facilitate communication among students, parents, and teachers by means of a "lifestyle diary" (*seikatsu dayori/nōto*) in which students record their daily activities — including study time and time spent watching television. Teachers review these journals daily or weekly. The journals, teachers explained, allow students a more private means of communication than having to come to the teacher's desk to discuss some problem. In this way, teachers provide students with a private means of discussing problems before the child exhibits aberrant behavior.

Finally, teachers place a great deal of emphasis on and spend much time on preventing problems from arising. They attempt to diffuse or interrupt what they believe to be the inevitable progression of negative behavior. As Mrs. Kawaguchi explained, teachers try to catch or pick up students who are falling from the precise routines laid down for them in school. The responsibility of the teacher extends far beyond the bounds of the school. Furukawa teachers patrolled the city at intervals during the summer break to observe local hot spots. They discussed how to alert parents to an adult talk line number and toyed with the idea of taking down the registration numbers of bicycles parked outside a local *karaoke* establishment where students might consume alcohol. Teachers are supported by local counseling centers and the police in these efforts, creating a highly effective prevention network, but one that demands long hours from teachers.[5]

### United States: The Referral System

In the United States there is more diversity in how schools organize discipline and guidance procedures, and overall there is far greater reliance on such outside professionals as the police, psychologists, and counselors. Greater numbers of students are referred to health care agencies and social workers. How schools organize to connect with these outside support systems depends partially on the initiative of the administration and partially on the funding available to the school. In figure 6.2 I have tried to schematize how students are referred to various specialists. Note that there are distinct referral

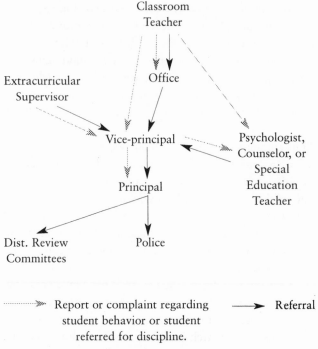

Report or complaint regarding
student behavior or student
referred for discipline.

→ Referral

Figure 6.2. Discipline Referrals in Oak Grove Schools

processes for discipline, testing for learning disorders, or other disabilities and referrals for suspected physical or sexual abuse. Since the discipline referral is the most common and since many other problems are often first recognized as discipline problems, I have used this referral process to illustrate basic patterns.

In Oak Grove teachers often were the first professionals to discover evidence of sexual or physical abuse, depression, and other emotional problems among students. In most cases of severe disruptions in the classroom, examples of extreme behavior, or suspicions of underlying problems or traumas, teachers in the Oak Grove schools referred students to staff within the school, who then decided whether or not to contact outside authorities. For example, one teacher at Wade noticed that a girl in his sixth grade class had drawn some disturbing pictures. He turned these pictures over to Barbara Lane, who talked with the family. The girl's father had kidnapped her brother when she was a child, and the girl, her brother, and mother now lived alone in hiding from the father. After learning these facts, Barbara did not pursue outside intervention. This situation was typical in that the teacher who referred the student turned over responsibility for investigating the situation and contacting outside authorities to the counselor.

At Pleasant Meadows, the budget allowed the school to hire a counselor, Mark Jerome, who visited the school three full days a week. Working through the Oak Grove Regional Counseling Center, Mark came to the school to run individual and group sessions, a job which had been carried out by a teacher until the previous year. Students were referred by teachers (75 percent), parents (10 percent) and administrators (15 percent) to Mark's groups. The groups ran for ten weeks and most focused on conflict resolution or on developing social skills among students labeled as social isolates. Students could stay in the groups for more than one quarter, and about 50 percent of the students in Mark's groups had been in groups the previous year. Most of his work, Mark said, focuses on conflict resolution and developing social skills. Most are socially introverted, but many of his individual students are clinically depressed. In his work with the children, Mark often uses sand-tray therapy — a common technique in which the child plays with a tray of sand and a set of toys under the counselor's supervision. The underlying psychological theory is that the figures in the tray have symbolic meanings that give cues to the child's inner world. One boy, Mark said, kept recreating the fights going on at home:

"The dad is divorced and remarried, and has a one-year old. This boy pairs up the good guys and bad guys. The child buries the world in the sand. The children dolls were the good guys, the bad guys were the monster images. The parents were put with the monsters. He's gaining mastery over something. His grades are up. When he's mastered these things, he'll move on."

Mark approached his work from the view that many children had a variety of internal conflicts that they needed to work out under professional supervision. He also helps organize the "natural helpers," students who are selected by peers and trained in peer counseling. At all of the Oak Grove middle schools, variations of this program are in place, and the program at Martin, another Oak Grove middle school, has been a major success.

At Wade, Barbara Lane's teaching load was reduced to facilitate her work as a counselor. Whereas Mark's work was oriented toward traditional counseling techniques (sand-tray therapy, group process), Barbara tended to focus on conflict resolution. Barbara also served as the major mediator between teachers and the schools' growing Spanish-speaking population. Few of Wade's teachers spoke Spanish, and Barbara was often called to the front office to translate. Barbara and several other teachers who had received certification also ran group sessions like Mark's aimed at helping students learn how to deal with school and their peers.

Students were also involved in schools as mediators and counselors. At

Pleasant Meadows, selected upperclassmen received training in conflict resolution and listening to peer problems. These students were often called on to
help incoming students deal with adjusting to life at a new school. At Martin,
teachers had supported a peer-mediation program in which students could
elect to talk to peer counselors about conflicts that arose in their lives.

The role of counselor in the Oak Grove schools in the 1990s was in flux.
Many schools, I was told, were having to do without counselors, and the
workload for school psychologists, administrators, and teachers was corre-
spondingly increased. Already, in the Oak Grove district, the school psychologists had to make the rounds of several schools. Ann Jacobs, who worked at
Wade, also worked at an elementary school with 850 students. She noted that
her caseload had basically limited her to giving diagnostic tests and working
with special education teachers to develop Individual Educational Programs.

Wade and Pleasant Meadows approached the organization of counseling in
different ways but had fairly similar relations with other outside sources of
support in dealing with crises.

The procedures used in Oak Grove tend to maximize the (professional)
attention given to an individual student but minimize the teacher's control of
the process and the kind of information the teacher receives. During my fieldwork I did not find any formal mechanism by which teachers were notified of
the results of these inquiries. That is to say, in most cases teachers did not learn
the outcome of the referral or heard about it only through informal channels
such as conversations in passing in the halls. The opposite is true in Kotani,
where individual students rarely met with trained counseling professionals
and where teacher control of the process was strong. The ways in which these
systems functioned can best be seen by examining some specific examples. At
Wade, these decisions were largely in the hands of Barbara, Emily, and Ralph
Forest, the vice-principal. At Pleasant Meadows, there was a committee system that dealt with the most severe cases on a weekly basis.

In cases in which students had a diagnosed problem or a record of problem
behavior, Oak Grove teachers were also involved with Child Study Teams,
which consisted of teachers, counselors, and often the school psychologist.
(Students with chronic attendance problems were referred to the district Attendance Review Panel.) Students were given a review at the district office, at
which the student, parent, and teachers involved with the student were allowed to attend. These Child Study Teams functioned much like Japanese
committees, but they were convened on an ad hoc basis.

The Team Leaders Committee at Pleasant Meadows functioned in a way similar to the School Governing Committee at Furukawa. A representative from
each grade, the team leader for that grade, the vice-principal, the principal, the

counselor, and a representative from special education met once a week to plan events and to deal with any current problems that had occurred. This committee was a permanent part of Pleasant Meadows School and afforded a more consistent channel for information flow than did the Child Study Teams. This committee allowed Pleasant Meadows' teachers to attain a higher degree of integration and coordination as a staff when responding to student problems.

## Harming the Self

Suicide can be viewed as either the ultimate act of self-destruction or the ultimate act of individuality. In the West, suicide has been linked with the trials of youth and adolescence at least since Goethe's days. It has played a large role in Japanese history also and has been linked with images of youth in the modern era.[6] The romantic treatment of suicide in both European and Japanese literature stands in sharp contrast to the actual experiences which teachers encounter. In the United States and Japan, teachers are often called on to intervene when adolescents attempt suicide. The ways in which teachers see their actions as being efficacious provides striking insights into how they think about the selves of their students, and how schools function in the face of severe adolescent disturbance.

### ATTEMPTING TO RECONNECT

For several months, I followed the case of a young girl at Furukawa, Kaneko Yamanaka. Kaneko had a history of troubled behavior, including substance abuse and running away from home. By the time I met Kaneko, her mother had largely given up on her daughter, and through the work of the Furukawa teachers she had been placed in a group foster home.

During her first year at Furukawa, Kaneko posed a considerable puzzle to the teachers. She was chastised for wandering the halls and failing to show up for school on time. As she did not respond to teachers' guidance, the staff began to interpret her actions as indicative that she didn't want to be adult. Unfortunately, Mrs. Kawaguchi explained, an older physical education teacher had slapped Kaneko for talking back, and this had given her a general distrust of teachers.[7] It was, Mrs. Kawaguchi later explained, another case in which Kaneko felt her connection to others was broken.

Mrs. Kawaguchi took an active role in trying to counsel both Kaneko and her mother. All teachers agreed that despite her stressful situation at home, if she were reconnected to her class she might be able to graduate and get on with her life. When relations between Kaneko and her mother deteriorated, the teachers took on even more responsibility. Mrs. Kawaguchi also tried to arrange counseling sessions between Kaneko and her mother at a regional counseling center in the capital. Several times during the study the senior teachers at Furukawa met to discuss Kaneko's case. During these sessions I learned that she had attempted suicide (by cutting her wrists) sometime prior to the beginning of my fieldwork. During her stay at the foster home, the Furukawa teachers acted in loco parentis by talking with the foster home staff on at least a weekly basis. Kaneko had difficulty adjusting to life at the home, and her school performance continued to deteriorate. The teachers expressed concern that she would be drawn into gangs (*bōryokudan*) as well as negatively affect other students. During her final year at Furukawa, when Kaneko began to exhibit even more extreme behavior, the foster home mother called the teachers when she was rushed to a local clinic after going into convulsions, the cause of which was unclear. Mrs. Kawaguchi, Mr. Hamanaka, and Mr. Mizuno, not her mother, arrived in the wee hours of the morning to oversee her care. As I have described elsewhere, working with Kaneko put an enormous strain on the Furukawa teachers and showed the inadequacy of teachers to care for such severe cases and the lack of a mental health care infrastructure in this part of Japan. When I left Japan, Kaneko had been reunited with her mother, and the family was seeing a local monk/spiritual medium.[8]

## CONCERN AND REFERRAL

Francice Rohnert, in her last year of middle school, was a popular girl, a girl who, according to one of her teachers, Sandy Briotte, "set the trends." Francice, like Kaneko, tried to commit suicide. During her time at Wade, Francice tried twice to commit suicide, once by slicing her wrists, once by taking an overdose of some kind of medication. Teachers reported that Francice had written a note to friends in which she stated, "You won't have to worry about me in a couple of weeks." Her friends also said that she showed them medication in her purse. At one point in Adrian Norris's class, she emptied out a pill bottle on a desk and told her friends she was going to take them all and overdose.

After a pill incident, Adrian referred Francice to Barbara. When Barbara heard about this she called Francice's mother and said, "You need to get her to a hospital." As Barbara related the story to me, "If the parents wouldn't have acted, I would have had to put a seventy-two-hour hold on her. Chambers [a local hospital] gave her a psychological evaluation and they took her up to Portside [a psychiatric facility]. Her parents pulled her out before the counselors got any info out of her. Portside can only keep them a certain amount of time—the counselor from Portside said that she was sullen."

In discussions with Barbara Lane, I found out that Francice's mother was considered to be an alcoholic and that Francice had suffered from depression for some time. In April of her last year, the mother and the school staff agreed that Francice should be placed in the care of a psychiatric unit. The mother, however, apparently did not follow up on the suggestions.

After leaving Portside, Francice returned briefly to Wade and then left to finish the rest of eighth grade in self-study at home. Barbara was worried that Francice would not receive proper medical attention and that she would not complete her self-study work. Barbara was also unclear as to just who was in Francice's home. Although a stepfather was supposed to be living in the house, Barbara had not actually met him. At one point, Barbara expressed her fear about possible sexual abuse but said she had no evidence to go on. After Francice's mother decided to pull her out of school, Barbara was effectively cut off from Francice. While Francice was formally a student at Wade, Barbara had tried to push the family to get professional treatment for Francice: "She wasn't seeing the psychiatrist. I had to check with the parents and make sure she was going, but now I won't have the time to check."

The cases of Francice and Kaneko were emotionally painful for all of the teachers involved. In both cases, teachers felt emotionally close to the students and wished to help them. Indeed, in both cases, the school staff tried to get outside professional help, but in Japan senior teachers essentially supervised the process, and the homeroom teacher was involved in major decisions about Kaneko's care. While the system supported teachers in trying to care for Kaneko, the Furukawa staff simply did not have the training or resources necessary to effectively treat her case. And while some teachers took positive steps toward getting outside psychiatric help, others (such as her physical education teacher) engaged in behavior that was clearly detrimental to her mental health. The quality of outside school care available to her was, in comparison to that available to Francice, totally inadequate. In this regard, Kotani appears to fall well below the level of social services available in Japan's large metropolitan areas.

In Oak Grove, at each step of referral, from Adrian to Barbara, from Barbara to the Portside facility, the teacher's control over the process was attenuated and information generally was not conveyed to teachers. Both the hospital and psychiatric facility were limited by law in terms of the type of information they could provide to the school. Within Wade, Barbara freely shared her knowledge of the case with Adrian and other teachers when opportunities arose. But in the absence of any formal mechanisms to support this communication, the information flowing to the teachers was sporadic. Having heavy class loads and other duties, teachers at Wade and Oak Grove had to make an effort to follow up on students like Francice.

## *Loss and Grief*

Adults and young adolescents must deal with the loss of loved ones, expressing grief in appropriate ways. Early adolescence is often the time when young people experience the first loss of a close family member. Coming to terms with the finality of human existence is difficult for both Japanese and American adolescents. Teachers in both countries expected that by middle school, students would have an understanding of death. But when faced with the death of a fellow student, the teachers mobilized the schools' resources in different ways to provide support for students.

During my fieldwork in Kotani and Oak Grove, two students, one in each district, died, prompting the staff to organize special events to deal with the loss. Mark, a sixth grade boy at Wade was killed in a car accident, and Junko, a girl at Aratamachi, died as the result of a terminal illness.[9] I had not met either student prior to their death and have few details about their lives or their role in the school community. In Mark's case I have notes on how the teachers and administrators reacted to his death and was able to observe the counseling processes that went on. Junko's death occurred during my pilot study, and I have only limited information on the range of events that went on in the school. Other differences were that Junko's death was not unanticipated. Teachers at Aratamachi knew that there was a high probability that she would succumb to her illness in middle school. Mark's death, by contrast, was totally unexpected and may have had more of an emotional impact on his schoolmates and teachers.

The primary response of the teachers at Aratamachi to Junko's death was to organize a schoolwide ceremony that all students and teachers took part in. At about ten o'clock in the morning, the entire school lined up by homeroom class in single file along the streets leading to Aratamachi. The students were extremely quiet and subdued. As some students began whispering, "It's coming," the entire student body bowed as the hearse slowly drove by. Afterward, walking back to the school, Mrs. Kawaguchi explained that Junko's class was allowed to leave school to attend the funeral ceremonies held later in the day.

At Pleasant Meadows, there was no schoolwide ceremony. Mark's death was announced at an emergency meeting of teachers in the staff room — a significant departure from the usual procedure whereby Emily would make important announcements over the loudspeaker during morning assembly. Emily asked teachers to "Let kids know your feelings" and to inform students that if they were upset by the event they could go to the office to talk to someone. Emily had arranged for a counselor from a local crisis center to be at the school to talk with staff and students.

After listening to the usual notices over the loudspeaker, Sandy's class was surprised to hear Emily say that each teacher had "a private announcement." Sandy then talked about Mark's death. Sandy allowed the students to talk about the incident for five minutes. Many of them wanted more information. Later in the day an outside counselor, Debbie Hoffman, came to Wade to talk to any students or staff who wanted to see her. Debbie said that she had worked with schools before and was "impressed that the principal asked teachers to make an announcement" and had organized the crisis counseling so quickly. She noted that "kids need to get back to normalcy" and that events like Mark's death "trigger feelings around deaths in our own families." Students were given individual passes to go to speak with the counselor.

INDIVIDUAL GRIEF IN A PUBLIC PLACE

The Kotani staff tended to deal with loss and grief, as with responsibility, by diffusing the significance of the loss to a wide range of people and creating a ceremony (as in the money returning ceremony in the Murata case). In Oak Grove, loss and grieving were treated as an individual concern. The school offered support in a way that made the students responsible for determining the degree of grief they would show and the degree of counseling they would need. Kotani teachers were supported by committees of teachers that advised and often took responsibility for various students. Oak Grove teachers were supported by being given significant latitude in determining what students were to be referred for special counseling and by having special support staff brought to the school.

In Kotani, the school as a social unit organized a mass, formalized expression of grief for Junko's passing. All school events were suspended and the entire faculty and school staff mobilized to say a last farewell. In Oak Grove, administrators and teachers worked to allow students to deal with their grief in an individualistic way. Great emphasis was placed on allowing students to deal with the loss in a personal way. Students in any class were allowed to leave class to talk with the special counselor, if *they themselves* felt a need to do it.

Both sets of teachers worked hard in response to these deaths, and both deaths resulted in organized reactions that were significantly out of the day-to-day norm for the operation of the school. The emphasis in the United States was one of personal loss and coping. A trained counselor was provided at Wade. There was significant emphasis on counseling and professional work with the emotions. In Japan, the emphasis was less on personal dealings with the loss than on organizing a way for all to participate in a ceremony that was at once one of respect and one of grieving. At Aratamachi, the teachers dealt with the incident themselves.

There was no denying the emotions in either school. Students and teachers openly wept as Junko's hearse passed by. Students in Sandy's class, although they did not know Mark, were shaken. And I am sure that many tears were shed in the group sessions that Debbie Hoffman led. But grief was a personal matter in Oak Grove, one that every individual was required to deal with and seek outside help with on a case-by-case basis. The institution's role was to provide the help or support individuals might need. In Japan, the ceremony almost seemed designed to provoke deep emotions. The sight of nearly a thousand students bent in formal bows, many weeping, moved me to tears even though I did not know Junko. Individual grief was expressed in solidarity with a group in a public display.

The emphasis on group versus individual displays of grief is clear, but this dichotomy must not be overdrawn. In all likelihood, individual students conveyed their feelings about Junko's death to their teachers via the lifestyle diaries they filled out, and the dedication of a memorial to Mark provided a public ceremony for Oak Grove students. Both individual and group expressions of grief occur in each nation. Rather, the most significant difference was the use of professionals from outside the school. This suggests that American teachers saw themselves as less able to deal with the emotional and psychological reactions of the students. The Kotani teachers saw themselves as able to meet this task.[10] The events following Mark's death suggest that American teachers must deal with adolescent grief by seeking professional referrals. The events following Junko's death suggest that teachers must take responsibility for organizing a schoolwide response to the tragedy. In a similar way, American teachers responded to fighting in the school by utilizing external actors.

### External Actors and Intervention: Violence

Shortly after counseling one boy, Dave, the vice-principal at Wade emerged from his office to discover that two boys had gotten into a fistfight on the playground and that Emily had called the police. Emily reasoned that since one boy appeared to have broken the other's nose the matter was technically a case of assault. If the school did not call in the police, they could be held responsible for negligence. Dave had another opinion: "Emily directed that the police be called in. That probably comes from the district. Annette (the superintendent) thinks the police should be called all the time. She wants CPS [Child Protective Services] in here every time we have a fight."

In Kotani, police will turn juvenile offenders over to the custody of teachers if the parents cannot be reached, but in Oak Grove teachers have little control over or responsibility for student actions that might legally be considered a crime. Problems on or off schoolgrounds — such as one student physically attacking another — were regarded as crimes and therefore under police jurisdiction. School administrators were required to call police in the event of physical attacks or theft of expensive items.

Teachers saw the use of police on a more frequent basis as evidence of a tendency to treat physical confrontations between young adolescents as crimes rather than violations of school rules. Many Oak Grove teachers believed this removed teachers' or administrators' authority to deal with student problems that happen on campus. Media reports about litigation in schools in California strengthened teachers' perceptions that playground fights may now be considered felonies.[11] The perception among teachers in Oak Grove is that when parents are willing to press charges against students, the school has no choice but to call in the police or face lawsuits for negligence. The media attention to legal action by parents appeared to heighten teachers' sensitivity to these issues.[12]

In Kotani, police presence on campus appeared to be by invitation only.[13] I recorded no police visits after reports of student problems during my study. During my three years of teaching in Japan, the only time police appeared at a school where I worked was when windows were broken by someone throwing rocks at night. Fights between students, Kotani teachers said, were dealt with by the school, and teachers in the past had forced students who injured others to make a formal visit to the victims' home in order to apologize and pay for any hospital expenses. In some cases, teachers reported, the homeroom teacher would accompany the offending students.

Differences in how teachers responded to fights among students probably reflect differences in beliefs about the adolescent personality but are also affected by levels of crime in the society. In the United States, violence played a strong role in shaping teachers' beliefs and organizational routines.

## VIOLENCE

A disgruntled schoolteacher handed in her resignation with the following comment: "in our public schools today, the teachers are afraid of the principals, the principals are afraid of the superintendents, the superintendents are afraid of the board, the board members are afraid of the parents, the parents are afraid of the children, and the children are afraid of nobody.
— [Newspaper article copied and posted in the Wade teachers' room]

Fear of violence permeated the Oak Grove schools. Even in the suburban parts of Oak Grove weapons incidents occurred. In the year prior to the study, a boy was suspended for bringing a knife to Pleasant Meadows. In the late

1980s, an Oak Grove middle school student was under investigation for murder. Rumors of students bringing guns into school or planning to shoot other students or teachers only served to increase the general climate of fear of violence. While no weapons were brought to either school during my study, student and teacher worries about such a scenario were clearly evident.

Fear coupled with a lack of good information increased the spread of rumors and misconceptions. For example, a boy named Roy in Gretchen Jondervag's class was rumored to have been seen with a handgun at his home and was reported to be coming to school to shoot a teacher. For several days, this topic buzzed around the lunchroom. Dave indicated that the story was started by a student, and his questioning led him to the conclusion that the story was a pure fabrication. A similar rumor at Wade suggested that an unnamed boy was planning to come to the school to kill Emily with a shotgun. I heard the story from several Wade teachers, some of whom said that Emily had had to go into hiding; but when I talked with Emily about it she confirmed that the rumor was false. She thought that the story had started from a rumor that a boy had been seen playing with his father's shotgun while home on suspension.

The fear that students might bring a weapon to school and turn it on teachers seemed to be intensified by the use of violent gestures among students. In both Nancy Carrither's and Janice Leitskov's class, I saw boys stare at one another and make punching gestures with what appeared to be open hostility.[14] In one of Sarah Martin's classes, two boys, Gilbert and Andrew, made punching gestures toward her when she turned her back to the board. One of the boys then turned to a classmate, saying, "I'm gonna beat your butt." Their talk continued in whispers. I caught fragments of talk about plans for a "jumping," in which several people assault an unsuspecting victim and pummel him or her.

Oak Grove teachers' sensitivity to violence was strongly linked to a fear of gangs. Nick Brisbane told me that local gangs "jumped in" kids right on the Wade campus.[15] Families like the Ramirez (of whom Dave Jarvis said, "They've supplied our special ed. classes for years") were considered gang families, and their children considered potentially violent. Teachers were not the only ones worried about violence. The students themselves expressed a fear of violence, and students depicted certain families and neighborhoods as dangerous, although they did not use the label "gang" as teachers did. Rather, adolescents tended to focus on behaviors or actions that might put them at risk of violence. In Nancy Carrither's class Raymond told Chico, who had flashed about forty dollars in cash before his peers, "You don't live East Side. If you did you don't be here." Fights among students were also a common topic in the classrooms of Oak Grove. Girls as well as boys discussed who was involved in fights at school and out. Mary, in addition to her confrontations with Janice, would brag in class about beating up other girls after school.

In Kotani, violence was considered an unlikely threat.[16] Mrs. Chino noted that about ten years earlier some students at Furukawa had hit teachers during the height of the "in-school violence" period (*kōnai bōryoku*). She also said that such incidents had virtually disappeared. Teachers at Furukawa and Aratamachi referred to school violence as something that had passed. Other teachers that I spoke with had fresher memories. One teacher I interviewed for the TIMSS study described his experience with school violence while he was teaching at one of the more rural schools in the prefecture:

> It was just like on *Kinpatsu-sensei* [a popular television show]. The students took up posts before the teacher's room and blocked the hall. They broke the glass. This confrontation in front of the room escalated, and it turned into a mess in the teacher's room. I was hit in the nose with a drawer. They were mad at the teachers because the teachers weren't working together. And, in that area, there was a lot of divorce. So the kids were very upset. Some weren't studying and the whole school was tense. The school and parent relations were disputed; no real PTA relations. That is why it happened.

This teacher's account of school violence in Japan demonstrates why, although school violence is of concern to the Japanese, it does not impact teachers' lives and attitudes the way it does in the United States. This teacher, like the Kotani teachers, saw violence flowing out of a lack of human relations: gaps in the involvement between parents and children or teachers and students. But these were gaps that the school could (and should have) worked to mend: the school was not perceived as being besieged by a violent surrounding culture.[17]

## Summary

The organization of school, police, and social welfare institutions in the United States reflects a belief in the necessity of specialists to deal with mental and emotional problems. Suicide is a breakdown in the psyche or personality; suicidal tendencies are personality disorders and are the province of medical specialists. It would do no good for Oak Grove teachers to attempt to treat these problems and might even make things worse. In Kotani, however, students like Kaneko were seen as having a fundamental flaw in their upbringing that prevented their character from developing. There was a pervasive belief in the power of teachers to correct such defects. If the same beliefs in personality, identity, and mental illness were highly institutionalized in Japan, then the doctors at the hospital where Kaneko was first brought would never have released her to the teachers. The doctors, however, were actually relieved that the school personnel were willing to take over the case and work with Kaneko.

In caring for Kaneko, most teachers at Furukawa displayed extraordinary care and were deeply concerned with all the details of the girl's life. The Japanese teachers were more informed about the personality of Kaneko than the teachers at Wade were about Francice. This difference was largely a result of the organization of mental health care systems of referral. The teachers at Wade had little access to Francice's case. In contrast, the Japanese system allowed Kaneko's teachers to be major actors in her care. The diffuse nature of the teacher's role as well as the linkages among school, hospitals, and formal counseling centers opened up avenues for Japanese teachers, but in the end these limited resources were insufficient to effect positive change in Kaneko's life.

There appear to be striking similarities between the theories employed by Japanese teachers and the neo-Confucian philosophy which developed in the latter half of the Tokugawa era. Kaibara Ekken wrote, "Human nature is originally good, but in ordinary people this goodness is lost by the obscuration of the physical disposition and by human desires.

The nature of all people is good and, based on this fact, they can be induced to activate their innate goodness" (Tucker, 1989:146).

Teachers regularly tried to activate students' good inner nature. They saw that unrestrained expression of personal preferences can lead to undesirable socialization and breakdown of the correct development of the child. Current Japanese worries about school violence, school refusal, and bullying are similarly linked to beliefs that modern, commercial society and school competition have destroyed children's ability to connect with and care for others.[18]

In the face of the U.S. media coverage of adolescent violence in the early 1990s, it would have been difficult for any teacher to retain faith in the innate goodness of human nature. The levels of violence and teachers' perceptions of violence reinforced a belief that many young adolescents were raised in social circumstances in which personality or emotional problems disrupted the basic process of maturation. The Oak Grove teachers did not believe that they alone could address these deficiencies or disruptions. They believed that specialists — psychologists, social workers, and the police — were essential in dealing with these problems and in keeping the school safe.

In all of the counseling taking place in American schools, be it group or individual, the goal is to allow the individual to navigate his or her social and emotional world successfully. Conflict resolution, internal or external, is a crucial task that American middle school students need to learn how to do. The individual must learn to clearly think about duties and responsibilities as well as rights. More important, the individual must learn what he or she believes is true and stick to it. The struggle is an emotional or mental one. And the atmosphere most conducive to facilitating the growth of the individual is one that is caring (supportive) but well defined (well ordered). In this age of identity crisis the adolescent needs professional attention.

## Implications

In Oak Grove, criminal acts resulted in a referral out of the school's system of discipline to the police, Child Protective Services, or other agencies. In Kotani, teachers continued to play a significant role in working with the adolescent. This pattern of expulsion of students from the system versus teachers' working with outside authorities was common for acts of violence as well as for substance abuse. The autonomy of the school in Japan is stronger and the boundaries of the organization more tightly maintained. In the United States, the school's organizational boundaries are loosely maintained, and any disruption in the community — real or perceived — can strongly impact the school.

From a strictly organizational point of view, American teachers were highly buffered from responsibilities for dealing with student crises. In most cases, teachers referred students out of the classroom, and in many cases were required by law to contact other professionals. This was not the case in Japan, where teachers tended to be made central participants in dealing with treatment of student problems. The fact that teachers in Japan were less buffered from these kinds of demands increased their workload, but also appeared to increase both the kind of information they received and their input into the decisions of school committees or outside authorities. It also meant that teachers were often faced with situations well beyond their capabilities. In the United States, individual teachers could also have substantial input into such decisions, but only if the teacher took the initiative to attend the meetings and make time to meet with or telephone the authorities working with the students.

Structural forces clearly play a significant role in determining overall patterns of adolescent deviance. The access to educational advancement is much more limited in Japan than in the United States. At the same time, teachers' perceptions of juvenile problems show far more consistency and a far narrower range of expected behaviors. In Japan, student disruption and problem behavior are tightly linked to the schooling system. Juvenile delinquency is signaled, in Japanese middle schools, by a strikingly narrow set of physical displays and follows a course of events that is recognized by teachers and students.

Violence, disruption, and rebellion are linked, in U.S. culture, with a prolonged and pervasive adolescence and with stereotypes of ethnic and linguistic minorities.[19] Beliefs in the disruptive nature of puberty coexist with beliefs that poor parenting results in defiant, disruptive, and often violent adoles- cents. Ethnic differences in family structure, parenting styles, and life course expectations all acerbate miscommunication between family and school, making teachers less able to receive accurate information about the lives of the adolescents they work with. As a result, many U.S. teachers from middle-class backgrounds perceive themselves and their schools as being under siege.

The adolescents of Oak Grove had access to far more professional health care than did the adolescents of Kotani. And the lack of training in counseling and psychology among the Kotani teachers appeared to severely limit their ability to respond to serious cases. The tight communication and committee support was effective in dealing with small problems in Kotani, but overwhelmed teachers when students had major problems.

Overall the Oak Grove system was far superior to the Kotani system in getting professional care to students.[20] The system was hampered by the fact that teachers were not adequately supported in their work in recognizing and referring students with problems. Schools like Pleasant Meadows captured the more positive elements of the Japanese system (i.e., its strong preventative component and high level of teacher integration) but were still constrained by funding. Rather than increasing the time teachers have to meet and deal with student problems, budget cuts in the Oak Grove district have reduced the support for teachers. The cutting of such services at this time appears to be a short-sighted strategy.

# 7

## The Disruptive Adolescent, Defiance, Delinquency and the Family

In the United States teachers believe that puberty destabilizes young adolescents, while at the same time they expect them to begin to control their behavior. The Oak Grove teachers appeared willing to give young adolescents the benefit of the doubt (such as in the examples from Hattie Sonval and Janice Leitskov's class) when disruptive behavior appeared to be directly caused by hormones. But in other cases, the Oak Grove teachers held students responsible for their actions. If teachers thought the behavior was defiant, it received a particularly harsh response. Problems like theft or persistent patterns of antisocial behavior were linked to problems in the student's basic upbringing and socialization, that is, the family. In these cases, teachers were most likely to refer adolescents to such outside agents as the juvenile authorities, social workers, or even the police.

Puberty was not considered a source of major disruption in Kotani. Teachers believed that, given proper routines, young adolescents could control their behavior and organize themselves quite effectively in groups. Teachers did not often link lapses in individual behavior or classroom disruption to puberty and tended to hold groups or leaders of groups responsible for group actions. There was much less sensitivity to defiance, some teachers believing even that the resistant attitude associated with puberty was a positive thing. In cases of persistent patterns of antisocial behavior, however, the Kotani teachers appeared to make the same causal connection as Oak Grove teachers: they blamed the family.

Rebellion or resistance was associated with puberty by both U.S. and Japanese teachers. In both countries, teachers believe that pubertal processes initiate changes in adolescent capabilities and adolescent behavior that could increase adolescent tendencies to resist or rebel against authority figures. A certain level of resistance or rebellion was seen as part of the normal process of maturation, and both Kotani and Oak Grove teachers believed the middle school years were marked by more disruption (of classroom or school procedures) than either the elementary or high school years.

In this chapter I analyze what teachers think about disruptive behavior and how they respond to it. The distinction between resistance and rebellion made in chapter 4 is highly salient. Rebellion in the United States is linked with the concept of "defiance," a key factor in determining whether teachers ignore or downplay acts of disruption or not. When Oak Grove teaches perceive defiance they are far more likely to react in a severe manner. The story line of defiance is far weaker in Kotani; this is consistent with the general perception in Japan of the adolescent as being resistant, but not hostile or rebellious. Both U.S. and Japanese teachers link repetitive or severely disruptive behavior with problems in the adolescent's family or upbringing. What is striking is the convergence of opinions between the two sets of teachers on the role of the family in the most serious cases of juvenile delinquency.

Given the very different beliefs about development that these teachers expressed about other aspects of development, I am struck by how similar they viewed the role of the family in serious cases of disruptive behavior. In the final section I analyze how teachers view the role that families (or communities) play in juvenile delinquency and juvenile gangs. Many U.S. teachers, though not all, also appear to associate defiant and even violent adolescents with ethnic or linguistic minorities or poor families, whereas many Japanese teachers appeared to associate troubled adolescents with single-family homes. Perceptions of violence and beliefs about adolescent gangs in Oak Grove were a major factor in shaping teachers' awareness of and reaction to disruption in the United States

## Classroom Disruption: Definitions and Responses

What kind of act disrupts the learning process in a classroom? To a large extent, it is an act that draws the teacher's attention and causes him or her to change her behavior, thereby interrupting the flow of the lesson. For example, as a graduate student, I trained teachers in cooperative group-work techniques. As part of the process, we recorded each time the teacher verbally reprimanded, admonished, or threatened students with punishment and used these charts to provide feedback that helped teachers to lower their rates of disciplining.[1] Many experienced teachers learn how to discipline without interrupting the flow of the classroom lesson. Gretchen Jondervag, like an experienced orchestra conductor, was able to verbally engage her class, use physical proximity to quiet a pair of students, and direct another student with a gesture.[2] Most teachers in Oak Grove encountered many student behaviors that distracted them and disrupted the lesson.

Vignette 1: Oak Grove
[Condensed from field notes.]

At 11:53 Lynn is into her second period of science. She spends the first ten minutes of class going over the class's last test. She admonishes one boy who is talking, "Adam, that's two strikes."

By 12:14 Lynn has written four students' names on the board as part of her discipline system. Students get three strikes before receiving a punishment — usually after-school detention. "People are not responding to the lights and we're wasting time," Lynn says. "Robert, shhh."

Robert responds, "I wasn't talking." [He was talking, and both Lynn and I saw him directly.] Lynn ignores this remark and responds, "Sit right!"

"I am!" he responds and moves from being sprawled across his desk on his belly to a sitting posture while glaring at Lynn.

Four-person groups now begin to get the dirt for the class terrarium project. The students are seated in groups of four, and one student from each group is supposed to get the material, but sometimes two or more come up. Lynn has handed out a paper that describes how to make the terrarium. Lynn moves from group to group responding to student requests for help and demonstrating how to set up the terrarium. Robert keeps calling to her saying, "Mrs.! Mrs.!" One or two students in each group appear to dominate the activity while others get bored and drift off.

Many students are talking and appear to be ignoring the lesson. Lynn puts a check by Monica's name on the board — this means that she will get detention. The bell rings and students hastily pack away their materials. Monica comes up to Lynn and with tears in her eyes says, "I didn't say it to you."

"We'll talk about this later," Lynn responds. [Apparently the girl used inappropriate language, but I could not record what it was.]

After the girl leaves, Lynn turns to me and says, "She wants to negotiate."

The room is now empty of students, and Lynn begins preparing the materials for yet another class.

Lynn's class was fairly typical of the Oak Grove classrooms I observed during my pilot and main study. The class periods were filled with student behavior that caused small disruptions in the flow of the classroom. In the next section I have selected field notes from an Aratamachi classroom that was atypical in that it contained a large amount of the kind of student activities (talking, moving about, playing with materials) that Oak Grove teachers found disruptive. From the standpoint of looking for disruptive behavior, the typical Kotani classroom is incredibly boring. I attended classes day after day, but in my notes I remarked that most teachers made only sporadic requests for quiet. Although some Kotani teachers (including one veteran teacher like Noriko Tanaka) used as many verbal admonitions as Oak Grove teachers, on balance teachers would admonish students once or twice during the entire period.

Vignette 2: Kotani
[Condensed from field notes]

At 9:36 Mr. Hori enters the lab at Aratamachi, and the students, who had been talking noisily, stand and bow. The day's lesson is precipitating solids in a solution, and Mr. Hori will teach it three times today. Mr. Hori diagrams the steps students are to take on the board. Twice he tells the students, "Don't talk." Each time the students quiet down for a moment and then resume talking. At 9:48 he tells the students to get the equipment: Bunsen burners, salt, other chemicals, and water. The students are already in groups (*han*) and apparently know where all the materials are. Mr. Hori gives them no instructions as to where they can find the burners and test tubes. The students work quickly to collect the materials and get the experiments set up, yet continue to talk. The snippets of conversation that reach my ears do not appear to have any relation to the lesson or the task at hand. Mr. Hori stands up front distributing material as the students continue to chatter away while working on the experiment.

Mr. Hori circulates among the groups. He advises some groups on how to get the salt to dissolve faster, adjusts the burners for others. Some groups proceed at a much faster pace than others do. There is a great deal of noise and talking, but now most of the student talk appears to be focused on the task. Mr. Hori continues to ignore virtually all student talk except direct questions to him.

As the experiments progress, more and more students engage in off-task behavior. One boy squirts a girl with water, and she cries, "Teacher!" but, to my surprise, Mr. Hori has left the room [to get more materials]. Students in several groups are boiling the material away over the Bunsen flames. One group boils off the mixture too fast, sending bits of hot precipitate flying onto the desk. Another boy has no hot mitts on and attempts to use his hand-kerchief to remove the solution, inadvertently setting the handkerchief on fire. In neither case does Mr. Hori reprimand the individuals or groups.

Mr. Hori gives a ten-minute warning before the class is over, but some groups are already packing up. Mr. Hori does not seem angry with the class; indeed he appears amused and exchanges fake karate chops with a group of boys who have been particularly rambunctious in their movements around the classroom. The bell rings as cleanup is still in progress. Mr. Hori calls for quiet, which the students generally follow. After Mr. Hori explains the homework, the class bows, puts their chairs away, and leaves for their next class.

I briefly talk with Mr. Hori as he hurries back to the teachers' room to prepare for his next class. While he felt this class was perhaps disorganized, he also thought the students had understood the basic principle of precipitates.

DEFINING DISRUPTION

Mr. Hori and Lynn are both experienced teachers of science. Both classes were engaged in lessons that required the manipulation of various materials. Although both lessons were group-based, hands-on lessons, the teacher's re-sponse to student actions varied significantly. These two vignettes were not chosen to provide typical examples of levels of classroom disruption. I chose them because they illustrate the difficulty of defining just what disruption means. During my fieldwork I tried to construct a rubric for identifying inci-dents of disruption in order to systematically compare the Oak Grove and Kotani schools. I was ultimately forced to abandon this attempt because the most important factor in determining if an incident was disruptive was the teachers' reaction.

Defining classroom disruption proved to be a matter of understanding not only the teachers' basic attitudes toward teaching and students but also the implicit norms present in the school cultures of each country. There were few behaviors — except for acts of physical violence and loud verbal abuse — that both Kotani and Oak Grove teachers would agree was disruptive.[3] How teachers dealt with classroom disruption and rebellion revealed much about how they perceived the nature of the students they were working with.

There was considerable variation among individual Oak Grove teachers. Some, like Nick Brisbane, tended to see any talking in class as a disruption, whereas others, like Sandy Briotte, did not. Oak Grove teachers also believed that it was their duty as teachers to intervene when students were having a disagreement in class or engaging in behavior that was off-task. In Oak Grove, off-task behavior — from writing notes to talking in class — could be construed as an act of disrespect or an attempt to undermine the authority of the teacher, depending on the individual students and teachers involved.

In general, Kotani teachers simply did not appear to interpret students' off-task behavior — talking, playing with a pen, staring out the window — as a sign of disrespect or an attempt to undermine their authority. Kotani teachers usually described these acts as exaggerated attempts to attract attention and support.[4] Students who rebelled or acted out in extreme ways in Kotani tended to be viewed as hurt, sad, or confused. Such incidents were rare, and teachers in both Furukawa and Aratamachi spent little time on what U.S. teachers call classroom management.

Kotani teachers tended to react like Mr. Hori. They utilized strategies that minimized direct confrontation and redirected students back on task. Teachers in each nation varied in their use of these techniques, with young teachers more likely to stop a lesson and admonish students than older ones. In this regard Mr. Hori's behavior was more typical of experienced teachers in both countries. While years of teaching did appear to affect how teachers reacted to their classes, however, it was not a perfect predictor of teacher behavior: cultural expectations appeared to have a larger effect.[5]

Teachers' perceptions of disruption impacted the way class was taught, creating national patterns. Lynn's pattern of interrupting the flow of the lesson to comment on and redirect behavior was quite common in Oak Grove but very rare in Kotani.[6] Although it is an overgeneralization, at times the teachers in Oak Grove spent more time on student behavior modification than on the academic subject, despite their stated belief that they should be academic specialists and not baby-sitters.[7] Compared to the Oak Grove teachers, Kotani teachers were far less likely to stop class to admonish a student for individual behavior.[8] The teachers in Oak Grove appeared far more likely to interpret student behavior as disruptive than their Kotani counterparts.

Much of the difference in the amount of teacher management appears to stem from the fact that each teacher in Oak Grove had a distinctive teaching style and used various kinds of instructional techniques (e.g., group work as opposed to cooperative groups). In Kotani, the core subject teachers all used the same basic instructional pattern the vast majority of the time.[9] Similarly, each Oak Grove teacher had to get the students into his or her classroom after each period change and get them settled. The fact that Kotani teachers moved from classroom to classroom (instead of the students) appeared to considerably diminish the potential for students to become overly boisterous in their play. Nonetheless, Oak Grove and Kotani teachers differed significantly in what they believed caused disruptive behavior.

## Defiance and Authority

At Wade, I watched Janice Leitskov engage in day-to-day battles with Mary over her behavior.[10] Janice attempted to redirect Mary to her seatwork or group project. Mary's stock reply was, "You can't order me around." And if the fight escalated, Mary inevitably called Janice a bitch! This was an act that Janice could not ignore, and Mary was off to the office to see Dave.[11] These incidents generally led to widespread class disruption.

Mary's behavior was quintessentially defiant in the Oak Grove system because she verbally rejected the teacher's authority to orchestrate the learning tasks in the classroom and she used disrespectful language. In the Pleasant Meadows official discipline policy, the first behavior listed is "failure to follow instructions." Oak Grove teachers perceived that noncooperation, a failure to follow instructions, constituted attempts to defy the authority of the teacher.

Pleasant Meadows' vice-principal Dave Jarvis attempted to formally differentiate between minor and major disruptions:

> *In all classrooms there will be times when students interrupt the learning process and the students.
> *In the classroom and on the school grounds major disruptions will occur, infractions such as: defiance of authority, weapons, fighting or threats made to others.
> — Vice-Principal's Handout on Discipline

His delineation is striking. Defiance of authority is classed as a major disruption in the same category as threats, fighting, and even weapons. Dave wrote, "Certain behaviors call for expulsion, and most times involve police intervention: possession of drugs or alcohol, *exceptional disruption or defiance,* repeated endangerment to staff or other students" (emphasis added). While "exceptional disruption or defiance" is never defined, it is clearly *not* dangerous behavior *or* the use of drugs — both of which are covered separately. Yet, "exceptional defiance" constitutes grounds for expulsion from school — the most severe punishment the school can inflict.

Mary's behavior was considered a major disruption. She was suspended but never expelled, perhaps because while she used abusive language, she did not physically attack Janice. And, more important, when ordered to leave the classroom and go to the office, she complied. Other behaviors that were considered defiant, but not exceptionally so, were repeated note passing, drumming or banging on the desk, throwing material, making noises, repeated movement out of one's seat. Because teachers had very different rules as to what constituted inappropriate or disruptive behavior, defiance was largely determined by whether or not the student followed the individual teacher's classroom guidelines.

The most defiant adolescent I worked with was Kaneko Yamanaka, whom I described in the last chapter. When Kaneko called Mrs. Kawaguchi an "old hag" (*oni-baba*), Mrs. Kawaguchi originally dismissed this as her childish inability to control herself; she did not take it as a personal assault. It was, Mrs. Kawaguchi later explained, another case of Kaneko feeling her connection to others was broken.

The refusal of Mrs. Kawaguchi and most other teachers to interpret Kaneko's insults, disruptive behavior, and even delinquent acts primarily as ones of defiance was remarkable in my mind. The teachers clearly thought Kaneko often had a resistant attitude, but they usually attributed this to her family problems. They believed that Kaneko, whose father had divorced her mother, felt discarded (*tsuterareta*). "She feels that she has been thrown away," Mrs. Kawaguchi said. Not all teachers agreed with Mrs. Kawaguchi's interpretation, and some saw the need to discipline Kaneko's behavior in a severe manner, actions which further alienated her from school.

But such teachers were in the minority. Mrs. Chino and the principal in separate interviews emphasized the causal link between the absence of her mother's love and Kaneko's behavior. They expressed the idea that because she never received a sufficient amount of love as a child, Kaneko was unable to grow and develop in the natural way a middle school student should. Mrs. Kawaguchi mused, "The essential human relation between Yamanaka and her mother was broken, maybe when Yamanaka was a baby or in her mother's belly."

Such dramatic differences in United States and Japanese definitions of and causal attributions of disruption were reflected in school discipline policies.

SCHOOL DISCIPLINE POLICIES

The school discipline policies in Oak Grove prominently noted but did not clearly define "defiance," leaving individual teachers much leeway in how they interpreted the term. Individual classroom discipline practices, then, effectively defined what defiance was.

The Oak Grove teachers fell into two major camps in terms of classroom discipline policies, the largest number of teachers using what is generally labeled positive or assertive discipline.[12] This is a system of external punishments and rewards such as writing student names on the board, sending students to the office, providing rewards for valued behavior, or excluding students from classroom activities or trips. Sanctions and rewards are distributed for both poor social behavior and academic performance. Failure to follow a teacher's instructions or warnings leads to increased sanctions, the final sanction being a trip to the office.

The other camp of teachers used a variety of cooperative discipline and cooperative group work strategies for classroom management. Tom Brabeck, a former principal, even taught college classes in alternative discipline strategies. For years he had tried, unsuccessfully, to engage district-wide training in these measures. Teachers like Adrian Norris, Hattie Sonval, and Opal Lorella as well as Emily Saunders worked to bring cooperative group-learning strategies into the school. Both Emily and Stan Proud encouraged teachers to investigate alternative programs for discipline and classroom management. These teachers and administrators rarely used the term "defiance" and instead assigned causality for the individual adolescent's disruptive behavior to underdeveloped social skills or emotional problems or both.

These teachers appeared similar to Kotani teachers in how they regarded and dealt with student problems. The majority of Kotani teachers basically tended to ignore a great deal of behavior that would have been labeled disruptive in Oak Grove. During periods when students were assigned to individual work at their seats or to group tasks, Kotani teachers generally allowed students to talk and rarely distinguished between on-task and off-task discussions. Interactions between students, such as one student snatching a pencil away or a boy squirting a girl with water, were most often ignored. And sometimes, when one student complained to the teacher about another student's behavior, Kotani teachers ignored the incident.[13]

As I have written previously, Japanese teachers generally attribute persistent disruptive behavior to a lack of social maturity, emotional problems, and a demand for attention.[14] Homeroom teachers, as discussed in previous chapters, believe that they can effectively modify student behavior and nurture social and emotional maturation. As shown in chapter 6, homeroom teachers occupy the center of a highly coordinated system of information in Japanese schools. When a young adolescent's behavior is seriously out of line, the homeroom teacher is notified. The principal and vice-principal are rarely involved in the actual counseling or guiding of the student but are called in when the student needs to be referred to an external agency or when the disruptive behavior occurs outside of the school.

In contrast, the largest camp of teachers at Oak Grove followed a form of assertive discipline in which teachers asked students to leave class at some point. Some teachers might simply ask students to step outside to cool down, others would send them directly to the vice-principal. In serious cases — using vulgar language, breaking equipment, threatening the teacher or another student, ignoring teacher's warnings — all teachers were supposed to send students immediately to the school office for discipline.[15] This resulted in the "Fast Food Discipline" system that Dave Jarvis jokingly summarized as "You run 'em in and you run 'em out."

Oak Grove teachers varied in the number of students they sent to the vice-principal's office. The office staff and vice-principal worked to track student misbehavior and assign punishments, often with little or no information flowing back to the teacher. Table 7.1 records the discipline referrals to the office at Wade on a morning that the secretaries considered to be medium.

By the end of the third period, the vice-principal was unable to keep up with the students sent down by teachers, and students were lined up in the halls and sitting on the benches. This meant that teachers received comparatively little information about a student whom they had sent to the office. Because the vice-principal handled most of the referrals at both Wade and Pleasant Meadows, they were often forced to deal with each case in a hurried manner, which meant that individuals did not always receive the treatment they deserved.

There is no equivalent table for Kotani because individual teachers dealt with discipline in the classroom or asked homeroom teachers to speak to disruptive students after school. During my fieldwork I recorded only one incident — students had been turning the hall lights on and off — in which a student was asked by the homeroom teacher to report to the teachers' room.[16]

The Kotani and Oak Grove discipline policies highlight key differences in how young adolescents are perceived. Disruptive behavior in Kotani is left to the teachers because teachers believe that they know their students best and can best redirect student energies. Teachers believe that young adolescents may be disruptive and even display resistant attitudes, but they rarely characterize young adolescents as defiant. Disruptive behavior is interpreted as a signal or sign by the students that they want attention. Consequently, discipline policy in Kotani is largely based on preventative strategies. Teachers are highly motivated to work to monitor student behavior in order to prevent problems.

In contrast, there was no universal routine that applied to classrooms in Oak Grove. Even within Wade or Aratamachi, each teacher implemented very different routines. Some used a flash of lights to signify the room was too noisy, other teachers counted down to some target number. Some teachers used group work, others never did. The period bells provided the only overall structure, but even this order was commonly disrupted — often on a daily or weekly basis.

Table 7.1 *Discipline Referrals Handled by Vice-Principal*

---

Number of students sent for discipline: 29

Discipline referrals by period:
    First: 0
    Second: 0
    Break: 2
    Third: 10
    Fourth: 9
    Lunch: 8

Time on each discipline case:
    Shortest — 3–5 minutes
    Longest — over 2 hours

---

The Oak Grove schools were also far more likely to experience shortened days or days with special periods than Kotani schools. This meant that teachers had to constantly alter their teaching patterns to accommodate the time allotted that day. More disturbingly, administrators in Oak Grove routinely interrupted class time with announcements, sometimes simply to call a student down to the office for a telephone call. In many classes, I observed several interruptions from the main office in the same period. Japanese classrooms have speakers like American classrooms, but they are rarely used.

And in Kotani schools, students are not removed for remedial or special education classes, as is the case in Oak Grove. During the course of observing lessons in Oak Grove, I noted that several students in any given period leave or enter the classes, adding to the general instability of the classroom. Teachers in Oak Grove also allow students to go to the rest room — using some kind of hall pass — whereas in Kotani teachers did not. This is most likely due to the fact that Kotani students have ten-minute breaks between classes, whereas Oak Grove students have two or three minutes.

The general organization of the school day in Kotani buffers classrooms from outside interference and tends to reduce the amount of work that teachers spend in directing students' actions. Disruption of classroom routines seemed almost to be built into the Oak Grove schools. At the same time, teachers' attitudes appear to make Oak Grove teachers sensitive to off-task behavior and to interpret this as disruptive of the classroom process. Compared to Kotani, Oak Grove teachers had to exert far more effort to maintain the classroom process.

## The Influence of the Family

As I have already shown, Oak Grove teachers believed that some kinds of disruptive behavior — talking, acting odd, being distracted, and so forth — might be the result of hormones. In these cases the teachers generally tried to redirect student attention but did not mete out any form of disciplinary action. Teachers believed that maturity was "the internalization of self-control," according to Urma Baxter. She and other fifth grade teachers already expected a high degree of internalized self-control in their students during class time. They seemed to believe that there was little they could do to advance this maturity aside from presenting a clear and consistent set of rewards and punishments.

Oak Grove fifth graders do not change classrooms as often as the older grades, but in other ways they are very similar to classes for older students. In his fifth grade class, Bill Joiner established an elaborate system of external rewards — volume levels, names on the board, group minutes for detention, stars for reading — that was similar to those used in sixth, seventh, and eighth grade classrooms.[17] This gaining of self-control is a highly individualistic process in teachers' minds — some fifth graders possess it in a high degree, some eighth graders lack it entirely.

In Oak Grove, teachers believed that a child's home life and sense of self-esteem were the most important factors in creating or undermining this internalization. Young adolescents who come from alcoholic homes, who shuttle back and forth between divorced parents, who have no parental supervision are all less likely to internalize this self-control. In the lunchrooms of Oak Grove, Wade, and Pleasant Meadows teachers frequently discussed the "video generation" who had lost respect for adults. Most teachers believed that strict sanctions (including sending students to the office) were one of the few effective ways they had to exert control over the classroom. Furthermore, in cases of extreme defiance, like Mary's, teachers and administrators alike felt that parents would not support the teachers in dealing with the defiant adolescent.

In discussing the most disruptive students, teachers and administrators in Oak Grove consistently mentioned problems in the family. In talking to me about a boy who was often sent to the Wade office, Barbara Lane said, "He had an argument with his aunt, who took the house key and said, 'You'll have to live somewhere else.' You can't teach through those sorts of things." In discussing Stephen, a boy that I often saw in the Pleasant Meadows office, Lynn Jing said, "The father didn't want him and made this known to Stephen. The whole family is in counseling. The mother is scared to talk to the father. When the father comes in he's like a rock. No reaction."

In looking at the aspects of the family that seemed most detrimental to young adolescents, the Oak Grove teachers appeared to have assigned a loose hierarchy to family conditions that caused problems for young adolescents. Starting with the least disruptive, the teachers mentioned such factors as (1) parents with unrealistic expectations for their child (academic or social maturity); (2) parents unaware of what their child is doing; (3) families that are emotionally distant; (4) families disrupted by divorce or separation (including incarceration); (5) a family member who was an alcoholic or drug addict; (6) a sexually or physically abusive family member.

In the last two cases, teachers were required by state law to report knowledge of such incidents to the local social services (the Child Protection Service). In the teachers' opinion, however, these referrals were often not effective. Most of the Oak Grove teachers had several students in their classes who they thought were strongly affected by a negative family situation.

In a very similar way, Japanese teachers saw the family as the key reason for severe or repetitively disruptive behavior among young adolescents. If adolescents did not come from a loving (*aijyō*) home, teachers reasoned, they would have great difficulty developing the empathy and sense of responsibility needed to manage themselves. Americans saw the outcome of problem families to be defiant adolescents who lacked self-control or had emotional problems, while Japanese saw the outcome of such families to be disconnected adolescents who disrupted school life in a demand for attention. Though they interpreted the outcome very differently, both groups of teachers consistently identified families as the source of severe or persistent problems in adolescent behavior that affected their self-control (i.e., their will).

The absence of a loving, supportive family was identified by both groups of teachers as a major cause of disruptive or even delinquent behavior on the part of young adolescents. In both countries, teachers were sympathetic to the plight of the young adolescent, but in Oak Grove, the number of problems appeared to overwhelm the capacity of many teachers to cope. Like the Kotani schools, most Japanese middle schools I have worked in have perhaps a handful of children whose families are so dysfunctional that the children have been removed to social services. Moreover, the Kotani teachers did not worry about violence or the prospect of violence when adolescents turned disruptive. My analysis suggests that the community violence that surrounded the Oak Grove schools made teachers and administrators alike hypersensitive to defiance because they feared that disruptive, defiant adolescents might injure other students or even the teachers. Fear of violent adolescents was part of life in Oak Grove. In Kotani, it was not.[18]

## Delinquency and Gangs

During an internal school review day at Wade, I spoke about gangs with three older white, male teachers who had come to evaluate Wade as part of district-wide evaluations. One teacher described for me the "classic Mexican gang look" — Pendleton shirt, white T-shirt, very baggy pants whose crotch might sag to the knees, sneakers, and slicked-back hair. This same style was described in an article originating in Los Angeles on school bans on clothing.[19] The following alternative description of Latino gang appearance appeared in a paper published by the county sheriffs' association and was reprinted in a pamphlet on drugs and gangs that was widely distributed in regional public libraries:

> The uniform of Hispanic gangs is an easily recognized standard. Most gang members adopt a basic dress style: sparkling white T-shirts, thin belts, khaki pants with split cuffs, a black or blue knit cap (beanie) or a bandanna tied around the forehead similar to a sweatband. They refer to the bandanna as a "moco" rag.       — County Sheriffs Association Newspaper

Stereotyped images of Hispanic gangs are pervasive in California. Teachers believed that gangs and gang-related problems (violence and drugs) were intricately intertwined with racial and ethnic stereotypes. Teachers in the Oak Grove District area largely believed that gangs were a Hispanic or Asian problem — there was little talk of white gangs or black gangs — although some young adolescents that teachers pointed out as sporting gang clothing appeared to be European-American or African-American. The sheriffs' association newspaper also notes that "black gangs do not follow a continuing dress style as Hispanic gangs do." Gang clothing was usually a problem when it was Hispanic students who wore the clothes.

The difficulty in identifying symbols or styles that are indeed markers of gangs lies in the complexity of what gangs are and what teachers perceive them to be, and it is compounded by the fact that adolescents actively manipulate the symbols used by gangs. The use of gang symbols by students who do not live in economically depressed neighborhoods and who might be called middle class by their teachers is augmented by movies, apparel, accessories, and music, which market a gang image to adolescents. As active participants in various school subcultures as well as consumers of gang image paraphernalia, young adolescents appeared to be far more aware of the uses of these images than adults.

Students at Wade found teachers to be both hypersensitive to and naive about gang clothes and colors. For example, in several middle schools in the Bay Area, I observed students wearing crosses made of beads. At Wade students told me they were made by one boy who is involved with a Christian antidrug group. The necklaces were popular, and many students wore them. When I asked Adrian Norris about them, she said, "Oh, they're probably gang related." The same week, a seventh grade girl interrupted our conversation to plead with Adrian to tell Mrs. Lorella that the crosses weren't gang related. Mrs. Lorella, the student feared, was going to send one of her friends to the office.

At the same time, teachers seemed oblivious to the fact that many of the objects that students wore, (i.e., pacifiers), were part of a gang image. The pacifiers — bright green or blue plastic replicas of infant pacifiers that appeared to have been expressly manufactured as decorations — were associated with a character from the movie *Boyz N the Hood*. This character portrayed a youth who had been shot in gang fight. I asked several teachers about the pacifiers, but only Emily Saunders, the principal, had noticed them previously. She said that they were technically forbidden as they constituted gang paraphernalia.

Other symbols or fashion devices were subject to similar conflicting interpretations. Teachers drew my attention to several things they connected with gangs. At Pleasant Meadows several boys put playing cards, such as the four, five, and six of diamonds, inside their baseball caps. Outside of school, students would wear hairnets or bandannas over their heads in a way that imitated the look portrayed by some gangster rappers. Other students, primarily African-American males, wore hooded sweaters or workout tops with the hoods pulled over their faces, in ways that mirrored images from movies and music promotions. Yet it was not clear that any of these styles or paraphernalia would have been viewed as symbols of gang affiliation in the students' homes or neighborhoods. The students, moreover, never talked about these styles as gang related.

Some students at Pleasant Meadows found with cards in their hats in one class were sent to the principal's office, but others were not. At Wade some teachers insisted that boys take off their hoods, but other did not. Similar conflicts also appeared over the wearing of baseball caps in class. While not identified by teachers as gang paraphernalia, some teachers demanded that students take off the caps — even sending recalcitrant students to the office — whereas others ignored the wearing of these caps.

In March, Dave Jarvis and I were walking during his yard duty time at recess. We watched several boys playing basketball on the outside court, in what appeared to be a mixed age–range group of Latino and Anglo students. Dave saw that one eighth grade boy was, as he described it, "flying a flag." The boy had a dark blue and white bandanna sticking about three inches out of his pocket. Dave called the boy over and grabbed the bandanna. Shouting ensued and the boy and his friends walked away, despite Dave's ordering them to go to the office.

Dave took the bandanna to the office. When he showed it to Stan Proud, the principal, Stan got agitated and asked the secretary to get a camera: "Yup, he's flying a flag. This is the evidence we need to send to the district that gang activity *is* in this area. We've had indications that gangs were moving into the northern end of the district." Stan made a loudspeaker announcement for the bandanna's owner to come to the office. The boy was suspended for three days for violating the antigang clothing rules.

When I discussed this incident with Barbara Lane at Wade, she offered a significantly different interpretation of the events. She told me that gang members had long ago given up flying flags, and the use of a bandanna was indicative of a kid who wanted to look cool.[20] The boy might be a "gang wannabe," in her words, but was not really aware that hard-core gang members did not want to attract attention to themselves. Barbara expressed similar opinions about the baggy pants and large black sports jackets (San Jose Sharks or Oakland Raiders) that some teachers saw as a sign of gang involvement.

At the time of the study, teachers and administrators all over California were extremely sensitive about gangs. Conflicting opinions about gangs and gang involvement appeared to be heightened by media coverage that focused on the possibility of gang wars and gang violence in high school.[21] One story described police efforts to educate *elementary* school students about gangs.[22] Dave and Stan's reaction to the boy's bandanna appears to have been influenced by a climate of political pressure from parents in Pleasant Meadows' largely white, middle-class district, anxious for schools to be tough on gangs. As part of her job in counseling students, Lois, the only Wade teacher fluent in Spanish, had close contact with Wade students who had a juvenile record. Her reaction appeared to reflect the views of the working-class Hispanic community. The ethnic tensions around gang violence in the San Francisco Bay Area during the early 1990s strongly affected the Oak Grove Schools and appeared to strengthen teachers' beliefs in the idea of adolescent proclivity to rebellion and disruption.

While American teachers made strong connections between certain clothing and membership in or desire to be a member of a gang or proto-gang, Japanese teachers seem to see violations of the dress codes as indicators that a child's motivation to study was slipping. Teachers in both countries expressed concerns over the propensity of their students to be swayed or influenced by peer groups. But the Japanese teachers usually did not associate the disruptions in dress code as a challenge to their authority, their safety, or the immediate safety of other students.

In most instances, the Japanese teachers took deviations in school dress as indicative of the *individual's* character being in trouble. Japanese teachers were highly conscious of students' dress and vigorously punished any infractions in the dress code. Mr. Shimoda warned the Furukawa teachers at a November morning meeting that a few girls were wearing thread bracelets and asked that it be stopped. Mr. Shimoda expressed concern that they were symbols of distraction — an indicator that students might be thinking too little of their studies.[23]

Clothes and accessories could also be signifiers of how students were being affected by their peers. The greatest fear of teachers was that students who smoked or associated with dropouts would pull (*hipparu*) other students into illegal behavior. Although Japanese teachers expressed confidence in their students in other ways — by allowing frequent unsupervised behavior — they kept very close watch on clothing and any sign of deviation from the dress code. They did not, however, attribute fashion-consciousness or a preoccupation with clothes to natural adolescent tendencies. Rather, they saw these things as the negative effects of a material culture.

Although some former students from Furukawa were rumored to be involved in the local mafia (*yakuza*), teachers generally determined mafia involvement by family association rather than by clothing. Mafia involvement in Kotani was considered to be mostly a problem with late high school boys and boys who had dropped out of school. Students from mafia families were reputed to be concentrated in the local Industrial High School. One of my former students was rumored to be in training as a leader of his family's branch of the mafia, according to the teachers. The teachers also said that boys in these proto-gangs might have elaborate (and illegal) designs sewn into their jackets. The young man sported a highly elaborate purple dragon on the inside left breast of his jacket. He also openly bullied other students into giving him rides on the back of their bicycles.[24]

But the most conspicuous thing about gangs in the Kotani middle schools was their absence. Whereas students in urban centers may be more likely to form groups that ride motorcycles, Kotani middle school students did not appear to become involved with these activities until high school. Neither did teachers appear worried that gang activities would invade the middle school; rather, they worried that certain students, like Kaneko, would be pulled into gangs. Part of this security probably stems from the fact that Kotani teachers actively policed student behavior in and out of school and had good access to information about students' outside school activities.

In both the U.S. and Japanese schools, clothing that violated school rules was associated with students from lower socioeconomic classes or students from different ethnic backgrounds. In the South Bay area, the styles of young working-class Hispanics does not differ much from what the school rules deem gang clothing. In Kotani, boys from poor homes — whose fathers might be laborers or work the fishing boats — similarly wore clothes or adopted habits that my teaching colleagues thought of as delinquent or mafia related. In both countries, the styles of minority or economically marginalized groups were the target of school restrictions.

The definition of gangs and their activity is highly charged with ethnic and racial conflict. The media have played a role in the Bay Area by portraying gang activity in working-class Hispanic neighborhoods. The fact that only one or two teachers at Wade and Pleasant Meadows during the study could speak Spanish meant a further distancing between the worlds of student and teacher. Like staff at many schools in California, the Oak Grove District staff appear to link certain styles or apparel with gang membership even though this link is not made in the community at large. Yet teachers in Oak Grove were not able to articulate just what gangs were.

The application of gang to styles primarily common to the Hispanic community suggests both a gap in communication between the teachers and the communities they serve as well as underlying prejudices which link Hispanics and gang activity.[25] During the study, significant media attention was given to racial conflict among younger children in a case in which eight elementary school boys were arrested for beating an African-American boy while using racial epithets.[26] Yet neither the media nor the Oak Grove teachers labeled the behavior of these boys as "gang related." Many California school districts have banned certain clothing, but the rationale appears more based on stereotypes of ethnic gangs than on actual information about organized crime.

In Kotani, teachers had direct access to a wide variety of information on student life. Teachers tended to see patterns of problem behavior emanating from families or groups of families, not from an autonomous and hostile peer culture. Despite the problems that Japanese teachers have faced in the past, Kotani teachers did not fear their students. They did exhibit stereotypical or prejudiced views of families from the lowest socioeconomic stratum.

## Summary: Disruption and the Adolescent

Japanese teachers did not tend to see disruptive acts as intentional acts of aggression in the way American teachers did.[27] They tended to ignore most disruptive acts and relied on school routines to guide student behavior. In more serious cases, the homeroom teacher — the person with the strongest emotional contact with the adolescent — took charge of investigating the situation and administering a mixture of guidance and punishment. The teachers rarely saw students as openly defiant, and when they did, they were most likely to attribute the behavior to family problems. Rather, Japanese see resistance. The related terms *hankōki*, the period of "resistance," and *hankōshin*, a "resistant heart," relate to an obdurate quality of will thought to be characteristic of middle school students in modern Japanese culture. Kotani teachers did not see young adolescents' boisterous or obstreperous behavior as a threat to themselves or a challenge.[28] Most commonly Kotani teachers attributed students' misbehavior to a lack of love, respect, or thoughtfulness (*omoiyari*).

Teachers at Furukawa and Aratamachi were inclined to see student misbehavior as extended immaturity caused by the lack of emotional attachment or connection to the social group. The data from Kotani suggest that Japanese teachers see juvenile behavior in a far different light than their American peers. As with the discussion of clothing cited above, Japanese teachers were very ready to interpret various illegal acts as signs of a student's inability to adjust to his or her surroundings.[29] Yamanaka's behavior would, I am sure, have been defined as "exceptional defiance" at either Wade or Pleasant Meadows. Why then was it tolerated at Furukawa?

A common theme emerging from my analysis is the lack of love that these young adolescents suffer from. As I discussed in the case of Yamanaka, Japanese teachers often cited lack of parental love (*aijyō*) as the crucial factor causing a child to resist teachers' guidance and school rules. Children deprived of love (caring) at an early age experience a breakdown of the "essential human connection" and are not capable of maturing. They resist the responsibilities each new year brings — numerous committee duties, being a senior and instructing juniors, bearing down on their studying.

Resistance was regarded as a sign of immaturity — a failure to accept the adult responsibility of a mature volition, that is, a volition simultaneously more powerful and subtle but requiring great effort to use. Yamanaka's behavior (and the behavior of virtually all students I observed in various counseling situations in Kotani) was described by teachers as one betraying lack of connection, immaturity, and a refusal to accept more adult/mature attitudes. Indeed, several teachers described the middle school student period of rebellion (*hankōki*) as evidence of the child's refusal to grow up and take on the responsibilities of a more mature self. Teachers in Kotani appeared to associate the increased energy of adolescents with an increased capability for mature acts of volition — acts that a child would not be able to perform.

This difference suggests that student behavior in the United States is framed as rebellion — any disruptive behavior is seen as potential defiance. In Japan, disruptive behavior tended to be framed as showing a child's *nayami* (worries) and was interpreted as resistance — the child was not ready to be mature and resisted growing up and taking on responsibility.

Many, though not all, American teachers thought that disruptive students were actively undermining the teacher's authority by their behavior. In the United States many teachers feel that a growing number of adolescents are out of control. While occasional disruptions were tolerated and often attributed to the changes of puberty, persistent disruptions were defined as defiance. In most cases, teachers made a direct link between the adolescent's upbringing and their behavior.

Both groups of teachers saw families as key players in the lives of adolescents with severe problems. The underlying causal story line is invariably that young adolescents who lack a sense of love or connection feel outside the social atmosphere. They cannot make a link with the school and channel their energy into rebellious or delinquent acts. These students often have a weak sense of identity or weak wills (*ishi ga yowai ko*) and are easily pulled into problem behavior by students who have already moved into a path of rebellion. In the United States, family problems were seen to somehow inhibit the maturation process: students were not able to develop self-control.

In both cultures there is an underlying tone of lack of self-control or self-restraint among adolescents or middle school students. And in both countries, families were seen as a major force in affecting students' propensities toward disruption and crime. But Oak Grove teachers tended to reaffirm their belief that it was not their job to engage in counseling and that providing a clear set of rewards and consequences would stimulate students to develop self-control. A minority of the Oak Grove teachers adopted a view similar to that of the Kotani teachers: disruptive behavior was a sign of a lack of human connection or a problem in human relations.

Problem behavior (*mondai kōdō*) or worries (*nayami*), teachers reported, are first exhibited in some disruption of daily routines. Beginning with offenses like missing school or wearing modified uniforms, students move on to smoking at home, truancy, and perhaps petty shoplifting. As students become more distant from school routine they inevitably get more involved with juvenile delinquents. They exhibit more defiant behaviors — sleeping over at a friend's house (forbidden in Japan) or running away. Involvement with other delinquents usually involves substance abuse: inhaling paint thinner or glue. Clothes and other outward forms of appearance are considered by teachers to express the inner emotional state of the child. Minor lapses in decorum — even the use of seemingly innocuous clothing or accessories — can be taken very seriously.[30] The teachers at Furukawa and Aratamachi saw a straightforward progression from lapses in the proper uniform to association with juvenile delinquents and acts of delinquency. Mrs. Chino, the head of the Furukawa second-year teachers, believed that there was a direct progression from cigarette smoking to substance abuse at the middle school age.[31]

In Oak Grove, classroom management is left to individual teachers, but when students break certain rules or the teacher feels unable to manage the student, they are sent out of the classroom. The autonomy of teachers and schools in dealing with student problems is restricted by state law, and teachers have little incentive to become involved in guiding or counseling students. Furthermore, little information flows back to Oak Grove teachers from either the school office or outside agencies. The office staff coordinated discipline referrals. Students wait for the vice-principal, have a brief meeting and are assigned detention, are referred to another staff member, or sent back to class. Only rarely did classroom teachers in Oak Grove receive any information about what had happened to the student. In more serious cases, teachers would participate on teams with administrators or other staff and would report to the district board in expulsion cases. The weak organizational boundaries of the U.S. school and the lack of coordination between classroom and school discipline make U.S. teachers more vulnerable to rumor and misinformation.

The realities of school organization and the work norms for teachers made the system draining on administrators, counselors, and teachers alike in Oak Grove. The staff at Pleasant Meadows and Wade are caught in institutions in which they themselves have little power to affect the lives of adolescents outside of school and are significantly constrained by a host of laws and regulations as to what they can do inside of school. Facing families that are poorer, less likely to speak English, and more likely to have a member suffering from some form of addiction, both schools were experiencing significant strains on their ability to deal with segments of the student populations.

The inherent instability of life in American middle grades schools has been previously documented. While Japanese middle school students can readily anticipate their daily and weekly schedule, many American middle school students have great difficulty knowing just what the schedule for the day is and how it will be modified. Most significantly, the practice of sending disruptive students out of class (required in Oak Grove for certain offenses such as the use of foul language) tended to increase the overall disruption of school routines in general.

Most of the classrooms in Kotani followed the same basic instructional process. Kotani students were well versed in a range of group behaviors and classroom routines that reduced the need for direct teacher intervention. These skills are developed in elementary school, and when Kotani students first enter Aratamachi or Furukawa, they are already highly socialized to participate in a variety of routines that organize the flow of classroom life. Teachers in Kotani were then able to engage in intense counseling of students around future life choices and also direct students who broke rules to intensive counseling sessions. The argument could be made that middle school is the time that Japanese constrain the child's behavior the most and that schools are organized in ways that support this control. Having both social and legal support, Japanese teachers can implement prevention strategies that essentially stop problems before they happen.

## Implications

From an outsider's perspective, the organization of the Oak Grove school day made it easy for young adolescents to be disruptive. Students were exposed not only to a wide variety of teaching styles, but to a daily schedule that was frequently disrupted. Few Oak Grove teachers, however, saw adolescent behavioral problems as arising from the chaotic atmosphere. Oak Grove teachers were more likely to cite social factors, adolescent turmoil, hormones, or lack of self-control as the sources of disruption. The Oak Grove school discipline policies supported a cycle that increased disruption and student disobedience. Teachers employed various management strategies in class, but when student behavior or teacher patience reached a certain point, Oak Grove teachers all used the same method: expel the student from class. This simple policy had complex effects, the most significant of which was that the vice-principals were unable to attend to all of the problems they were faced with in a day.

The Oak Grove schools are quite typical of U.S. middle schools with regard to disruptive behavior. Robert Everhart documented that truancy, food fights, swearing at teachers, and fights were relatively common in the middle school he worked in. He argued that for some students, disrupting classroom routines had become a daily activity. In Oak Grove, particularly at Wade, students and teachers engaged in daily confrontations about basic school and classroom routines. This kind of constant challenge to the school or class routines was absent in Kotani. A Japanese student in Bill Joiner's fifth grade, whose family had just moved into a neighborhood near Wade, quietly came up to me the first day I observed the class and asked in Japanese, "Don't you think that Mr. Joiner is having a rough time?"

Several teachers at Wade and Pleasant Meadows were keenly aware of how discipline policies work to keep young adolescents out of class and in the office, further undermining their ability to succeed in classrooms. As Hattie once remarked to me, "By the time we get them in seventh grade, its just too late." The majority of American teachers vigorously resist the idea that they should take major roles in counseling, guiding, and disciplining students. Administrators also play a key role.

Toward the end of my fieldwork in Oak Grove, I presented my findings at the Oak Grove District Office. I gave a basic overview of how the discipline process was organized in Kotani and Oak Grove. Two of the district staff, Barbara D'souza and Charlotte Girdeaux, had been enthusiastic about my findings. They had put together a proposal that would link social services and health services and coordinate both at the elementary school level. The superintendent and the director of in-service training, however, seemed to take offense at my comparison and made long comments about how the comparison was unjust as the Japanese have a "brutal system of discipline" and a "high rate of suicide among teens."

When I attempted to list the top problems that teachers had told me about, the superintendent stopped me and said, "We don't have problems in this district. We're doing a great job. There are areas we need to progress in, to take the lead in . . . "

Teachers, however, saw the situation quite differently.

Classroom management was a major concern of Oak Grove teachers. Oak Grove teachers and administrators often expressed frustration with the system and with students who appeared indifferent to cycling from the classroom to the office to detention and back to the classroom. They did not believe the system was working to effect changes in the behaviors of the most disruptive students.

Japanese teachers were, on balance, far more positive about their system and prospects for change with regard to disruptive behavior. Japanese teachers are most concerned with the negative effect of increased academic pressure and academic competition (see chapter 5). Nonetheless, some teachers complain that the demands of guiding, disciplining, and counseling students require too much of them. Both younger teachers like Mr. Shimoda and older teachers like Mrs. Chino also expressed the concern that the Japanese system of guidance undermined a student's sense of self. By applying minute rules to all aspects of student life, the Japanese system might prevent major disruption but at the cost of students being able to think for themselves.

# 8

## *Creativity and Self-Expression*

Both American and Japanese schools instruct young adolescents in art, aesthetics, and the creative process. Teachers hope to promote adolescent creativity within certain areas, while regulating it in others. The middle grades are a time in both nations when young adolescents learn what modes of self-expression are tolerated or even encouraged (e.g., playing the trumpet, painting with oil paints) and what are prohibited (e.g., listening to vulgar song lyrics, painting gang symbols on school walls). Conflicts over student clothing or dress styles arose in both countries when adolescents attempted to create an image that was perceived as dangerous or defiant. That is, one could argue, when adolescents asserted their right to self-expression outside predefined limits, teachers reacted by curtailing adolescent choices.

Such conflicts map out the limits of autonomy that teachers in the two nations are willing to grant to young adolescents and highlight teacher beliefs about the role of creativity and self-expression in adolescent development and the relation of the will and creativity. In this chapter I examine how teachers try to control and encourage adolescent self-expression in the classroom and in the school, beginning with the formal curriculum and then discussing events and extra-curricular activities. Next I focus on the ways in which schools and teachers try to regulate adolescent self-expression and show that students channel consider-able creative energies into music, dress, artwork, jewelry, and makeup. These outlets are not only a means of creative expression, but also ways of displaying who the adolescent is or hopes to be. Creative expression is a way to create or recreate self-image and associate with others who have a desired image.

In conclusion, I argue that American and Japanese schools are remarkably similar in that both countries offer a range of courses, clubs, and activities purposely designed by adults to promote creativity, stimulate self-expression, and enhance a sense of aesthetics. The Japanese schools appear to provide more cohesive practice in the basic skills needed in creative exercises like drawing, singing, and playing a musical instrument, but informally American school policies and teachers' beliefs foster a far broader range of self-expression. This informal facet of American education is far more crucial to the overall development of adolescent self-identity than the formal curriculum. And, while a range of creative activities are incorporated in the formal curriculum, the restrictions placed on Japanese adolescents have a deleterious effect on individual capacity for self-expression. Although traditional Japanese beliefs equate long-term effort and the exertion of the will with creative accomplishment, such emphasis on practical exertion appears to have a negative impact on young adolescents' creativity and on their ability to exercise their will.

## Teaching Creativity

Art, music, and creative writing are typical curricular elements in both U.S. and Japanese middle schools. Teachers believe that these activities promote adolescent creativity and offer outlets for self-expression. In addition to art and music courses, students can take a variety of electives such as shop, home management, or even composition classes, all of which include projects that use materials in a creative fashion. In some schools, depending on how individual teachers organize the work, classes on the use of computers can be forums for creative expression.

### THE FORMAL CURRICULUM

There are significant differences between Japan and the United States in terms of the types of classes offered and the ways in which students select such courses. The Japanese curriculum offerings in art and music, like those in academic subjects, are derived from national curricular outlines. In the United States, such offerings are affected by state and local regulations, local demand, and budget constraints. The classes available to students in Kotani occupied a much narrower range from school to school and were far more consistent in terms of materials across schools than in Oak Grove.

Elective classes were limited in Kotani. Students at Furukawa and Aratamachi may take drawing or watercolor classes, calligraphy classes, music, and home management classes. The curriculum for these classes was remarkably similar in both schools. For example, in music class, students learn how to play recorders. Classes in other instruments, such as guitar, were not offered in the Kotani district. The only foreign language offered was English. Moreover, as students generally stay together with their homeroom, Kotani students had no opportunity to individually choose classes that they preferred.

The emphasis in the Oak Grove schools, by contrast, was on providing a diverse set of classes that individual students could pick from. At Pleasant Meadows, the students could choose from a variety of classes offered in the "exploratory wheel," including two foreign languages and a selection of music, art, and writing courses. Block scheduling allowed students considerable freedom to manage their schedule. The electives were, for the most part, predetermined by the school.

On the most general level, Oak Grove teachers and administrators strove to provide a range of choices of activities, support services, and optional classes so that students might sample from this spectrum and pick what they need or like. Teachers expected that in this unconstrained atmosphere the students would discover their predilections and talents. Kotani teachers attempted to create many structured (i.e., teacher guided) *school* or *grade* activities in which young adolescents performed or exhibited works of art. The Kotani teachers often employed guided exercises in self-reflection both in class and in extracurricular activities. Although these exercises appeared to increase student thoughtfulness, they also may have hindered students' ability to take independent action and make individual decisions.[1]

The course offerings in middle schools like Wade and Pleasant Meadows suggest that teachers believe students become developmentally ready for expanded curricular choices between fifth and eighth grade. While fifth graders in these schools were cocooned in one classroom with one teacher for much of the school day, eighth graders were negotiating electives and streamed classes, changing classes and teachers every hour. Many eighth graders had little contact with other students in their homeroom, sharing only one class, a common core of language arts or social sciences. The philosophy of curriculum presentation in Oak Grove (which coincides with that promulgated by advocates of the middle school movement in general) is to offer as great a range of choices as the school and district can support: "A major focus is to insure that all students have a language arts/social science core program, a goal that has become a reality. A second area of emphasis is to continue to develop programs at our school that assist students develop [sic] their potential, improve study habits, communicate effectively, and function at high level in today's complex society"—Pleasant Meadows "School Report Card."

Student options to take creative courses were emphasized as individual choice in Oak Grove, as opposed to Kotani, where some kind of creative or physical activity was a required choice. In the elective courses at Pleasant Meadows, class performance was sometimes remarkably high, suggesting that those students with an interest in these subjects were more motivated to master the subject material. In Kotani, all students in middle school were expected to be able to read music with a fairly high degree of proficiency, though the general level of performance in music classes was low. The Kotani system produced students with very similar musical capabilities, whereas the Oak Grove system produced students with very different musical capabilities.

And as Kotani students moved into the ninth grade, options to study elective courses were drastically curtailed, and teachers exhorted students to prepare for the entrance exams.[2] Teachers expected young adolescents to suspend their interest in creative activities in order to attend to the immediate task of getting into a good high school. The young adolescent in Japan is expected to learn to postpone or restrict his or her interests in art and other kinds of self-expression in order to attain long-term academic goals.

Differences in the general curriculum for middle schools in Kotani and Oak Grove show a strong American concern for providing the widest range of classes possible for students. Students in Oak Grove, for example, had a broad range of courses to choose from and autonomy to choose between academic courses and electives. Kotani's course offerings reflect the Japanese concern with offering a uniform curriculum to all students. The Japanese curriculum at the middle grades level suggests that instruction in artistic creation is considered an important element, but providing a wide range of options for individual selection is not a priority in the curriculum. The Oak Grove curriculum suggests that venues for creativity and self-expression are assumed to grow in importance as the young American adolescent matures, whereas in Kotani the curriculum suggests that artistic expression plays a diminished role as the young Japanese adolescent matures. The young American adolescent was expected to become mature enough to balance academic studies that may lead to better school and job prospects with creative studies that foster artistic expression. The young Japanese adolescent was expected to become mature enough to control or limit his or her involvement in creative, self-expressive acts.

CREATIVITY IN THE CLASSROOM

In any given teacher's classroom, however, there was considerable variation in how teachers approached the task of encouraging creativity. Compare the differences in the following four classrooms:

Vignette One: Wade

In Hattie Sonval's art class, the room is decorated with reproductions of various artists interspersed with charts depicting such specific art techniques as creating a three-dimensional perspective. The class has difficulty getting under way. Hattie has to carefully note who gets what paints because she must collect these at the end of the period. There is very little money in the art budget, and she noted that in the past "paints and markers have a way of walking off." Some students work quietly on their paintings, some work on projects for other classes; a few simply talk. Three boys at a central table are using their mirrors to explore their faces instead of drawing their face, the project for the day. In what seems a mocking voice one says to another, "Wow, look at my picture, love that background." Not one of the boys has progressed much beyond rude sketches. One boy starts doodling and says to another, "Will you come right to my house after school?" Hattie stations herself at the front desk, and students come to ask advice about their drawings. She is unaware of what the boys are saying.

### Vignette Two: Furukawa

As soon as the bell rings, the students begin pulling out the canvases they have been working on. Mr. Shimoda lingers in his office and does not go out and bow in front of the class as is customary. All around the room are pictures painted by previous classes. After about ten minutes, Mr. Shimoda gets up and goes into the classroom. He wanders around and comments on each painting, inevitably expressing appreciation for some aspect of the picture. Abut half-way into the class, a student asks him how to draw eyes; he asks the class to stop and briefly sketches a few ways to draw an eye on the board. Then as abruptly as he started talking, he resumes chatting with me and walking around the classroom.

### Vignette Three: Pleasant Meadows

In Winnie Rawler's class they are preparing for Friday's class, to which students will bring food that represents German cuisine. Every quarter, as part of her German classes, Winnie has the students bring in food. She explains to them where they can buy German bread. They begin watching a videotape. Winnie stops the tape at one point when the students don't understand the narrator. The class begins to try to decipher the tape as a group. Winnie allows them to shout out answers or ask questions without raising their hands.

### Vignette Four: Furukawa

Mrs. Tanaka has already told the students three times to quiet down and the class is not even under way yet. Students are still fumbling with their calligraphy cases.[3] Now she begins to describe the correct stroke order for the characters they will practice today. She orders one boy to sit down. Every detail of the character is explained and demonstrated on a water-board by Mrs. Tanaka. She has the students lift their hands in the air and follow her. She asks students to critique each other's work. After asking students to quiet down a fourth time, she tells them to bring their sheets up when they think they have finished. Some students borrow paper or ink from her. Seated at the front desk, she uses orange ink to redraw the places where students have made mistakes or to circle parts of the characters that are drawn well.

CLASSROOM CONTROL AND THE CREATIVE PROCESS

Maintaining classroom order and fostering the creative process proved difficult for many teachers. Both Hattie and Mrs. Tanaka were highly concerned with making sure that all students got equal attention and equal access to the material. Moreover, they were concerned that students learn the basic techniques. Therefore students who were not very interested in the lesson or who were careless with materials became a problem for each teacher. Both teachers reacted to such students as if they lacked self-control and were disruptive of the creative process. In interviews outside of class, both Hattie and Mrs. Tanaka expressed concern about students' ability to master basic techniques, and both expressed the belief that creativity flows from rote practice of basic routines. For both teachers, students who could not draw with precision would not be able to proceed to more complicated works of art. Both tended to focus on aspects of self-control and basic techniques in the classroom.

Mr. Shimoda and Winnie expressed opposing beliefs. They said that their students lacked the spontaneity needed for true creativity. Neither teacher provided much work on basic technique (grammar or sketching drills) unless students specifically asked for instruction. Both appeared willing to supplement materials supplied by the school with materials they themselves had purchased. In the two classes described above, the teachers tried to let student interest drive the classroom process. Creativity was viewed not as flowing from routines but as generated in a desire for expression and the willingness to experiment.

Hattie and Mrs. Tanaka emphasized equitable distribution of attention or materials and instruction in basic techniques. Winnie and Mr. Shimoda emphasized fostering individual opportunity and experimentation with various forms of expression.

Teachers like Hattie Sonval did believe that lack of basic skills hampered adolescent attempts at creativity. She believed that more emphasis on basic skill building (drawing techniques, use of special tools, etc.) would help adolescents to unleash their creative powers. In Kotani, Mr. Shimoda believed that Japanese learning was altogether too heavy on rote learning and endless perfection of basic patterns and hoped to bring out life (*iki-iki*) in his students' work. When asked what he meant by *iki-iki* in describing how the students should be painting, Mr. Shimoda said that young adolescents' pictures should be *kawaii* (simple and cute). This kind of naiveté or simple drawing style was a desirable quality. Mr. Shimoda remarked that up until fourth grade Japanese students produce rather good pictures, pictures that he compared favorably with children's art from other countries. In later grades, he thought, young adolescents' artwork declined. This decline was linked in his mind with the increased use of routine and drill in Japanese schools.

Mr. Shimoda had both a definite artistic opinion as well as a general opinion about young adolescents' art. As a member of a movement aimed at allowing greater appreciation for and expression in young adolescents' art, he was an advocate of simply letting young adolescents draw as they would without teaching them too many techniques. Young adolescents could, he said, become quite skillful at copying cartoons (*manga*) and learning various set conventions, but this made their drawings *umasugiru* (overly stylized). Middle school student art should, he believed, be simple (*kantan*). Hattie, on the other hand, thought her students limited by a lack of basic skills.

The opposition between the mastery of basic skills ability and individual expression was a powerful dynamic in both countries, bringing to light a concern that American and Japanese teachers shared: as instructors, do teachers emphasize control and mastery or innovation and individual expressiveness? This dilemma was not restricted to artistic classrooms but was found to some degree in other subject areas as well. Even within mathematics teachers had to balance practice on drills with lessons that emphasized the creative application of mathematical equations.

Concern about the use of materials and the safety of students was a much stronger concern at Wade than at Pleasant Meadows. Schools like Wade experienced keener budgetary constraints than Pleasant Meadows, and these constraints forced teachers like Hattie to be very cautious in the use of materials. The problem was compounded by the fact that in the past some students had stolen materials or broken equipment in art classes. Hattie stated that she had great difficulty in keeping protractors in her class. The fear that some students might indeed steal art equipment and later use it as a weapon increased Wade teachers' concerns for unstructured art classes. At Pleasant Meadows, where both the school and individual families had budgets which afforded leeway in terms of material expenditures, teachers had the freedom to engage in more open-ended activities in which students could use a variety of materials and were more likely to allow students greater autonomy in art classes. Concerns for the safety of the class when using tools like X-acto knives and heating materials were absent in Kotani.

Creativity, narrowly defined as the ability of students to use material and create works of art with minimal teacher control or intervention, was linked with the ability to demonstrate self-control in the classroom in Oak Grove. Teachers noted which students were capable of working with materials on their own and which had a tendency to misuse or break materials. Teachers thought that those students who came from homes that were dysfunctional in some way lacked the basic self-control or discipline necessary to safely carry out individual artistic projects. While all students in Oak Grove were given access to films, ethnic food days, and other events that offered opportunities for creative participation, in classes with students who were perceived to be disruptive, the carrying out of these classes was constrained. Some teachers made these days treats or special privileges that a class could earn by good behavior, instituting a reward and punishment system similar to those described in chapter 5.

Wade and Pleasant Meadows teachers rarely emphasized mastery of basic forms as a way to instill a foundation of creativity in all students, a belief common in Kotani.[4] This basic difference in belief resulted in markedly divergent attitudes among teachers about how to instill and encourage creativity. In the Oak Grove schools, teachers believed that some students were simply uninterested in artwork. They did not believe, as many Kotani teachers did, that mastering basic skills through repetition would increase students' creative capacity.

### EXTRACURRICULARS, EVENTS, AND EXCURSIONS

Extracurriculars, events, and excursions (I will use "extracurriculars" throughout this section to refer to all three) were also offered by the schools as part of the formal curriculum or as a supplement to it. As they did with regard to classes, the Kotani schools offered a set of extracurriculars that varied little from year to year and from school to school. The Oak Grove schools enjoyed an assortment of extracurriculars that changed substantially from year to year.

Extracurriculars (i.e., club activities) are mandatory in most Japanese public middle schools, and schools do offer a substantial number of clubs. Students may choose any club they like at the start of the year, but after that, it is difficult to change. Extracurriculars in the United States tend most often to be sports teams, which are popular in American schools, but there were music, drama, and a variety of craft groups as well. Students are free to pick the club or team they like, and being on a team is an individual choice that can be changed at any time in most schools. It is, however, also a privilege in most schools that teachers can rescind at any time. Bad grades or bad behavior means being suspended from a team or restricted from attending a school dance. This is not the case in most Japanese schools.

In the United States, the individual student, from the first offense onward, is held responsible for his or her individual behavior and is punished accordingly. While Japanese teachers also punish students for infractions, they place themselves in positions of responsibility for the students. It is the teacher's duty to spot minor infractions and investigate to make sure they are not the manifestations of deeper troubles. As in the Murata case, infractions do not result in automatic suspension. On the contrary, they most often result in more intense involvement with the club — extra time spent writing reflection papers or working for the benefit of the club.

In addition to clubs, schoolwide events are a type of activity organized for students to express their creativity as well as to demonstrate their responsibility. Schoolwide events in Japan, like the curriculum, vary little from region to region. Yearly sports and cultural festivals are held in virtually every school in the nation. Many schools like Furukawa have a choral competition as well. Occasionally, some schools sponsor idiosyncratic events, such as the homeroom art contest at Aratamachi.

Schools in the United States exhibit more diversity of schoolwide events. School plays and concerts are quite common, but most schools organize several special days — for example, dress-up day, dress-down day, or stuffed animal day — which vary from school to school. Larger middle schools may have pep rallies for the eighth grade sports teams that allow for considerable creative expression in the cheers and music played. Trips to local museums, parks, and other sites are also common. Wade and Pleasant Meadows hosted very different events even though they were in the same school district.

U.S. teachers and administrators often try to incorporate a schoolwide event into the school day, setting aside a morning or an afternoon for it to take place. Japanese staff use such schedules much less, preferring to reserve an entire day for an event. American middle schools also host functions in the evening that promote the nonschool social life of the adolescent, including school dances and trips to recreation centers. These kinds of affairs are rare in Japan, where teachers prefer to deemphasize social interaction outside of school.[5]

As discussed in chapter 3, when Japanese teachers organize schoolwide events they put a premium on intense preparation. The Kotani teachers provide a frame, a complicated set of expectations or forms for the activities, within which the students can express their creative energies. In conjunction with students, teachers meticulously plan how the event will be structured.

Teachers do not openly contradict students' desires, but they are continually present and steer students toward activities that will be generally acceptable. On the day of the event, teachers tend to move into the background, allowing students to engage in creative or spontaneous acts within the framework of the event.

For example, the following is a description of a school festival I recorded in my field notes:

> For at least a month and a half before Furukawa's Culture Festival (*bunkasai*), students and teachers have been planning the events that each homeroom would sponsor. During the long homeroom periods, students and their home-room teachers noisily debated, brainstormed, rejected, and finally came up with plans. 2–1 class would sell noodles, 2–7 would put on a haunted house, 2–3 would have games. While teachers made sure that students made plans, and did indeed pay attention to certain restrictions concerning fire codes and cleanup, the teachers I saw did not attempt to limit or direct the class's decision.
>
> On the day of the festival, the energy in the hallways was palpable. Students raced by me at full tilt — an act which received a halfhearted "Don't run" from the usually active and voluble Mrs. Kawaguchi. Several students literally grabbed me by the arms and dragged me to their class to see the displays or engage in games.
>
> Out in the courtyard, 2–1 had set up its noodle service. One of the parents had donated freshly split green bamboo logs that had been sectioned together to form a sluice. Customers paid a set fee and then grabbed noodles that periodically flowed down the sluice in a free-flowing stream of water. Occasionally the cooks sent noodles down when no one was waiting just to watch the beautiful flow of the water and noodles. Water and noodles sloshed onto the courtyard and clogged the drain. An elderly male teacher and the principal — who both had lived through the famine of the postwar years — looked on with smiles and laughed when the noodles plopped on the ground. They appeared to be, as I was, delighted by the ingenuity that these young adolescents had displayed in creating an event that was both commercially successful and highly innovative.

The above example highlights the tension between order and spontaneity in Japanese schools. Such tension did not exist in the same way in the United States. In Oak Grove, individuals students were held accountable for their actions during special events just as they were in the classroom. What was different was the autonomy teachers had in deciding their role in the events. Teachers and administrators in each school decided the extent to which they would plan and manage an event. At the time of the study, Wade and Pleasant Meadows provided stark contrasts. At Wade, teachers oversaw most aspects of school functions, and student input was considerably less than at Pleasant

Meadows. At Pleasant Meadows, students took significant initiative in organizing, planning, and running events.

The teachers in Oak Grove varied markedly in the degree to which they allowed young adolescents to take control of planning and running school events, but they did not try to frame each activity in the way Kotani teachers did. What was particularly striking in the case of Pleasant Meadows was the willingness of teachers to let each student or group succeed or fail according to the merits of the performance. Schoolwide events in Oak Grove were characterized by an amazing range of performances that drew both applause and boos from the audience. The act of allowing students to openly express disapproval of their fellow students' performance would be anathema to Japanese teachers.

By their actions, Oak Grove teachers evinced a belief that young adolescents are capable of a wide range of actions. In some circumstances, they must be strictly supervised and controlled; in others they can virtually plan and execute events on their own. When individual students who demonstrate self-control can be found, they are allowed by teachers to largely determine their own performance and to reap the applause of admirers and the catcalls of detractors. This can lead to social differentiation between students who are perceived as worthy to engage in less restricted work and those who must be continually supervised.

In Japan, part of the effect of the teachers' enormous organizing efforts is to assure that all students participate and that all groups carry off a creditable performance. In Japan, events are run the same as classes, grades, and clubs: teachers carefully plan and organize the basic structure of the event and then allow students to make decisions within that structure. Students perform in the context of the group event, even when engaged in ostensibly individual events like painting a picture, singing a song, or running a race. Individual creativity is constantly negotiated through a group decision-making process. This doesn't mean, as is obvious from the noodle sellers at Furukawa, that individuals or groups are lacking in creativity or spontaneity, but it does mean that individual initiative is eventually embedded in events orchestrated by adults to achieve group consensus and group goals.

In the United States, individual students are more likely to be given leeway to express their opinions, but in some cases individuals are given little or no say in determining how they will engage with art or performance. Prior demonstration of self-control appears to determine the degree of autonomy that teachers allot to students. Japanese teachers would find Pleasant Meadows' talent show remarkable because of the degree to which students were made responsible for their own success or failure. In Japanese schools maximizing individual freedom would disrupt the careful organization of groups that form the basic structure of life in Japanese schools.

## Regulating Self-Expression

Abiko thought that the freedom in dress, makeup, and expression given to American middle school students was the way that schools made American adults out of children. Clothes were, in American culture, *watakushigoto* (personal affairs). Dressing in a certain way was not obligatory for participation in school, but rather was the "responsibility of the will of the parent or child."[6] To his mind, the Florida school he observed strove to further individual attention on every level. Every young adolescent in this middle school had a different personality.

The same is true in Oak Grove, where I could recognize some students at Wade or Pleasant Meadows by their clothing alone. Clothing plays an important part in expressing one's preferences or one's personality. Much of what young American adolescents carry around with them expresses their personality. And Oak Grove teachers believe that students should be mature enough to select their clothing appropriately.

In Kotani, students are expected to demonstrate maturity by conforming to the school's dress code with precision. Middle school students wear uniforms that on the surface are identical but by means of badges, collar pins, and other markers teachers can easily discern what school, year, and class a student belongs to. Figure 8.1 shows the uniforms and haircut requirements for a Nagoya middle school. Boys dress in a modified Prussian uniform: black pants and white shirt, black jacket in winter. Girls' uniforms vary more in that the color of the kerchief or cut of the blouse can deviate slightly from school to school. Some middle schools even allow drab brown or green outfits instead of the ubiquitous navy blue. Knapsacks and briefcases are also nearly identical from school to school.

Each day when Kotani homeroom teachers meet with their homeroom class — at morning meeting, cleaning period, and end-of-the-day meeting — they have an opportunity to observe how young adolescents are acting and behaving. Dress and deportment are crucial clues. Is Yabushita's jacket unbuttoned? Is Yamanaka's skirt too long? Did Murata remember to wear his name tag? These were all issues that teachers discussed with me.

Lapses, even minor ones, are treated severely. A missing name tag, gym sweats rather than a skirt, a bright-blue rather than a dull-blue headband were reason enough for a child to receive a scolding not only by the homeroom teacher but by the head of the guidance section (*shidō buchō*). What I as an

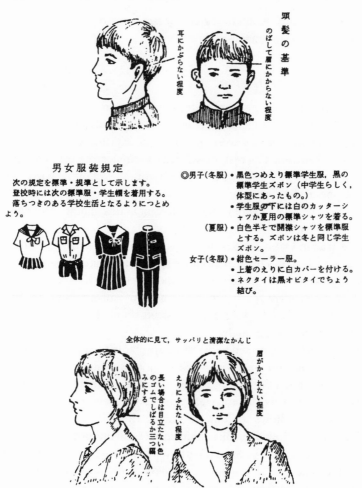

Figure 8.1. Regulations for Student Uniforms and Appearance in a Japanese Middle School

American saw as a normal caprice owing to personal preference or merely forgetfulness were warning signs to Japanese teachers.

In Oak Grove, students wore a wide variety of clothes, makeup, and jewelry. Teachers noticed dirty clothes (a sign of neglect), sexually provocative clothes (a possible sign of abuse), and symbols they associated with gang affiliation or drug use. Young adolescents who violated the school dress codes at Pleasant Meadows were sent directly to the principal's office. Gang-related items or drug paraphernalia were grounds for an automatic three-day suspension from school. The rules, the vice-principal told me, are clearly read to students at the start of each year and copies provided to parents. "It's their responsibility," he said. Oak Grove teachers did not appear to believe they had played or could play a large role in promoting students' social maturity and sought to sanction only items of dress or adornment that were perceived to be indecent or connected with illicit activities.

SCHOOL RULES

In industrialized countries around the world, young adolescents use clothing to express allegiance to certain groups or to project an image of a certain style or look of groups and individuals they are drawn to. They often find themselves at odds with adults over control of their appearance. Schools in particular may have a large number of rules regulating adolescent clothing and self-decoration, rules that teachers are called on to enforce. Enforcement of these rules tends to vary considerably within any given nation and may even vary within a school district, as was the case in Oak Grove.

Despite this variance, national patterns can readily be identified. Only a small percentage of U.S. public schools mandate uniforms, while only a small percentage of Japanese schools have abandoned them. For Kotani students, full expression of personal style could be realized only on weekends and after school. At such times, when shopping with friends, going to movies, or even attending cram school, young adolescents in Japan adopt a wide range of fashion. Students in the ninth grade might wear clip-on earrings and use lipstick. Designer labels were clearly evident in Kotani, indicating that students were aware of fashions in both Japan and the West.[7]

This restriction to weekend wear might not seem overly onerous to many educators and parents. What I found more striking than the use of uniforms in Japan were teachers' attempts to control peer identification and peer groups through the control of dress and adornment. Whereas Oak Grove teachers would send a student to the office for wearing gang symbols, Kotani teachers did not tolerate any visible sign of group belonging that was not officially allowed by the school. In other words, Oak Grove students might wear sports jackets or shirts demonstrating their membership in a fan club or other social group. Kotani students could not.

TEACHER CONTROL OVER IDENTIFICATION WITH PEERS

The ways in which Kotani and Oak Grove teachers constrained student self-expression via clothing and decoration are indicative of different general concerns as well as of dissimilar levels of tolerance for freedom of expression by individuals. Japanese schools deny students the right to express their religious or political affiliations at school, whereas schools in the United States have frequently been forced to change or drop policies that have been ruled to restrict student expression of speech. The lack of free expression in Japanese schools has been amply discussed, especially in relation to teachers' use of alternative texts. What I found most disturbing is that even teachers like Mr. Shimoda — who were critical of the controlled nature of Japanese education — strictly prohibited students from decorating themselves in ways that would express friendship groups.

In Kotani the teachers vigorously regulated any clothing, marking, or other adornment that could signal special friendships or liaisons between students. As demonstrated in chapter 4, any kind of marker — even a sign of friendship between same- or different-sex peers — was cause for concern among teachers. Despite the fact that all Kotani teachers stated that young adolescents were innocent, the teachers simply did not allow the public declaration of close boy-girl relationships. Furthermore, the Kotani teachers regulated any marking that would create special peer groups with clubs not sanctioned by the school. That is, students in the Japanese fencing (*kendō*) club might be permitted to form special relations around fencing, but membership in independent clubs, groups, or even cliques was strongly controlled. Students were free to participate in such groups outside of school but could not openly display membership in such groups through clothing or adornment.

There were some exceptions. Students in Kotani were not allowed to decorate their notebooks or other articles in the way that Oak Grove students were, but students were allowed to buy commercial pencil cases and other classroom implements that were highly decorated. For example, writing pads decorated with the image of a popular cartoon character, media personality, or singer were purchased by groups of students who all liked the same character, thus forming a semipublic expression of friendship. Students also exchanged pictures but at the time of this study were not allowed to have picture albums out during class.[8] Other than these limited forms of expression, the Kotani teachers did not permit adolescents to openly symbolize individual preferences for friends or popular icons.[9]

Oak Grove teachers placed few or no restrictions on this kind of activity, and Oak Grove students occupied the opposite end of the spectrum from Kotani adolescents. Backpacks, notebooks, textbook covers, lockers, the margins of mimeographed worksheets were all used by Oak Grove students to adhere or inscribe symbols that marked group belonging and friendship patterns. Girls in the same friendship group might engage in an ongoing exchange of pictures of a media or musical personality they both liked. Although this practice was forbidden during class time, I observed many instances of surreptitious exchange during classes, something that was very rare in Kotani. Both Wade and Furukawa girls frequently exchanged pictures of each other and used them to decorate their locker doors and notebooks. Students were also free to exchange pictures with students of the opposite sex.

From designer shoes to sports jackets to jewelry, Oak Grove students expressed interest in or allegiance with a myriad of teams, individuals, and musical groups. T-shirts were ubiquitous and displayed everything from biblical quotations to pictures of heavy metal bands. Makeup (for girls) and jewelry (mostly for girls, but also for boys) were common. Very few students wore outfits that were devoid of some trademark, logo, or symbol.

But this did not mean that Oak Grove students simply dressed for school like Kotani students dressed for the weekend. The use of clothing with trademarks, symbols and logos and the use of makeup or jewelry were typical on weekends among Kotani students, but they made no attempt to alter the clothing or accoutrements they purchased. Oak Grove students, on the other hand, actively altered their clothing, backpacks, and virtually every other item they possessed. Not only did students add stickers or prebought symbols, they manufactured symbols of their own by clever use of markers, cutouts, and glue. The result was an intricate culture of highly personalized symbols and decoration that almost escapes description.

For example, one girl had the Nike corporate logo (the swoosh) carefully manicured on each fingernail. I observed boys carefully coloring in extra lines on their running shoes with permanent markers they were supposed to be using for a social studies group-work lesson. I saw girls carefully cut and paste friends' photos into a collage during similar activities. During mathematics lessons, I observed students carefully practicing "tags" — the stylized ways of writing names or initials that can be seen almost anywhere in the United States. Sometimes parents were enlisted to sew special sports symbols on a favorite piece of clothing. Oak Grove middle school students created a rich world of fashion and decoration for themselves, filled with symbols and icons absorbed from advertising, the media, movies, music, sports, religion, and local traditions: symbols that students actively manipulated.

Although students did use a variety of symbols, the focus of clothing and adornment was decidedly social. Both Latino and African-American students occasionally wore shirts celebrating leaders of color in the civil rights movement, but clothing or adornment related to political expression was uncommon. (I recall seeing one campaign button during an election.) The teachers tolerated this kind of political expression, and I did not observe or hear of any incident in which students were reprimanded or restricted from wearing political or religious symbols.[10] The vast majority of Oak Grove students simply seemed uninterested in these kinds of things.

I was struck by the fact that Oak Grove students did not simply manipulate commercial symbols or inscribe their belongings with creative and innovative decorations: they inscribed each other, commonly marking each other's belongings and bodies. Most often this took the form of writing one's name on another's backpack or binder cover, but frequently students helped to actually decorate each other. Ink tattoos were common, and I observed many students giving each other tattoos, even during class time. In many cases, students wrote their names on other students. Sometimes students would use their tags, which made the marking indecipherable by most teachers or even other adolescents.

Girls tended to engage in this behavior more than boys did. Girls also exchanged bracelets and small articles of clothing. Girls also would groom each other — most commonly snipping off the split ends of hair of their friends sitting in front of them, but I observed even minimanicures during periods when students were allowed free time to talk or study. In the upper grades, girls occasionally groomed boys and vice versa. Boys and girls sometimes exchanged articles of clothing or jewelry in class.

Young adolescents in Oak Grove spent a significant amount of time (including class time), money, and effort to convey a highly elaborated sense of self as well as a vivid and complex set of peer-group relations. The considerable alteration of book bags, jackets, and shoes that American students engage in would simply not be tolerated in Kotani schools. And while I did sometimes see Kotani girls brushing each other's hair, I never observed the elaborate interactions characteristic of Oak Grove students either during my fieldwork or my years of teaching in Japanese classrooms.

### The Creative Adolescent: Summary

Creativity in both cultures presumes a basic kind of order, routine, or form of control which is necessary to prevent chaos but which stifles expression if there is too much of it. Teachers want their young adolescents to be creative, but how they go about engendering creativity — how teachers construct the basic order, control, or routine in the classroom or school — diverges according to how they see the capacity of young adolescents. In Japan, there is a fear that lack of order will create sloppiness or waste: without a solid base in routine and order young adolescents will lose their way. American teachers worry that they will lose control of their classes and that some adolescents will run wild.

The Kotani teachers clearly saw the need for adolescent creative expression and went to great lengths to provide organized outlets for such expression. Many of the older teachers appeared to hold the view that learning artistic pursuits was an essential part of a humanistic education. Some teachers thought the disciplined style of artistic instruction in such traditional Japanese pursuits as calligraphy, *ikebana,* and ink drawing produced pictures without life (*iki-iki*). Japanese teachers were in frequent conflict over how they should encourage creative expression among students, and this suggests that they saw the early adolescent years as developmentally special in terms of instilling basic creative values.

Although Oak Grove teachers were concerned with a lack of creativity — some saw their students as undisciplined and unable to produce carefully crafted pictures or products — by their daily actions they encouraged a culture rich in creativity and self-expression. Teachers tended to adopt a laissez-faire approach to basic skills in music and drawing but actively helped those who showed interest or made a persistent effort to learn some artistic skill. Most significant, the school provided enormous leeway for individual students to determine their interests, whether it be a sports team or developing their skills in drawing. The extent to which any adolescent could pursue a particular avenue of self-expression or creative interest in Oak Grove was largely determined by the students themselves. Teachers appeared to believe that students could not be made to learn creativity: they had to be mature enough to have the self-control needed to pursue a given artistic pursuit.

The basic structure of schooling tends to constrain what teachers offer in the way of creative expression, making teachers more likely to offer classes that reinforce dominant paradigms of creativity and self-expression. Japanese teachers emphasize harmony in group relationships, often at the cost of individual initiative. While students in clubs are given significant levels of responsibility, the daily life in Japanese schools is so organized that there is little opportunity for individuals to exercise self-expression outside of a set pattern. In the United States, the emphasis is on freedom of self-expression, not on harmony. Students are expected to control themselves, and much time is spent on organizing order among a heterogeneous group. This meant that Japanese students rarely exercised their decision-making power. Making choices or decisions requires an element of volition. In limiting student choice, Japanese teachers appeared to limit students' ability to exercise their will.

## Implications

Neither American nor Japanese teachers appeared to draw the same connections among individual dress or adornment, creativity, and self-expression that I did. For teachers on both sides of the Pacific, self-expression in personal decoration was associated with potential problems or disruption (as shown in chapter 7). Indeed, some of the Kotani teachers who seemed most critical of the restrictiveness of Japanese education were the most proactive in controlling student self-decoration.

Although the Oak Grove teachers were extremely sensitive regarding any symbol connected with gangs or drugs, the freedom of expression given to U.S. students was truly remarkable. The statements that students in Oak Grove made through their dress were proclamations of individuality. That most ubiquitous article of American clothing, the T-shirt, was a veritable sign of who one was, wanted to be, or what one believed in. And despite the qualms of many teachers, Oak Grove adolescents appeared to be aggressive and creative in their manipulation of images and logos drawn from the media and the marketplace.

The conflict over clothing in Oak Grove was linked to regional and social conflict between social classes or ethnic or racial groups in the United States. As in the case of the student carrying the bandanna at Pleasant Meadows, teachers and administrators were more likely to misinterpret (and often sanction) the symbols used by adolescents from different cultural and linguistic groups than those used by students from middle-class, European backgrounds. Yet compared to the Kotani teachers, the Oak Grove teachers permitted a wide range of behaviors, symbols, and adornments that young adolescents themselves had chosen. And the Oak Grove teachers allowed young adolescents to create strong peer groups by themselves and rarely intervened in the formation of these groups or sanctioned the public display of solidarity in these groups.

Though Kotani teachers deeply believed in the positive effect of creative activities, they systematically limited students' avenues of self-expression. In Oak Grove, student choice and self-expression — the free enactment of individual volition — were expressed in daily activities. In Kotani, student choice and self-expression were constantly encapsulated in group goals — the interaction of individual volition which melded to form a group consensus or plan. At the elementary level, this aspect of Japanese schooling has received much praise for the strong academic motivation it builds in young adolescents. When used on young adolescents, however, the same techniques appear to have negative consequences.

In attempts to preserve students' innocence, promote studying, and increase students' sense of responsibility to the group, Japanese teachers systematically limit venues for the spontaneous display of self-expression. Despite the views of some Oak Grove teachers that the media influence on adolescents has undermined morality, leaving our schools in chaos, Oak Grove students appeared far more ready to challenge and defy modern consumer culture than their Japanese peers. While the Kotani adolescents had ample opportunity to be creative within group boundaries, Oak Grove students were essentially given daily lessons in managing an acceptable balance between self-expression and group approval. The boundaries of their self-expression were broader and more fluid, and most important, they were left up to the individual. Oak Grove adolescents had to make many decisions each day (e.g., engage in an act of volition) about how they would express themselves. Day-to-day life in schools provided Kotani adolescents with little opportunity to exercise choice in how they express themselves or in how they choose to display their sense of self in public.

# How Adolescence Gets Institutionalized

In previous chapters I presented various story lines connected with young adolescents in the United States and Japan and examined how they affect the day-to-day functioning of the schools. Some story lines have a specific impact on how Japanese and Americans decide how to organize the school, what behavior is appropriate, and how the school personnel should respond when problems arise. So far, most of the analysis has been focused on observations and interviews, with brief references to school policies or procedures. In this chapter I present an analysis of policy documents to show how adolescent story lines are institutionalized at the regional and national levels. I found that at the national level, U.S. and Japanese educational policy documents are similar in the way they represent adolescence. There is significant difference, however, at the regional levels. I show that in the United States adolescent story lines are strongly institutionalized at the regional and national levels and that these story lines are closely linked with local-level documents. In Japan, adolescent story lines are weakly institutionalized at the national level, and even these story lines do not appear to be linked to regional or local-level documents.

## Educational Texts

Between 1992 and 1996 I conducted systematic comparisons of U.S. and Japanese educational texts to see what was being written about adolescence in U.S. and Japanese educational policy literature at different levels. Traditionally, sociologists have used legal documents to prove that such phenomena as children's rights are institutionalized around the world.[1] But this analysis leaves unanswered the question of whether or not these phenomena are institutionalized within national organizations or at the local level. By combining an analysis of policy documents with the ethnographic data, one can assess which adolescent story lines are institutionalized at various levels as well as investigate how closely the depiction of adolescence at each level resembles depictions at other levels. Such analysis allows one to see whether adolescent story lines are institutionalized widely within each nation or at just one level.

One problem in using texts or legislation as an indicator of the impact of a given concept on behavior is that many texts are read only infrequently and some laws are not enforced. In selecting which national texts to analyze I began by determining which texts had actually been read by teachers or administrators. Furthermore, I decided not to compare academic journals, not only because they reflect an international level of scholarly discourse, but because few teachers or administrators ever referred to them. This method of selection does not include the full range of statements about adolescence extant in the policy documents; one could probably find more adolescent story lines in Japanese policy documents, but it is unlikely that these documents would have much effect on how teachers think or how schools are organized.

A second problem in conducting this analysis was how to identify national policy documents in the United States. Because the United States has a decentralized educational system, no one national agency sets policy or standards for middle schools in the way the Ministry of Education does in Japan. Several U.S. organizations, however, do specifically make adolescence and middle schools their primary object of interest and have produced works that promote specific practices and policies for middle school organization and middle school curriculum. These include the Carnegie Council on Adolescence and the National Middle School Association; and at the regional level the California Superintendents' Middle Grade Task Force.[2] These texts represent constituencies that work to impact middle level education, and they have slightly different agendas for young adolescents. The documents I selected were *Turning Points* (Carnegie Council), which has been widely circulated in the United States and often cited in media reports; *This We Believe*, the basic position paper of the National Middle School Association; and *Caught in the Middle*, which was published by the Superintendents' Middle Grade Task Force and is the text most cited by teachers in California.

Within Japan's highly centralized system, the Ministry of Education produces a set of curriculum guidelines that lay out specific policies for instruction, guidance, and management in Japan's middle schools. I surveyed ministry publications that focused on middle school students and had topics ranging from curriculum to counseling.[3] I chose three texts that dealt with guidance and counseling in the middle school: *Guidance for Students with Problems, Prevention Measures for Problems Arising in Student Guidance*, and *Techniques for Furthering Counseling in Middle School*.[4] To counterbalance the Ministry of Education's views I reviewed a variety of reports and teacher guides published by the Kotani Prefectural board of education, prefectural guides from Nagoya and Kanagawa, and issues of the teachers' magazine *Chūgaku Kyōiku* (Middle Level Education) dealing with guidance and counseling.

HOW MUCH DID TEACHERS READ?

There were clear differences in how much the U.S. and Japanese teachers referred to these texts. Teachers in Oak Grove routinely referred to *Caught in the Middle* and *Turning Points*. The Oak Grove teachers stated that they had read parts of these documents and had been affected by them. Japanese teachers rarely referred to any text at all, and several Kotani teachers stated that they had never read the Ministry of Education official guidelines. Teachers in the United States, then, were far more likely to have been impacted by policy statements at the national level than teachers in Japan.

When Japanese teachers did refer to a text that specifically dealt with the education of adolescents, they usually referred to the curriculum plan for middle schools published by the Ministry of Education. This curriculum plan *(chūgakkō shidō yōryō)*, however, discussed only the details of curriculum and had virtually nothing to say about the characteristics of the young adolescent. Kotani teachers who worked as counselors or who had had experience with emotionally disturbed adolescents referred to other Ministry of Education texts, suggesting that among Japanese teachers there were degrees of exposure to theories of adolescent development.

These differences are salient for the analysis that follows. While I found that some Ministry of Education texts contained elements of Western story lines of adolescence, my fieldwork shows that these texts had only a small impact on teachers. In contrast, the U.S. texts had a far greater impact. Teachers in the United States tended to have read more national level documents than their Japanese counterparts, and a broader range of teachers in the United States had read these documents. Thus while Japan does indeed have a national set of curricular objectives and is in many ways a highly centralized system, the Kotani teachers were influenced less by national policy directives than their Oak Grove counterparts, at least in regard to how they thought about adolescence.

THE ADOLESCENT IN U.S. EDUCATIONAL TEXTS

In U.S. documents, the general characteristics of adolescence are elaborated in detail, and there is a high degree of correspondence between the selected texts at the national, regional, and local levels. These texts define the young adolescent as having "special learning needs" that differ substantially from those of children and older adolescents. In the two national level documents analyzed, the unique traits or characteristics of adolescence were put forward as the rationale (i.e., are the rational myths) for why there need to be special schools and special curriculum for young adolescents. That is, these texts point to the special characteristics of adolescence in order to legitimize the concept of the middle school.[5] For example, a passage from *Turning Points* (Carnegie Council, 1989:12) reads, "The onset of adolescence is a critical period of biological and psychological change for the individual. Puberty is one of the most far-reaching biological upheavals in the life span. For many young adolescents, it involves drastic changes in the social environment as well, foremost among them the transition from the elementary to secondary school. These years are highly formative for behavior patterns in education and health that have enduring significance."

In *This We Believe, Caught in the Middle,* and the Oak Grove District Guide for Middle Schools, the degree of elaboration is extensive, including lists of special emotional, psychological, physical, and social needs characteristic of the young adolescent. In table 9.1 I have listed *only* the intellectual/emotional and physical changes presented in three texts from the local, regional, and national level, respectively. Each trait may be looked at as one story line of adolescence.

Adolescents are characterized by a wide range of mental development, curiosity, and ability to reason abstractly; they are attracted to real-life problems and are egocentric. Physically, they exhibit a similar disparity in rates of change and are awkward, subject to fluctuation in basal metabolism, and self-conscious of their body image. Mental and physical predilections or processes are portrayed as being interlinked in an organic whole. At this formal level of discourse, the concept of adolescence and the specific characteristics associated with adolescence are encoded as a cohesive tale about why kids are the way they are.

The degree of elaboration is remarkable. Each of the texts contains detailed descriptions of what kinds of changes or behaviors are normal for adolescents. They also portray the American adolescent as facing particularly stressful social circumstances: "The young adolescent is moving from dependency to interdependency with parents, as well as with friends, relatives, and other

*Table 9.1  Comparison of Adolescent Characteristics in Three Major Texts*

Intellectual Development

| *In This We Believe* | *Caught in the Middle* | *Oak Grove District Manual* |
| --- | --- | --- |
| Wide range of individual development | Wide range of individual development | Display wide range of skills and abilities |
| Concrete to abstract thinking | Propositional thought | Range from concrete-manipulatory stage to abstract |
| Intensely curious | intensely curious | transescent is intensely curious |
| Prefer "active" learning | Prefer active learning | |
| Prefer peer-interaction when learning | Favor interaction with peers | |
| Respond to real life situations | Learn things considered useful; solve real life problems | Learn things considered useful; solve real-life problems; organize curicula around real-life concepts |
| Preoccupied with self | Egocentric; argue to convince others | Egocentrism; argue |
| Need for approval/ easily discouraged | Personal-social concerns dominate thoughts and activities | |
| Developing understanding of personal abilities; Inquisitive about adults/challenge authority | | |
| Distrust conventional academics | Consider academic goals as secondary | |
| Developing higher levels of humor | | |
| | Are intellectually at-risk | |
| | Developing metacognition | Independent critical thinking |

Physical Development

| *NMSA* | *Superintendents* | *Oak Grove* |
| --- | --- | --- |
| Rapid, irregular physical growth | Experience accelerated physical development — weight, height, | Accelerated physical development; increased in weight, height, heart size |

*Table 9.1 Continued*

Physical Development

| NMSA | *Superintendents* | *Oak Grove* |
|------|-------------------|-------------|
| | heart size, lungs and muscular strength | |
| Awkward, uncoordinated movements | Experience faster bone than muscle growth, may result in awkwardness and bones lack protection | Bone growth is faster than muscle grown resulting in lack of coordination and protective covering |
| Varying maturity rates; girls mature earlier | Manture at varying rates with girls taller and more physically developed | Wide range of physical differences appear; girls mature faster; secondary sex characteristics: breasts enlarging and menstruation |
| Varied rates may cause disadvantage requiring understanding of caring adults | | |
| Restlessness and fatigue due to hormonal changes | Fluctuation in basal metabolism can cause extreme restlessness or listlessness. | Fluctuation in basal metabolism may cause students to be extremely restless at times and listless at others. |
| Need daily physical activity due to increased energy; develop sexual awareness as secondary sex characteristics appear | | |
| Concerned with bodily changes: sexual maturation, nose size, ears, long arms | Show changes in body contour — ears, arms, posture; disturbed by body changes | Display changes in body contour — have large ears, long arms, posture problems; self-conscious about bodies |
| Prefer junk food | Ravenous appetites and peculiar tastes — large quantities of improper foods | |
| Lack physical fitness — endurance, strength, flexibility | Lack physical health — poor endurance, strength, flexibility — | |

*Table 9.1  Continued*

Physical Development

| NMSA | Superintendents | Oak Grove |
|---|---|---|
| | fatter and un-healthiness | |
| Physically vulnerable due to poor health habits; engage in risky experimentation with drugs and sex | | |
| | Reflect a wide range of individual difference. | |
| | Experience biological development five years earlier than adolescent in last century | |
| | Face responsibility for sexual behavior before socially ready | |

**Source:** National Middle School Association, 1995: 11; Superintendent's Middle Grade Task Force, 1987; Oak Grove Guide for District Middle Schools.

persons outside the home. While renegotiating relationships with parents and other care-givers, often in outwardly stormy ways, the young person simultaneously seeks to maintain strong ties with exactly those people" (*Turning Points,* 22).

The elaboration of so many points of development (social, mental, and physiological) along with descriptions of adolescent predilections ("have ravenous appetites and peculiar tastes") means that as a whole the picture of adolescence drawn in these texts is one of contradictions.[6] Adolescents are striving for independence, yet want connection and authority; they are bombarded by pubertal changes, yet seek to create a stable identity. The correspondence between the three documents is less than perfect, meaning that even in terms of national policy documents, differences in focus or in interpretation of specific traits are officially codified. Young adolescents are characterized as lacking physical fitness or being vulnerable, yet are also depicted as having increased energy. Similarly, adolescent "restlessness" is attributed variously to "hormonal changes" and "fluctuations in basal metabolism." In terms of men-

tal traits, the adolescent is "intensely curious" but only about "real-life problems." These conflicting messages suggest that a belief in the sturm und drang
of adolescence is alive and well in modern U.S. educational policy.

Regardless of whether these adolescent story lines are currently supported
by research or not, they are strongly institutionalized at the national, regional,
and local (California) level. Adolescence has been written into policy documents at every level. While individuals or groups may debate whether or not
adolescents are restless because of hormones or because of metabolism, the
fact that adolescence is a time of stressful change and conflict is depicted as
fact. Moreover, the level of detail about adolescent development does not
become lower in regional or local literature. The Oak Grove district text gives
precise details about adolescent development and in fact even mentions the
term "transescent" — a term currently advocated by some educational psychologists to differentiate the stage between childhood and adolescence.

The evidence from policy documents in the United States shows that the
story lines of adolescence are found at the national, regional, and local levels in
very similar ways. Overall, adolescence is described in extensive detail at all
levels and is portrayed in contradictory images at all levels. Moreover, the
language of the documents is reflected in teacher and administrator speech
that is powerful evidence that, in the United States, adolescence is strongly
institutionalized at every level of the school system.

THE ADOLESCENT IN JAPANESE EDUCATIONAL TEXTS

The adolescent and adolescent development are discussed in terms of
Western psychological theory in the Ministry of Education materials I reviewed. For example, the following passage is typical of the kind of statement
of the characteristics of adolescence found in these texts:"Adolescence [*sei-
nenki*] is a time of problems, in the midst of which sexual worries and other
troubles are not exposed, rather the tendency is to turn them inward.

"For example, the characteristic adolescent demands of the budding ego
grow stronger as the student tries to solve problems by his own power. Furthermore along with this independent spirit, a sense of self-respect, a sense of shame
and sense of fastidiousness also become obvious" (Monbusho, 1977:78).

This document shares many adolescent story lines with U.S. educational
policy texts. Adolescence is a time of problems, sexual awakening, and issues
of identity. Terms like the "budding ego," and "characteristic adolescent demands" are found. Development of the identity is theorized to coincide with
rising sexual consciousness, and adolescents are depicted as caught in a period
of identity crisis. Conflicts over identity can produce a heightened sensitivity
and susceptibility to emotional problems as well as a tendency to rebel. All in

all, a classic formulation of adolescent development theory that could be derived from classic texts on adolescent development.[7]

Yet the chapter from which the above quotation is taken continues by describing a case in which a middle school boy attempted to rape a female student. The text provides specific details about how the school handled the problem.[8] The language is technical, almost criminalistic. Later in the text the teachers are described as discovering that the presence of the father's new and much younger girlfriend seems to have unbalanced the boy's state of mind. This example, then, although it presents a general theory of adolescent development, is clearly constructed around an idea of abnormality. Psychological theories in this text are linked to accounts of unexpected behavior, not to everyday problems. This was an account, not of the normal, but of the significantly abnormal. The link between theories of adolescent mental functioning and abnormal behavior is found in several places in these texts. The authors appear to be using these theories as ways to account for the problems students sometimes manifest rather than making manifest the conditions that account for students problems. In another section, the authors of *Mondai Kōdō* describe the conditions that can cause juvenile delinquency (*hikō shōnen*) *in every child*: "It is important to understand the problems that occur among 'preadults' [*miseinensha*], that is to say, those moving through the process of change from child to adult. We can think of the transient deviant acts that occur in this developmental process as actions of a kind of 'trial and error' nature. As students undergo such intense [*hageshii*] changes at the middle school stage, they are easily influenced by undesirable social influences, thus this quality of being easily affected is not limited to children with problem behaviors already" (Monbusho, 1977:9).

The Japanese text posits tremendous changes as a kind of base for why adolescents are "swayed by peers." All the upheaval of this stage puts all children at risk. The deviant acts are seen as a kind of experimentation: the child trying different things in the midst of an extreme time of transition. The text later goes on to link problems with inferiority complexes, blockage of individual growth, family and friend relations, and inappropriate guidance at school (10). Finally, in passing, the text mentions that when puberty is not proceeding naturally or properly it may pose an obstacle to the student's development. The text seems to indicate that when some natural developmental process occurs, the kinds of mental conditions that cause problems do not arise. Adolescents exhibit problems because of external factors (school stress) which appear to engage or aggravate an instability or susceptibility in the normal mental development process.

The depiction of adolescent problems in the other two Ministry of Education works, however, indicates a very different picture. Student problems are seen as arising out of mismatches between student's goals or hopes and the expectations of peers, teachers, and family. The influence of family and peers in pulling young adolescents into unhealthy behavior is emphasized at the same time that the power of the school to counteract these effects is also mentioned. Teachers are encouraged to establish ties with parents and the community.[9]

What is most striking about these texts is the absence of the idea, expressed in the Carnegie document, that "puberty is one of the most far-reaching biological upheavals in the life span." While texts at the national level in Japan have a distinctly psychological tone, they do not tightly link dramatic psychological changes with normal puberty or sexual development. Rather, problems in normal development or cases of extreme deviancy result in psychological disturbance. The link between physical change, emotional turmoil, and the identity crisis is mentioned only indirectly. The more prominent story lines are those that link social disconnection or family problems with delinquent behavior.

There are no adolescent story lines to be found in any of the regional or local documents in Japan. Neither of the school manuals from Furukawa or Aratamachi nor the various research publications from Yamagawa Prefecture or the Oda region make use of any systematic definition of adolescence. In an essay on "juvenile students with emotional problems" a teacher from a metropolitan area near Kotani wrote, "Historically, puberty has been discussed in terms of a troubled period of uncertainty." This lone reference to the disruption of puberty occurs in the preface to an article on students with emotional problems, written for teachers and administrators. The document evidence suggests that reference to American story lines of adolescence are quite rare at the regional and local level in Japan. And when they do occur, they reinforce beliefs that puberty or adolescent development is linked with problems only in exceptional cases.

Furthermore, the Japanese documents do not connect the developmental changes faced by young adolescents with the specific learning needs of middle school students. Both national and regional documents in the United States cite adolescent development as a rationale for having special schools and curriculum for young adolescents. The Japanese documents are void of this link between development and learning.

These documents suggest that story lines of Western adolescence occur in Japanese educational policy literature only at the national level. Furthermore, even in these documents, there is less elaboration of the storylines than is found in U.S. documents, and the story lines tend to be connected with abnormal cases. The story lines are infrequently presented as a set of normal expectations for the adolescent. An elaborated set of adolescent characteristics is simply not encoded in the Japanese policy literature reviewed in this study. There is significant dissimilarity in how adolescence is depicted between national and regional or local level documents. Moreover, the language of the national documents is *not* reflected in teacher and administrator speech, which is powerful evidence that in Japan adolescence is not institutionalized at regional or local level of the school system and only weakly so at the national level.

## Policy Documents and Teachers

In the United States there is a much tighter correspondence in the description of adolescent development between formal levels of discourse at the national or regional level (as exemplified in the texts cited above) and informal, local levels of discourse (as exemplified in teacher writings) than in Japan. American teachers appeared fluent in their knowledge of theories of adolescence, even if these sometimes conflicted with the latest academic research on the issues. The terms used in writings at various levels were similar. For the Japanese, the language at the formal level tends toward the abstract and incorporates elements of Western psychological theory not found in most local documents used by educators. This suggests that the cultural story of adolescence, the robust set of story lines that set forth the characteristics of adolescence in the United States, is, again, weakly institutionalized in Japan.

Why such disparity? Let us take for an example the connection between physical change and behavioral response. *Caught in the Middle* encodes the story line that tremendous physical changes in adolescence impact behavior and emotion: "restlessness or listlessness." The idea that adolescents are somehow more prone to illness is reiterated: young adolescents "lack physical health." Alternatively, these physical changes cause a ravenous appetite that may compel young adolescents to eat unhealthy food. These variant story lines all encode a belief that adolescents are experiencing rapid physiological changes that have, as a consequence, poor or fragile physical or emotional health or both. Although recent studies contradict this belief, such a belief has a long history in U.S. culture. Hall wrote about theories of "turgidity" of the blood as an explanation of adolescent behavior.[10]

Adolescence in U.S. culture has, since the days of the Puritans, been viewed as a time of instability and disruption. These beliefs have, over time, been reinterpreted and restated by a wide variety of social theorists. Starting with Hall, psychologists and psychoanalysts began to make theoretical connections between physiological development and psychological development, emphasizing the instability that puberty and adolescence bring on.[11]

Only within the past few decades have these theories been challenged and refuted. Such prominent psychologists as A. Bandura and sociologists like J. Rosenbaum have questioned whether there is any evidence to support a developmental link between adolescence and aberrant behavior and argue that social factors are far more likely candidates to explain adolescent behavior than developmental changes.[12] Other detailed studies of pubertal change and hormonal levels have found that there are only very weak links between puberty or hormonal changes and the disruptive or unstable behavior usually associated with adolescence.[13]

But teachers in U.S. middle schools work inside organizations whose institutional rational derives from highly elaborated descriptions of adolescence and the special learning needs of the adolescent. Although many of the specific characteristics, the story lines, of adolescence may no longer be supported by scholarly research, they are strongly institutionalized at the local, regional, and national levels in the United States. Moreover, a practitioner culture and literature has developed in which some psychological and developmental theories have been assimilated: "Adolescence today has become at its best a state of ambivalence, at its worst an identity crisis, and both states send young people into the adult world without knowing who they really are. They have not found themselves, have neither examined deeply what they can best do nor examined realistically what they cannot do well. Their years since puberty have been caught up in unresolved value conflicts, imposed conformity, sheer ennui, or frustrating attempts to escape."[14]

For example, generalized uses of Erik Erikson's developmental framework for adolescence are commonly cited as the basis for defining adolescence, sui generis, as a time of identity seeking, of physical change and turmoil, as well as self discovery: "Erik Erikson describes adolescence as a period of increasing conflict in the quest for self-identity. Middle school teachers can testify best about the transitory nature of early adolescent personalities, who may try on five roles in as many days. Life is always an extreme; all adjectives are superlative; emotions range from high to low but seldom in between."[15]

Associated with this use of Erikson's stage development are stories of adolescent depression, ill health, and at-risk behavior. In the words of the writer Niki Scott, "The worst news is that adolescent girls are twice as likely as boys to be depressed — and four to five times more likely to attempt suicide."[16] Such overgeneralized interpretations miss the original intent of the author: Erikson was keenly aware of the role that culture played in development, but such nuances were lost when Eriksonian stage development theory became institutionalized in the U.S. educational culture.[17] This version of stage development is found not only in practitioner writings, but also in popular writings on education and in the self-help literature: "Why is life so unhappy for many adolescents? One reason is that they get hit with an emotional double-whammy, a study suggests. Often, they not only face a pileup of distressing events, but they also react to those events more strongly than younger kids do, researchers found."[18]

The study of adolescence, in popular conceptions, focuses on the relation between the biological and the emotional, especially the relation between hormones and subsequent emotions. As one advice columnist wrote to the perplexed mother of an eleven-year-old girl, "You're right, hormones are starting to stir some new feelings in her. During adolescence, kids' motivation shifts from wanting to please their parents to wanting to feel more in control of their lives."[19]

Rather than seeing identity-seeking and identity crisis as a result of the interaction between a specific pattern of child rearing (i.e., white, middle-class Americans) and general human developmental tendencies, the popular interpretation makes adolescent instability hardwired: "The parents were worried by the marked changes in their 13-year-old son's behavior and were convinced he had a brain tumor. His personality had changed, they said. His use of language had grown odd. He had become uncharacteristically rebellious." Victor Strasburger, the chief of adolescent medicine at the University of New Mexico in Albuquerque, talked with the parents and examined the boy:"'The symptoms the parents thought were caused by a brain tumor were actually signs of a normal adolescence,' Dr. Strasburger said.

"The changes of adolescence often take parents as well as children by surprise. The teenage years are a time of flux, as children take awkward steps toward becoming adults."[20]

The sturm und drang of adolescence in the present popular and practitioner literature is linked to biophysical changes, much as Hall said it was nearly a century ago. Emotional change, depression, rebellion, self-centeredness, and a search for identity all begin with the onset of physical change. Adolescents are depicted as proceeding through a natural, indeed human set of changes, but these changes are not cultural: they are universalized and made to appear to be the norm.[21] In dealing with the suddenly "moody teen" parents are reminded to remember their own developmental trajectory. "Parents, do you remember when your hormones raged?" queries the writer of an advice-for-parents piece. What may be different is the time of onset — puberty and adolescence are no longer associated with juniors and seniors in high school. The "grades from hell" now come during middle school: "According to child care professionals, the middle school years mark the beginning of a very challenging time that kicks off years of spirited family confrontations built upon two clashing but simple truths: Adolescents are suddenly desperate for independence, and parents are still trying to cling to their babies."[22]

## Summary

The consistency of how story lines are presented in the local, regional, and national literatures in the United States, along with the fact that Oak Grove teachers used language that was similar to that found in policy documents, is evidence of the degree to which adolescence is institutionalized. Adolescence is strongly (some might prefer the term "highly") institutionalized in the United States and is specifically linked with middle grades education. The evidence from Kotani shows that this is not the case in Japan, where Western story lines of adolescence can be found only at the national level and where teachers in their day-to-day work do not use the language and theories found in those documents.

The rational myths found in any culture can be remarkably tenacious, and in the case of adolescence they appear to have withstood decades of scientific research. Although I routinely assigned articles which refute a hard link between physiology and adolescence in both my undergraduate and graduate classes, each quarter many students (both future teachers and veteran teachers) would, in their final exam, write about the traumatic effect that puberty has on adolescent behavior. This experience first suggested to me that teacher beliefs about adolescence were trapped in a kind of time warp. The "discovery" of adolescence at the turn of the century by G. Stanley Hall set off an explosion of studies — some of which were quite influential — that have become part of the general educational culture and the broader culture as well.

James Kett asserted that modern adolescence arose from an idealized notion of the middle-class life course and was forced onto other classes (or religioethnic groups) via the institutions of school, the factory, the reformatory, and psychological tests and treatments in general: "Attitudes and concepts which had appeared within the middle class in the 1880s and 1890s now pushed beyond the perimeters of that class in the shape of efforts to universalize and to democratize the concept of adolescence."[23]

Through pop psychology and pop sociology, we now have many story lines in U.S. culture about how identity, self-esteem, and personality are formed and influenced during adolescence. In the popular culture, adolescence is a continually evolving complex of meanings and stereotypes that describe or identify normal behavior or expected reactions for young people during the pubertal or postpubertal phase of development. Adolescence is important in our (American) modern life course. We are born, go through a whole series of ministages subsumed under the categories of infancy and childhood, and then *hit* adolescence.[24] The abrupt end to childhood, adolescence is crucial to Americans because it heralds the onset of maturity. Parents and teachers anticipate that the child's physical changes presage mental and emotional maturation.

In working with teachers in California, Georgia, and Pennsylvania, I have become aware that their beliefs about adolescence, far from being current, appear to be close to descriptions and theories from psychoanalytic and psychological writings of thirty years ago. Although many basic psychological texts now directly address the myth of adolescent rebellion and emotional turmoil, the prevailing beliefs and attitudes among teachers are that such rebellion and turmoil are facts with identifiable biophysical causes.[25] Hadley Dimeck was right to complain that there was "no end" to books about adolescence, but he missed the salience of this fact: the *elaboration* of adolescence in the educational culture and educational policy of the United States is what most distinguishes American conceptions of adolescence from those found in other countries, such as Japan. And it makes educational reform at the middle grades level very difficult.

## Implications

Ambiguity about the future, impossible ideals, and a fragile sense of self combine to insure that all adolescents are at risk in American middle schools.[26] In much educational literature adolescence is portrayed as a time of tremendous physical and emotional change: hormones rage and students rebel as they desperately seek out their true identity.[27] Teachers struggle to maintain control against twin tides of disruption: sexual awakenings and rebellious attitudes. Crisis, conflict, confrontation, and identity are inextricably linked with the notion of adolescence.

How, then, can young teachers implement new educational practices based on up-to-date theories and culturally sensitive pedagogies? My former student teachers left my classroom to enter a world of lunchroom gossip about raging hormones and defiant middle school kids. Lacking the support of a strong mentor, many of them began to adapt the same attitudes as their peers. This was not the case for students whose mentors were among the relatively few teachers that had a strong knowledge of current research. Some Oak Grove teachers, like Gretchen Jondervag and Adrian Norris, did not accept the adolescent story lines presented in the academic literature and actively sought out new methods of classroom instruction and classroom management to integrate into their classes.

The use of master teachers as mentors is not a new idea in U.S. educational practice, and it is standard practice in Japan. What this study tells us is that the selection of mentor teachers is crucial. The mentor teacher must help new teachers not only to learn how to manage a class and develop his or her teaching style, but also to deal with the negative stereotypes of young adolescents that abound in the lunchroom and the advice columns. In the United States, this will be no easy task, as teachers face a phenomenon that is widely regarded as a normal part of the life course.

# Conclusion: Adolescence, Self, and Life Course

Now if selves are defined by their preferences, but those preferences are arbitrary, then each self constitutes its own moral universe. . . . There each individual is entitled to his or her own "bit of space" and is utterly free within its boundaries. — Bellah et al., *Habits of the Heart,* 76.

What does adolescence tell us about our beliefs in the self, about our very identity as human beings? In everyday parlance, we use "adolescence" to gloss a range of physical, emotional, mental, and social changes (and of course expectations and beliefs) which are crucial in defining adulthood in American culture. Although Americans generally encourage individuality from infancy on, a strong story line in our general culture holds that after puberty the child can make decisions for him- or herself. The adolescent is expected not only to be responsible for his or her actions, but to make big decisions, express preferences, and defend beliefs. Children, we believe, should begin to display hints of their adult personality during adolescence.

## The Centrality of Volition in Defining the Young Adolescent Experience

On one level, it appears that Americans are concerned with willfulness and Japanese with willpower — the American story lines of adolescence are replete with themes of rebellion, disruption, and conflict. In the Japanese story lines we find concern with establishing patterns, harnessing energy, developing skills and endurance. But this dichotomy is too crude to adequately depict the wide variety of themes found in each country. In both Japan and the United States, teachers displayed a concern for the maturing volition of the young adolescent. The concerns of teachers at Kotani and Oak Grove took culturally different paths, but both were anchored by a common idea that at this time of puberty and ensuing change, the child's innocent or unformed volitional capabilities are replaced by mature capabilities; that this process was a central task in successfully making the transition to adulthood; that young adolescent volitional capabilities or capacities could or could not be developed by adults.

"Will" is not a word widely used in either country. Neither Japanese nor Americans use the term "will" (*ishi*) commonly, yet both are concerned with the volition of the young adolescent. How Japanese or American teachers focus on this concept of volition is key to understanding the basic model or core of the adolescent self that adults (teachers) perceive as experiencing the changes wrought by maturation on the adolescent. An analysis of Kotani teachers' beliefs about and actions toward young adolescents shows clearly that the expansion of Western institutional ideals of self and individuality into Japan has not displaced a core of very deeply held beliefs about the nature of human beings which is rooted in older sources of Japanese culture. Rather than seeing the developing volition of the child or adolescent as a movement toward some adult state of freedom, in cultures like Japan, volition is depicted as being progressively attached via a self situated in more diverse and complex social relations. Western elements are indeed present, but their expression (when and in what manner they are used) is modified by the social and cultural milieu of Japan. In the process of amalgamation over the past hundred years, Western story lines about adolescence have been only weakly institutionalized in Japanese schools.[1]

As stated in chapter 1, a variety of scholars, social theorists, and philosophers — Robert Bellah, Peter Berger and Thomas Luckman, Charles Taylor, and Anthony Giddens, among them — basically agree that the kind of reflective, autogenic, and inwardly turned self described in the epigraph to this chapter is dominant in the modern world system. The conditions of modernity, the institutions of the nation-state, a democratic constitution, modern factories and schools all work to transmit this modern sense of self and individuality.

The fact that Western social theorists have only recently become enamored of the idea of the self as autoreflective does not mean that this is any great revelation to the Japanese. As we gain more access to Japanese texts and as more studies of the Japanese nature of self are produced, Western views grow more complex. Differences in the concept of self between the West and East and between the present and the past are more subtle and profound than the core assertion that the modern self is an inward-turned entity can sustain.

In formulating theories about the modern self, Western theorists have tended to ignore the key facet of volition. Perhaps because the doctrine of free will is so deeply institutionalized in Western culture (and because a modern self is by definition autonomous and autogenic) there has been little consideration that conceptions of volition that lie outside a dichotomy of free and unfree could exist. The evidence provided in this study demonstrates that the way in which volition is conceptualized in a culture has a great deal to do with how basic ideas about self and individuality are conceptualized. The basic reality of life in Japanese and U.S. middle schools is a daily enactment (or contestation) of beliefs in the development of adolescent volition.

Volition, in the school contexts of Oak Grove and Kotani, was expressed as control: control over one's actions and the actions of others. And this control was a dominant issue in both Oak Grove and Kotani schools. The focus (or emphasis) given to an adolescent's volition in relation to more general assumptions or goals for the social order of the school proved to be distinctive in each culture. Despite the presence of certain Western story lines of adolescence which suggest that some elements of the modern self have become institutionalized in Japan, Japanese and American teachers displayed very different understandings of the self of their charges. "Who am I?" the central question of modern selves, was important to Kotani teachers and students, but how this question was phrased and answered shows that there has been a melding that transformed the story lines of adolescence in Japan.

Teachers work out an adolescence that is presented to students in the organization of responsibility, punishment, and counseling within the school. The preceding chapters support the idea that teachers in Japan and the United States are concerned with a number of developmental processes. Middle school encompasses a crucial time for students in both cultures. Students, after puberty, are on their way to maturity. Keeping in mind that maturation is an amalgam of many processes, teachers in both countries evinced a central concern about the developing *will* of the child/adolescent. In both nations, teachers engaged in dialogues with students, parents, and each other over issues of will, willpower, and willfulness.

## Inculcating or Exercising Volition

In both countries explicit and implicit goals of education deal with forming or encouraging the child's capacity for exercising volition — usually idealized or exemplified in big decisions, written expression, and opportunities for displaying mastery of some subject, art, or sport. The difference between forming and encouraging is significant because the first assumes that the human volition is permeable and subject to changes that can be controlled and manipulated ahead of time. The latter implies that the development of human volition can be promoted or retarded, but not educated.

In the goals (both social and academic) of the Japanese schools the child's volition is invoked in many ways. Kotani teachers displayed a preoccupation with endurance (*gaman*), tenacity (*nebari tsuyoi*), and perseverance (*gambaru*), which they saw as being directly linked with self-realization (*jikaku*) and a sense of independence (*jishusei*). Teachers encouraged behavior in adolescents that would increase their self-realization and capacities for endurance, perseverance, and tenacity. Self-expression and self-realization meant much more than identifying likes and dislikes — a person's preferences. Kotani teachers were concerned with increasing the volitional capacity of young adolescents, most commonly described as *yaruki* (motivation/determination), by the systematic inculcation of specific goals (*mokuhyō*). This, they believed, was a necessary process of maturation for young adolescents. If young adolescents could not persevere at difficult tasks, they would not become successful adults. In the words of Mrs. Chino at Furukawa, "*Will* [*iyoku*] is willpower/ambition [*yaruki*], to persevere, to turn toward a goal and encourage yourself from within."

To strengthen or raise this will, young adolescents must have a goal. Throughout Japan, the overriding concerns of third-year teachers (at high school and middle school) is to get young adolescents to make up their minds about future schooling or work. At Furukawa it was the subject of endless debates in the Guidance and Placement Section. Mr. Hamanaka and Mr. Yamagata as well as other teachers at Furukawa spent hours discussing ways to get young adolescents to think about what they wanted to be in the future.

To get young adolescents to have a clear goal for the future (and strengthen their resolve) was the central objective of teachers at Furukawa, Aratamachi, and the middle schools I visited in Kanagawa and Nagoya. The educational plans, activities, and concerns of teachers showed a clearly defined developmental schema in terms of educating the adolescent's volitional capacity and capacity to persevere or endure. The first and essential phase is to establish a sense of order and acclimatize the adolescent to the rigors of study. Various committees, clubs, and activities are organized so that a sense of the sacrifice of others and an understanding of the duties of a senior member are made clear. Awareness of others' work is intimately connected with understanding one's self, one's part in the group, and the contribution one makes. The adolescent should decide on future choices, in some texts what kind of *jinsei* (human life) the adolescent wants to pursue. By helping students to establish a clear goal, the teachers provide them with the tools needed to develop perseverance, patience, and volition. Teachers essentially work to form the developing adolescent volition.

Teachers in Oak Grove seldom talked or wrote about increasing an adolescent's capacity to persevere or endure. Their concern is providing an atmosphere in which the adolescent can freely exercise his or her preferences, discover more about his or her likes and dislikes, and feel safe. American ideals of volition focus on the individual's ability to clearly state his or her likes, beliefs, and aspirations and to defend those choices. School is the place where each adolescent can explore his or her potential. Teachers could encourage or discourage the development of adolescent volition but not form its course. Documents from the schools and district stated this belief in one form or another:

> The educational process at the school must assist the student to meet his/her full potential by obtaining skills needed to meet continued change. (Pleasant Meadows *School Report Card*)

> Wade is committed to educating and empowering students to achieve their full potential and contribute to an ever-changing world by actively involving them in a supportive, safe, and challenging environment. (Wade *School Report Card*)

> First, it would be appropriate for 5th and 6th grade students to experience short term — non-choice — courses and activities that give a "taste" of a more in-depth course that they may take at a later time. These prescribed choices in the early grades would lead to free choices in the later grades. (Oak Grove *Middle School Guide*)

The focus in Oak Grove — and in the United States in general — is on providing adolescents with the opportunity to make decisions and then account for why they made the choice they did. (In contrast, Japanese schools focus on training the will or increasing motivation through a set of formal activities.) The difficulty for Oak Grove teachers came in the form of collisions between self-expression or self-determination and teachers' imposition of order. After puberty, and certainly after they have entered their teens, students are expected to clamor for more control over what they can do, say, wear, and eat. The exercise of volitional capacity can often run counter to what adults want young adolescents to do. Discipline and rebellion against discipline dominate the lives of teachers and students in middle schools. The crucial task for maturation is to learn self-discipline.

A sense of will is also emphasized in terms of notions of self-constraint. The adolescent is expected to have self-discipline, that is, a developed capacity for self-control or volition. But Oak Grove teachers largely avoided working on actively developing student self-discipline. Teachers instead tried to increase student motivation, sense of identity, sense of self, and self-esteem, but they did so largely by allowing opportunity for the exercise of volition and the imposition of sanctions when students violated certain norms. In terms of volition, Oak Grove teachers treated young adolescents much as if they believed that the body and volition developed according to an immutable schedule: a schedule that teachers might retard or speed up, but not substantially alter.

## Implications: Teacher-Student Relations and the Self

In his ethnography of a Florida middle school (1987), Tadahiko Abiko wrote,

> Even in front of teachers, children coolly evade the truth. They equivocate about a variety of things, but will not admit and apologize for what they have done. With elementary school students it may be different, *however even though they are middle school students no one thinks [this behavior] amazing because they are children.* It was as if I were watching adults quarreling. However, the teachers permit this kind of speech/manner in children. If this were Japan, how would we handle such middle school students?[2]

Abiko's impressions of American middle school students were not very flattering. From a Japanese perspective, teachers interacted with children as if they were adults. The social relations seemed strained, and Abiko used the term "cold" (*samishii*) to characterize the school he viewed. The coldness refers not to a lack of social interaction, but to Abiko's perception of the highly individualistic manner — the lack of social connection — that characterized the social interactions he observed. Contrast this to the social denseness of the Japanese middle school conveyed by American and Japanese ethnographers alike.

American students, as viewed by Abiko, could readily express their will (*iyoku*) as preferences and desires, but they could not control themselves. They engaged in the inappropriate behavior (by Japanese standards) of lying to a teacher and showing little concern for each other. In contrast, Japanese students, as seen by Rebecca Fukuzawa and Hiroyoshi Shimizu and Kozo Tokuda, were vulnerable when removed from the dense social networks of the school and had difficulty expressing individual preferences and desires. Japanese students exhibited low self-esteem in the Western sense and an inhibition that might be alternatively characterized as too much self-control.

The consistency of these cultural stereotypes is striking: the Japanese are

passive and group-oriented whereas Americans are cold (*ronri-teki*), argumentative (*rikutsuppoi*), and independent.[3] But why are these stereotypes so
persistent?

Part of the answer lies in the ways in which the form of schooling facilitates
patterns of interactions between adolescents and teachers. To be stubborn or
argumentative is to display self-sureness in America. It is to stand up for what
one believes in, and this is a key sign of independence and a sign that the
adolescent now assumes responsibility for his or her internal values. You are
responsible for your own actions. If you do not follow the rules, you will be
punished. Furthermore, a sense of individuality is promoted by a belief that
your actions do not reflect on me and do not change my will. Like the young
adolescents who damaged the textbooks arguing with Dave Jarvis that "it
wasn't us," Americans are uncomfortable with the idea of a self or will that is
permeable or contiguous with others. As early as the late years in elementary
school, U.S. young adolescents are expected to stand up for their rights, to
follow rules of their own volition, and to display their individuality by directly
responding to their teachers and ignoring the actions of others.

The story line of rebellion in the U.S. context is both positive and negative.[4]
It reflects a cultural tension over how to deal with the will of the adolescent.
Battles over the will of the child, the breaking of a child's will, and the tor-
ments of a willful child are significant and recurrent themes in the history of
childhood and adolescence in the United States. At the same time, the maturation of an autonomous, free-willed individual capable of rebellion is one of the
most celebrated elements of U.S. culture. Particular kinds of student-teacher
conflict are thus almost inevitable in the United States.

Failure to do what teachers (or other authorities) said was taken as a sign of
lack of self-discipline and self-control in Oak Grove. These behaviors are
labeled defiant and generally supposed to be rooted in the immature ego of the
developing child. But in the cultural logic of American schools, it would be
almost impossible for an adolescent not to appear disruptive at some point.
Individual adolescents were given exceptional leeway to organize and pursue
certain activities in Oak Grove schools, but at the same time teachers frequently punished lapses in self-discipline. When there are school events in
America, such as dances and plays, teachers usually allow students considerable latitude in determining how they want things to go. Abiko was shocked
by this and noted in his book that teachers seemed unconcerned and laissez-
faire about school dances. However, when students cannot follow the rules as
individuals, they are perceived as literally out of control of the self.

The struggle with order is largely played out on an individual level. The
teacher is the arbitrator, and although groups are occasionally punished or

rewarded, this is usually ineffective. This struggle for control and the imposition of order at the individual level is evident from very early on in American schools. In fifth grade classes like Bill Joiner and Urma Baxter's, each visit provided me with long entries on discipline and regulation. A considerable amount of the time in class is taken up in waiting, giving instructions, admonishing students to be quiet or orderly as well as meting out detention or various other point systems.[5] Oak Grove teachers spent a considerable amount of their teaching day engaging in activities that dealt with issues of control and volition. Adolescents were expected to display a mature, independent self via acts of self-expression and self-determination but were frequently censured or punished if these acts appeared to be in defiance of adult expectations. Students and teachers daily engaged in a clash of wills.

The culture and organization of American schools predispose American teachers to demand that each adolescent learn to be responsible for his or her own actions, but U.S. classrooms tend to be a battlefield of wills. For American teachers there is tension and ambiguity in accepting the free will of young adolescents. Oak Grove teachers readily treated young adolescents as individuals with free wills yet commonly discussed a student's behavior as if it were purely the product of immutable forces. Students are seen to be at the mercy of social pressures and hormonal fluctuations, yet teachers also recognize that some students are hard workers. When a student disobeyed, he or she was disruptive and lacking in self-control, not manifesting self-determination. The institutionalization of adolescence in U.S. public schools means that often behavior an adolescent displays will be taken as confirmation of his or her instability or lack of control.

The structure of Japanese schools predisposes Japanese teachers to do everything they can to teach students to be responsive to others, but Japanese classrooms tend to become overly self-conscious and inhibited. For the Japanese, constraint of the self is indicative of a mature volition, but this leads inevitably to cultural contradictions. In teaching students to exercise constraint of self, Kotani teachers often found themselves undermining the young adolescents' ability to choose for him- or herself. In the Japanese tradition, will was a power that brought selfish or asocial impulses under control and allowed the individual to live in harmony with the social or natural environment, but in a modern democratic nation such control in schools may undermine the democratic process.[6]

A brief reading of the history of Japan's prewar schools immediately highlights the tensions between ideals of egalitarian participation and a clear social hierarchy. Many of the basic practices outlined in this book—mutual participation of teachers in student events, the organization and enactment of a variety of events and ceremonies, teacher imposition of sanctions for outside school behavior — were all used in the prewar period to inculcate an ultra-nationalistic ideology. The major difference (and hence the central factor in determining whether these practices work to promote democratic versus ultra-nationalistic ideology) was the degree of autonomy teachers had in choosing the focus and content of the classes and events they organized.

Teachers in Japan have tended to transmit their values and position in the social and moral hierarchy. In a cultural system in which will and even self are believed to be permeable and interconnected with the wills and selves of others, the institutional story lines of Japanese schools have reinforced teachers' impact on students. In times when teacher participation in school activities was controlled from outside (during the 1920s and 1930s), the teacher's and and the student's wills were expected to be one — and this one will or one heart was subject to the demands of the emperor and the empire. The important element of teacher identification with his or her students was deemphasized while the elements of hierarchy were emphasized. No wonder that one of my older informants in Kotani described the social relations in prewar classrooms as a "terrifying existence" (*osoroshii sonzai*).

When Japanese teachers have significant autonomy to exercise their own will — to make important decisions about curriculum or the running of the school — they not only foster strong identification of students with the teacher and the school, but also themselves become sympathetic to student beliefs and concerns. Mutual participation increases the likelihood that teachers will speak and act on students' behalf — often directly challenging the social hierarchy. Teachers take on the will of the students, that is, their dreams, goals, and aspirations.[7]

Thus, although some American writers have given Japanese education high praise, many prominent Japanese scholars seem to have formed a directly opposite view. Teruhisa Horio writes, "Japan's officially proclaimed policies for educational reform have systematically usurped the rights, constitutionally guaranteed to all citizens in a democratic society, to freely grow and develop into self-governing human beings."[8]

Such criticism may be owing to the fact that Japanese scholars can readily see how the practices and beliefs of Japanese teachers are focused in an institutional setting that can create either an egalitarian or an authoritarian system. Depending on whether or not teachers are receptive to the hearts of their students, Japanese schools can work to increase students' sense of choice and volition or to extinguish it. The current concerns among a wide range of Japanese intellectuals are that the increasing push for academic standardization and continued pressures on students to pass entrance examinations are having the same effect of depriving teachers of control over the curriculum as in the prewar period.[9] Dramatically speaking, some Japanese would argue that worship of the emperor has been replaced by worship of the examination. The result for young adolescents is similar: development of volition and choice is restricted while various forms of self-abnegation are encouraged. Teachers may either encourage the adolescent to harness his or her pubertal energy and seek new goals or insist that the adolescent direct his or her energy toward preordained goals that reinforce the existing social hierarchy.

The key to resolving this dilemma, K. Mochidzuki argues, is to revise the school/test system and concentrate on guidance.[10] The major goal of education, he argues, should be simply to answer the question What is a human being? This is a far different question from Who am I? but one that focuses on the question of the core or essence of identity. Parents and their children encounter set patterns of activities when the child enters middle school that influence the child's perception of himself or herself. Adults in school settings (teachers, administrators, and counselors) present a set of expectations for the maturation of the will and self that may or may not correspond to the expectations held by the child and his or her family. While any single interaction with a teacher may be inconsequential, sustained patterns of interaction over time have the potential for tremendous impact. The taken-for-granted assumptions educators have about the normal course of development, which are often institutionalized in school rules and policy, systematically direct teacher-student interactions and hence define student opportunities for emotional, psychological, or even spiritual development.

In an era when diverse forms of education (home schooling, charter schools, private schools, and public schools) are being explored with surprising intensity, educators would do well to reconsider parental beliefs or values about adolescent development in charting the course of new state or national systems. At the beginning of the twenty-first century, there is massive discontent in both Japan and the United States with public systems of education, yet most attention is turned toward issues of reforming classrooms, providing more computers, increasing hours spent on mathematics. My work indicates that many adults (both parents and teachers) are more concerned with general developmental issues: how best to improve an adolescent's skills at self-control and self-determination. Citizens of both societies appear less concerned with specific academic skills than with providing adolescents the capacity to act in a respectful, yet independent, manner.

To promote this behavior, adolescents need opportunities to practice, under adult guidance, making choices, controlling impulses, and ascertaining when group demands conflict with individual beliefs. Neither educational system does a good job all around of providing such opportunities, but Wade, Pleasant Meadows, Aratamachi, and Furukawa did allow students to engage in some activities that had positive impacts on developing adolescent volition. These practices can be modified and integrated into a more cohesive form of middle grades education that would give adolescents consistent practice in exercising their will under the guidance of informed adults.

We must reformulate our understanding of education as a formal method of transmitting knowledge and reconsider the rather old understanding that education is a form of self-development or self-improvement that can alter, for good or bad, our basic capabilities. The education of young adolescents is concerned with that most central aspects of our humanity: the exercise and development of the human will.

# Appendix 1: Field Sites

## The Oak Grove School District

The district is smaller and wealthier than the Bay Area average, but has significant low-income areas. The ratio of support staff to teachers is higher, on average, than in other districts. The majority of teachers are European-American.

At least one interview (approximately fifty minutes) was conducted with each of the following teachers, administrators, or staff. Teachers whose names are marked with an asterisk were interviewed multiple times and were observed for full days (i.e., shadowed) on a rotating basis over a period of three months. Teachers taught five to six periods per day, not including extra duties such as lunchroom supervision.

### DISTRICT AND LOCAL AGENCY STAFF

| | |
|---|---|
| Barbara D'souza | Student Services Supervisor |
| Charlotte Girdeaux | Curriculum Development Supervisor |
| Ann Lewis | Former Principal and School Board Member |
| Matt Arnett | Police Officer and Drug Awareness Coordinator |

### PLEASANT MEADOWS

| Name | Gender | Position | Years Teaching |
|---|---|---|---|
| *Stan Proud | M | Principal | 20+ |
| *Dave Jarvis | M | Vice-Principal | 20+ |
| *Charles Johnson | M | Mathematics | 3 |

| Name | Gender | Position | Years Teaching |
|---|---|---|---|
| *Mark Jerome | M | Counselor | N.A. |
| *Lynn Jing | F | Science | 20+ |
| *Gretchen Jondervag | F | Social Studies/Language Art | 30+ |
| *Winnie Rawler | F | Foreign Language | 15 |
| *Sid Bixby | M | Computers | 30+ |
| *Edna Bryant | F | Special Education | 15+ |
| *Tom Brabeck | M | Social Studies | 30+ |

WADE

| Name | Gender | Position | Years Teaching |
|---|---|---|---|
| *Emily Saunders | F | Principal | 20+ |
| *Ralph Forest | M | Vice-Principal | 20+ |
| *Barbara Lane | F | Advisement | 30+ |
| *Bill Joiner | M | Mathematics | 15 |
| *Sandy Briotte | F | Home Economics | 5–8 |
| *Urma Baxter | F | 5th grade | 20+ |
| *Janice Leitskov | F | Social Studies/Language Art | 2 |
| *Sarah Martins | F | Social Studies/Language Art | 8 |
| *Nancy Carrithers | F | Social Studies | 1 |
| *Hattie Sonval | F | Social Studies/Art | 20+ |
| *Adrian Norris | F | Social Studies/Language Art | 20+ |
| *Nick Brisbane | M | History | 25+ |
| *Opal Lorella | F | Social Studies/Language Art | 25+ |

PLEASANT MEADOWS

Located at the suburban end of the district, Pleasant Meadows is considered the best place in the Oak Grove District for middle school teachers to work. Most of the teachers at Pleasant Meadows are veterans; seniority in the district confers the privilege of working at the best school. On average, the staff have been teaching longer than the staff at Wade.

The school has received state and national honors for excellence in teaching. Most families are middle to upper middle class. Seventy percent of students are white, 13 percent Hispanic, 14 percent Asian, 2 percent black, and 1 percent "other." In the early 1990s enrollment was around eight hundred. The Oak Grove school district was experiencing rapid growth, and portable classrooms were installed. The school is staffed by thirty-three teachers, not including aides, secretaries, and custodians.

Pleasant Meadows has the largest grounds of Oak Grove's three middle schools. It takes three minutes to walk from the office to the opposite end of the grassy area and five minutes to cross the long way.

The staff at Pleasant Meadows are generally pleased with their school and themselves, but there are signs of stress. A bond initiative for the district failed recently. The last principal, widely admired by the staff, recently retired. Due to district enrollment growth nearly two hundred students were expected to be sent over from other middle schools in the district. These students, teachers remarked, will come from backgrounds and home lives far less affluent than the adolescents they were accustomed to teaching.

WADE

Wade lies at the opposite end of the district from Pleasant Meadows near a freeway artery and includes low-income areas of Sun City. The school has been considered a tough assignment by teachers in the area. The families range from working class to middle class. The school is 56 percent white, 26 percent Hispanic, 8 percent Asian, 7 percent black, and 3 percent "other." Over 10 percent of the students in 1991–92 were designated as limited in English speaking proficiency. Wade's population has been capped at about one thousand students; the overflow of students is being sent to Pleasant Meadows or other middle schools.

At the time of the study staff turnover was high. In one year fifteen teachers had come on board fresh, and many senior teachers left. This produced instability in policy and procedures that coincided with a heightened sensitivity to gang activity in the area. Following directions from the superintendent, the police were called in whenever there was a serious altercation, a significant departure, teachers said, from previous school policy. Increased police presence seemed to acerbate, rather than reduce, tensions.

By the spring of 1994 the atmosphere at Wade had changed dramatically and the teachers seemed to have a more positive attitude. They gave a general impression of confidence in the school and its leaders. It appears that Wade has weathered a stormy period, though the school continues to be viewed by teachers as a less desirable place to work.

*The Kotani School District*

There are six middle schools in the Kotani school district, as well as several high schools. The high schools are administered under the Kotani Board of Education, but the middle and elementary schools are governed by the City Board of Education.

Teachers are hired by the City Board and then rotated through the six schools about once every six to seven years. This is standard practice in Japan, and within fifteen years teachers have built up working relationships with their colleagues throughout the district. This rotation as well as the services provided by the Kotani Youth Counseling Center allows schools to pass information quickly and accurately. By a few phone calls teachers can contact their colleagues and pinpoint what students from any given school have been involved in incidents throughout the city.

Both schools are three-story ferroconcrete buildings, similar in shape and design to urban middle schools throughout Japan. The schools each had their own song, emblem, and special uniform. Furukawa had some reputation in the past for its brass band. Aratamachi was also known for its music and for its English department. At least one interview (approximately fifty minutes) was conducted with each of the following. Teachers whose names are marked with an asterisk were interviewed multiple times and were observed for full days (i.e., shadowed) on a rotating basis over a period of three months. Except for the principal, personnel (e.g., Tanomi Kawamura) assigned to section or grade chair positions also taught about fifteen periods per week. Two interviews were also conducted with teachers in neighboring middle schools, and I also observed Mr. Deguchi, though not as systematically as the other teachers.

DISTRICT OFFICE

Osamu Hatanaka          Education Supervisor
Tsutomu Yoshida         Education Supervisor

FUKUDA MIDDLE SCHOOL

Hidenori Nakamura       Teacher

SAKURAGAWA MIDDLE SCHOOL

*Takeo Deguchi          Teacher

ARATAMACHI

| Name | Gender | Position | Years Teaching |
|---|---|---|---|
| Mitsunori Maeda | M | Principal | 30+ |
| *Kōzo Kitabatake | M | Section Chief | 20+ |
| *Tanomi Kawamura | F | 7th Grade Chair | 20+ |
| *Tatsuko Egami | F | English Teacher | 15 |
| *Ineko Hatta | F | Teacher/9th Grade Chair | 20+ |
| *Yoshio Tategami | M | Social Studies | 10 |
| *Masami Hori | M | Science | 10 |
| *Kanako Miyama | F | English | 10 |

FURUKAWA

| Name | Gender | Position | Years Teaching |
|---|---|---|---|
| Keiji Arakawa | M | Principal | 30+ |
| *Yashiko Chino | F | 7th Grade Chair | 30+ |
| *Kiyomi Kawaguchi | F | 9th Grade Chair | 20+ |
| *Mitsuko Yamamura | F | 8th Grade Chair | 25+ |
| *Noriko Tanaka | F | Curriculum Chair | 30+ |
| *Setsuko Ritsukawa | F | Counselor | 20+ |
| *Seiichi Mizuno | M | Student Guidance Chair | 20 |
| *Eriko Banba | F | Nurse | N.A. |
| *Naoto Iehisa | M | English | 5 |
| Kimiko Hashimoto | F | English | 5 |
| *Kuniko Hashimoto | F | Home Economics | 12 |

| Name | Gender | Position | Years Teaching |
|------|--------|----------|----------------|
| *Hidenori Shimoda | M | Art | 12 |
| *Sachiko Hayakawa | F | Music | 20+ |

### ARATAMACHI

Aratamachi's current building was recently renovated, giving it a fresh, new feel. The school services children from new developments, farming families, and some apartments. Aratamachi is somewhat smaller than Furukawa, and the families more affluent.

Like teachers in the rest of Kotani's middle schools, most teachers at Aratamachi live outside the immediate neighborhood, and most commute in their automobiles. In an attempt to promote contact between teachers and the neighborhood, each teacher is also assigned an area (a few *cho*, or "blocks") for which they are responsible. The extent of these responsibilities is not onerous; teachers are required to be familiar with the shops, dangerous intersections, and the like.

### FURUKAWA

At Furukawa, the atmosphere is stricter and slightly less personal than at Aratamachi. Teachers complained that they had to teach more classes than at Kotani's other schools. In particular, the grade chairs taught about eighteen periods per week whereas at other schools they might only teach fourteen or fifteen. Furukawa teachers appeared to spend more time counseling students. Informants from outside the school told me that a certain percentage of the students were from *yakuza* groups (mafia) or *burakumin* families that are socially discriminated against. Certainly, the dwellings of the residents along the river and railroad tracks were far more dilapidated than the new townhouses clustered near Aratamachi.

Furukawa's district straddles the Kotani River. The poorer dwellings are on the far side, while those clustered around Higashiyama are fine old farmhouses, often of exquisite design. Furukawa students along with the students from two high schools crowd the bridge along with the cars and trucks in the mornings and afternoons. The once pristine river is no longer graced with banks of rushes where night herons and cattle egrets could nest. In their stead the city has furnished a cement jogging path.

The teachers at Furukawa displayed a more assertive attitude than their Kotani peers. At a meeting at which they were requested to put on yet another research presentation at their school several senior teachers expressed sharply negative reactions. It was only the second time in my work in Japanese schools that I saw the staff debate the principal to a standstill on some issue.

Despite its past reputation, senior teachers think that Furukawa's problems are much less severe than five years ago. The last two principals have aggressively disseminated the impression that Furukawa is without serious student problems. It is difficult to gauge how much is the effect of image reinforcement and how much a change in the dynamics of the school. The residents of Kotani, at least, had a much better opinion of Furukawa in 1992 than they did in 1986.

# Appendix 2: Glossary of Japanese Terms

| | |
|---|---|
| adoresensu | adolescence |
| aijyō | love or compassion |
| akarui | bright or active (i.e., character or disposition) |
| amayakasu | to defer lovingly, to love passively |
| asagakushū | extra classes held in the morning |
| bōsōzoku | motorbike gangs |
| chikara | strength, power |
| chūgakusei | middle school student |
| daisotsu | college graduate |
| danchi | housing complex |
| enryo | reserve, restraint |
| furyō | juvenile delinquent (colloquial) |
| gakunenchō | head teacher for a grade, grade chair |
| gaman suru | endure, persevere |
| gambaru | persevere |
| hageshii | intense |
| han | small work groups of four or five students |
| hankō | resistant or rebellious |
| hankōki | resistant spirit |
| hankōshin | resistant attitude |
| hanpatsu | oppose |

| | |
|---|---|
| hanseisho | reflection paper, reflective essay |
| hikōshōnen | juvenile delinquent (formal) |
| hoshū | supplemental classes |
| ishiki | consciousness |
| ishi | will, volition |
| iyoku | will, desire |
| jikaku | realization, awareness, self realization |
| jinkaku | character |
| jinsei | human life |
| jishusei | independence, self determination, free will |
| juken benkyō | studying for an examination, especially an entrance examination |
| junsui | pure |
| ki | "spirit," mind, mood, disposition |
| kanri kyōiku | "managed" education, very strict discipline |
| kazokuteki | family-like |
| kōhai | junior, lower classman |
| kodomo | child |
| kōkōsei | high school student |
| kōnai bōryoku | school violence |
| kokoro | heart, mind, intentions |
| kōchō | principal |
| kōsotsu | high school graduate |
| mondai kōdō | problem behavior |
| majime | strict, serious, honest |
| manga | cartoons or cartoon books |
| mukiryoku | apathetic, lacking energy |
| mujyaki | innocent, childlike |
| nakama | peer, companion, associate |
| nayami | troubles, worries, concerns |
| nebari tsuyoi | tenacious, persistent |
| omoiyari | thoughtfulness, consideration, compassion |
| otonashii | gentle, good, obedient |
| ronri teki | logical |
| rikutsuppoi | argumentative |
| seishin | mind, psyche, mental state |
| seishōnen | youth, adolescent, juvenile |
| seinenki | youth, late adolescence |
| seishun | youth, adolescence |
| senpai | senior, upper classman |
| senpai/kohai | senior/junior relations |
| seikaku | character, personality |
| shidō buchō | teacher in charge of student guidance |

| shishunki | puberty |
| --- | --- |
| shūdan seikatsu | group living, guidance in group living or interpersonal interaction |
| shita machi | downtown, older part of city |
| sunao | gentle, obedient |
| tanoshii | fun, pleasant, enjoyable |
| tsunagari | connections |
| umasugiru | affected, insincere |
| yaruki | motivation, will power |

# Notes

## Chapter 1. What Is Adolescence?

1. Japanese psychologists, psychiatrists, and other social science researchers frequently use psychological and physiological theories of adolescent development generated in Europe and North America. The aim in this book is not to test how well Western theories of developmental psychology explain adolescent behavior or psychology in Japan, but to assess if beliefs based on these theories are established in the schools and educational policy literature. A critical analysis of the applicability of general psychological theory to Japan can be found in Robert Levine and Hidetada Shimizu's work on culture and psychology. Robert Levine and Hidetada Shimizu, eds., *Japanese Frames of Mind* (Cambridge: Harvard University Press, forthcoming). The effect of psychological research on education in the United States appears to be quite different from that found in other nations. Adolescence plays a major part in the modern life course in the United States because it is institutionalized in the schools via the impact of educational psychology — a history that can be traced back to the work of G. Stanley Hall at the turn of the century. The theories of Hall, Erik Erikson, Jean Piaget, and other prominent psychologists have been incorporated into a wide range of educational texts and policies but are used and defined in ways quite distinct from their usage in purely academic contexts. For a historical summary of how attributes of adolescence derived from psychology or medicine have been incorporated into U.S. schools, see James Kett, *Rites of Passage: Adolescence in America, 1790 to the Present* (New York: Basic Books, 1977). See also Youniss's work on the global spread of psychological theory. James Youniss, "Cultural Forces Leading to Scientific Developmental Psychology," in *Ethics in Applied*

198 Notes to Page 2

*Developmental Psychology* (Norwood: Ablex, 1990), 285–300. Major psychological or psychoanalytic texts which have influenced the popular conception of adolescence in the United States are G. Stanley Hall, *Adolescence: Its Psychology and Its Relation to Physiology, Anthropology, Sociology, Sex, Crime, Religion and Education* (New York: D. Appleton, 1905); Erik Erikson, *Childhood and Society* (New York: W. W. Norton, 1950); Erikson, *Identity: Youth and Crisis* (New York: W. W. Norton, 1968); Jean Piaget, *The Moral Judgment of the Child* (New York: Collier, 1962).

2. I use the term "life course" rather than "life cycle" to indicate the more specific meaning developed by such theorists as John Meyer. He and others argue that in the modern world system there is a universally recognized life course in which there are distinct expectations for behavior at each stage. "Western society is distinctively organized around the carefully sequenced age-graded system of child rearing, education, work and retirement" (243). See John Meyer, "Self and Life Course: Institutionalization and Its Effects," in *Institutional Structure*, ed. George Thomas et al. (Beverly Hills: Sage, 1987), 242–60. Meyer argues that individuals with a modern sense of self must give a rational account of their life history and trajectory. Similar ideas have been expressed by the sociologist Anthony Giddens and the historian Charles Taylor, who both argue that a modern sense of self, with a psychologically "deep" interior arose in the European context. Because none of these scholars seriously examined Asian philosophy or religious traditions, their attribution of a modern sense of self to Europe is understandable. A brief reading of the development of Buddhist or Confucian thought (see David Kalupahana, Sarvepalli Radhakrishnan, Tu Wei-ming, or Caroline Rhys Davids), however, reveals that most of the characteristics that these theorists attribute to a modern, Western self were present long ago in Asian philosophy and religion. Yet there are significant differences between Asian and European beliefs about the nature of the self. Hsu, Hamaguchi, and others argue that in Japanese belief systems the self exists partly in the individual and partly in the natural and social environment around the individual. See Anthony Giddens, *Modernity and Self-Identity* (Stanford: Stanford University Press, 1991); Charles Taylor, *Sources of the Self* (Cambridge: Harvard University Press, 1989); David Kalupahana, *A History of Buddhist Philosophy* (Honolulu: University of Hawai'i Press, 1992); S. Radhakrishnan, *The Dhammapada* (Madras: Oxford University Press, 1950); Tu Wei-ming, *Confucian Thought: Self as Creative Transformation* (New York: State University of New York Press, 1985); Caroline Rhys Davids, *Buddhist Psychology* (London: Luzac, 1924); Frances Hsu, "The Self in Cross-cultural Perspective," in *Culture and Self*, ed. Anthony Marsella, George DeVos, and Frances Hsu (New York: Tavistock, 1985); Eshun Hamaguchi, "A Contextual Model of the Japanese: Toward a Methodological Innovation in Japanese Studies," *Journal of Japanese Studies* 11 (1985): 289–321. For more detailed studies of the Japanese sense of self, see Takeo Doi, *The Anatomy of Self* (New York: Kodansha, 1985); Hazel Markus and Shinobu Kitayama, "Culture and the Self: Implications for Cognition, Emotion, and Motivation," *Psychological Review* 98 (1991): 224–53. Nancy Rosenburger, ed., *Japanese Sense of Self* (New York: Cambridge University Press, 1992.)

3. The definition of "institution" used in this book is derived from works by the new institutionalists. Like the older literature on the social construction of reality, institutional theorists tend to focus on how meaning is organized in mass society and place emphasis

on the role institutions play as central elements in ordering the conceptual world. See Paul Dimaggio and Walter Powell, eds., *The New Institutionalism in Organizational Analysis* (Chicago: University of Chicago Press, 1991); Richard Scott and John Meyer, eds., *Institutional Environments and Organizations* (Thousand Oaks, Calif.: Sage Publications, 1994). One of the most significant works on the social construction of reality is Peter Berger and Thomas Luckman, *The Social Construction of Reality* (New York: Anchor, 1966).

4. The terms "will" and *ishi* are primarily defined in relation to the individual's control over his or her mental and emotional faculties, particularly the ability to choose a course of action. The *American Heritage Dictionary* defines will as "the mental faculty by which one deliberately chooses or decides upon a course of action" (1465). In Japanese, *ishi* is linked to the power to make decisions (*ketsudan-ryoku*) and intentions (*ikō*).

5. Beginning with Philippe Aries a number of scholars have documented changing European and American expectations for stages in the life course, particularly how beliefs about childhood have changed over the past three centuries. Among the most significant factors affecting the conditions of childhood and early adolescence have been the rise of age-based norms, the banning of child labor, compulsory schooling, and psychological testing. See Philippe Aries, *Centuries of Childhood* (New York: Vintage, 1962); Howard Chudacoff, *How Old are You? Age Consciousness in American Culture* (Princeton: Princeton University Press, 1989); Joseph Hawes, *Children In Urban Society* (New York: Oxford University Press, 1971); Linda Pollock, *Forgotten Children* (Cambridge: Cambridge University Press, 1983); John Sutton, *Stubborn Children* (Berkeley: University of California Press, 1988); Vivianna Zelizer, *Pricing the Priceless Child* (New York: Basic Books, 1985).

6. Tadahiko Abiko's ethnography of a Florida middle school provides an excellent lens through which to view the implicit assumptions Americans hold about the function of the school. See Tadahiko Abiko, *Yomigaeru Amerika no Chūgakkō* (Revitalizing the American middle school) (Tokyo: Yuhikaku-sensho, 1987).

7. See Joseph Kett, *Rites of Passage*, and Alice Schlegel and Herbert Barry, *Adolescence: An Anthropological Inquiry.* (New York: Macmillan, 1991).

8. Which is not to suggest that *rites de passage* do not exist in the United States or Japan. August Hollingshead, James Coleman, and others have identified what can only be described as adolescent rituals among U.S. high school students. See August Hollingshead, *Elmtown's Youth and Elmtown Revisited* (New York: John Wiley and Sons, 1974); James Coleman, *The Adolescent Society* (New York: Free Press, 1962). A more careful analysis of these activities, however, suggests that they differ significantly from most of the puberty rituals documented in traditional societies. For classic anthropological analysis of puberty and adolescence, see Yehudi Cohen, *The Transition from Childhood to Adolescence* (Chicago: Aldine, 1964); Arnold Van Gennep, *Rites of Passage* (Chicago: University of Chicago Press, 1960); Margaret Mead, *Coming of Age in Samoa* (New York: Morrow, 1928); Margaret Mead, *Growing up in New Guinea* (New York: Penguin, 1954).

9. Yet in industrial society adolescents are marginalized as in some preindustrial societies. Most cultures have a stage in the life course between childhood and maturity typically characterized by a state of marginality or liminality. While liminal status is often

taken to mean a stage in a ritual phase, Turner effectively shows that certain social roles such as monkhood bear all the markings of a long-term liminal status. Many of the attributes of liminality defined by Turner in his classic anthropological study do apply to young adolescents in modern societies, especially in the sense that they are caught or lost in these middle years and considered disrupting or even dangerous. One could argue that the segregation into a special social organization — the middle or junior high school — is similar to age-segregated housing for pubescents used in some societies. In addition to works by Mead, Van Gennep, and Cohen already cited, see C. W. M. Hart. "Contrasts between Prepubertal and Postpubertal Education," in *Education and Cultural Process,* ed. George Spindler (Prospect Heights, Ill.: Waveland Press, 1987), 359–77; Victor Turner, *The Forest of Symbols* (Ithaca: Cornell University Press, 1967).

10. Some authors specifically state that schools are a primary institutional carrier of the modern sense of self and identity. Peter Berger, B. Berger, and H. Kellner, *The Homeless Mind* (New York: Random House, 1974).

11. Institutional theorists have used the spread of curriculum, rights of children, and school organization in the world as evidence that a modern sense of self and life course is rapidly being institutionalized around the world. While the evidence presented is strong, these theorists fail to take into account the degree of institutionalization. I show that while the Japanese Ministry of Education may use Western elements of adolescence in its publications, these have little effect on school organization or classroom practice. The work of Ramirez, Boli, and Meyer suggests that nations have rapidly adapted modern language with regard to school systems, but that this tendency toward isomorphism is one that takes place primarily at the level of national or even regional policy and may or may not be strongly connected to actual educational practice. John Boli, Francisco Ramirez, and John Meyer, "Explaining the Origins and Expansion of Mass Education," *Comparative Education Review* 29 (1985): 145–70; John Boli and John Meyer, "The Ideology of Childhood and the State: Rules Distinguishing Children in National Constitutions, 1870–1970," in *Institutional Structure,* ed. George Thomas et al. (Newbury Park, Calif.: Sage, 1987), 217–41; Francisco Ramirez, and John Boli, "Global Patterns of Educational Institutionalization," In *Institutional Structure,* ed. George Thomas et al., (Newbury Park, Calif.: Sage, 1987), 150–72.

12. Aaron Pallas has aptly summarized evidence from several nations on the role played by school in organizing the life course. Aaron Pallas, "Schooling in the Course of Human Lives: The Social Context of Education and the Transition to Adulthood in Industrial Society," *Review of Educational Research* 63 (1993): 409–47

13. There is a veritable plethora of studies from a variety of scholars that document the forms of "cultural resistance" displayed by ethnic or linguistic minorities or lower-class youth in school. Most of these works focus on the rejection of negative group or individual images that the dominant school culture presents to the student. These scholars do not address the more subtle, but more pervasive, presentation of life course norms through schooling, the problem I am concerned with here. For some of the most interesting ethnographic accounts of resistance in U.S. schools, see Jay MacLeod, *Ain't No Makin' It* (Boulder: Westview Press, 1987); Gerald Rosenfeld, *"Shut Those Thick Lips"* (New York: Holt, Rinehart and Winston, 1971); Robert Everhart, *Reading, Writing, and Resistance* (Boston: Routledge and Kegan Paul, 1983); Henry Trueba, George Spindler,

and Louise Spindler, eds., *What Do Anthropologists Have to Say About Dropouts?* (New York: Falmer Press, 1989); Harry Wolcott, *A Kwakiutl Village and School* (Prospect Heights, Ill.: Waveland Press, Inc, 1967).

14. See related work on education and the preservation of culture in Anabaptist communities by John Hostetler and Gertrude Huntington, *Amish Children: Education in the Family, School and Community* (New York: Holt, Rinehart and Winston, 1992); John Hostetler, "Education and Communitarian Societies—The Old Order Amish and the Hutterian Brethren," in *Education and Cultural Process*, ed. George Spindler (Prospect Heights, Ill.: Waveland Press, 1987), 211–30. The only works that I have encountered which address the question of basic conflict in expectations for the normal life course are Laura Thompson and Alice Joseph, "Adolescence the Hopi Way," in *The Adolescent*, ed. J. Seidman (New York: Dryden, 1953), 2–14, and Linda Burton, "Ethnography and the Meaning of Adolescence in High-Risk Neighborhoods," *Ethos* 25 (1997): 208–17.

15. Pallas, "Schooling in the Course of Human Lives."

16. See D. Eleanor Westney, *Imitation and Innovation: The Transfer of Western Organizational Patterns to Meiji Japan* (Cambridge: Harvard University Press, 1987); James Lincoln, "Japanese Organization and Organization Theory," *Research in Organizational Behavior* 12 (1990): 255–94. Other studies, however, have shown that national cultures may not have much impact on organizational practice. Work on manager training suggests that industrial sector is a far more powerful factor than national boundaries in terms of organizational procedures. Overall, technical factors affecting organizational production (i.e., the differences between supermarket chains and electronics manufacturers) will outweigh national cultures. However, as schools have large, often vaguely defined, "products" they are more likely to be impacted by national culture than other forms of organizations. See John Storey, Paul Edwards, and Keith Sisson, *Managers in the Making: Careers, Development and Control in Corporate Britain and Japan* (London: Sage Publications, 1998).

17. The rational myths of adolescence institutionalized in schooling can be analyzed just as anthropologists and folklorists have analyzed the myths and folktales told about adolescence in nontechnological societies. Elements or themes, the various story lines of folktales, have been transmitted across great distances through societies with very different languages and belief systems. In the course of their spread, some story lines were altered, dropped, or given different emphasis depending upon who was telling the story and who the audience was. I have chosen the word "story line" to refer to the common short descriptions or explanations people give (and texts provide) when the topic of adolescence is in the foreground. The story of adolescence is composed of many of these story lines—puberty, hormonal imbalance, identity crisis. The story lines mutually define each other and fashion a cohesive plot or coherent story. Each story line conveys certain elemental assumptions: metaphors or underlying rationales for what actions, behaviors, and even problems are expected at this stage in the life course. These story lines, then, are closely linked to the rational myths that institutional theorists believe provide the working assumptions upon which modern organizations function. See V. Propp, *Morphology of the Folktale* (Austin: University of Texas Press, 1979); Alfred Lord, *The Singer of Tales* (New York: Atheneum, 1978).

18. Thompson uses the term *motif* rather than *story line* but shows how folktale

analysis reveals that common motifs spread across a wide range of societies (368–69). The motif or story line is "the smallest element in a tale having a power to persist in tradition" (415). While folktale scholars have often documented the exact frequency of motif distribution in a given region, I have concentrated on analyzing adolescent story lines by assessing (1) the extent of their distribution; (2) their agreement with the overall story of adolescence; (3) the degree to which they are used to rationalize or account for school practices. Stith Thompson, *The Folktale* (Berkeley: University of California Press, 1977).

19. In addition to the institutional theorists cited above, see the work of the sociologist Richard Scott and the anthropologist Mary Douglas. Douglas argues that institutions play a crucial role in defining the basic analogies that are used to identify pertinent features of the social world. That is, we define who we are based on roles and expectations provided by institutions, such as the schools. She distinguishes between a convention and an institution by noting, "established institutions, if challenged, are able to rest their claims to legitimacy on their fit with the nature of the universe" (46–47). By this definition adolescence in the United States is clearly an institution, as teachers countered my queries about the sociocultural nature of adolescence by arguing that hormonal disruption was a biological fact of development. Mary Douglas, *How Institutions Think* (Syracuse: Syracuse University Press, 1986); Richard Scott, *Institutions and Organizations* (Thousand Oaks, Calif.: Sage Publication, 1995).

20. I have documented the fact that Japanese work roles and norms for teachers are organized along very different lines than those found in the United States. In particular, Rohlen and I argue that basic assumptions about the nature of learning in Japan are quite different from U.S. assumptions. Gerald LeTendre, "Guiding Them On: Teaching, Hierarchy, and Social Organization in Japanese Middle Schools." *Journal of Japanese Studies* 20 (1994): 37–59. Thomas Rohlen and Gerald LeTendre, eds., *Teaching and Learning in Japan* (New York: Cambridge University Press, 1996).

21. The theoretical role of rational myths in modern society is addressed by John Meyer and Brian Rowan, "Institutionalized Organizations: Formal Structure as Myth and Ceremony," in *The New Institutionalism in Organizational Analysis,* ed. W. Powell and P. DiMaggio (Chicago: University of Chicago Press, 1991), 41–62, and in John Meyer, John Boli, and George Thomas, "Ontology and Rationalization in the Western Cultural Account," in *Institutional Structure,* ed. G. Thomas, J. Meyer, F. Ramirez, and J. Boli (Beverly Hills: Sage, 1987), 12–38. Drawing on Berger and Luckman (*The Homeless Mind*), they start from the idea that institutionalized rules are "classifications built into society as reciprocated typifications or interpretations" (92) and reflect "widespread understandings of society" (44). However, while they note that such rules may derive from legal mandates or particular organizational practices, they ignore the fact that such roles may also derive from preexisting cultural beliefs. I.e., a belief in the disruptive nature of youth from colonial times supports the belief in adolescence as a distinct age (e.g., Hall's theories), which in turn legitimates the creation of junior high schools and later the middle school as a distinct organizational form.

22. Dimaggio and Powell discuss three distinct types of isomorphism that account for convergence among institutional forms. They isolate several factors that have played a key role in the rapid diffusion of Western schooling in the world system: the lack of visible

alternatives to Western mass education and the fact that educational "technologies" and goals are often ambiguous. Paul Dimaggio and Walter Powell, "The Iron Cage Revisited: Institutional Isomorphism and Collective Rationality in Organizational Fields," in *The New Institutionalism in Organizational Analysis*, 76–77. Their work, however, does not address the fact that rational myths and organizational forms are not all institutionalized to the same degree, i.e., institutionalization is a process. Jepperson takes up this argument. He notes that "institutions can be carried in different ways" (151), suggesting that there are higher order social forces that affect the growth, change, and depth of given institutions. I argue that institutions as social phenomena exist in a larger milieu of cultural beliefs or "social rationales or accounts," to use Jepperson's terms. Basic change in institutional forms arises when the rational myths (story lines) of a given institutions are in conflict with the most widespread cultural beliefs. What I found in Japan is that cultural beliefs affect which Western rational myths are incorporated as part of the rational account of the institution, and that core rational myths from outside Japan may be altered to become more in line with dominant cultural beliefs. See Ronald Jepperson, "Institutions, Institutional Effects and Institutionalism," in *The New Institutionalism in Organizational Analysiss*, 143–63.

23. One of the oldest questions in social science is, How do social systems persist overtime? Institutional theorists argue that institutions are the central mechanism by which social continuity and cultural persistence are explained. Zucker argues that cultural persistence arises from the fact that when institutional forms are deeply embedded in society, they tend to persist. My work confirms this tendency, but while the basic institutional form persists, there may be significant changes in the core rational myths over time, if these changes do not conflict with more general cultural beliefs. See Lynne Zucker, "The Role of Institutionalization in Cultural Persistence," *American Sociological Review* 42 (1977): 726–43; Lynne Zucker, "Organizations as Institutions," in *Research in the Sociology of Organizations*, ed. S. Bachrach (Greenwich: JAI Press, 1983); Lynne Zucker, "Institutional Theories of Organization," *American Review of Sociology* 13 (1987): 443–64.

24. Wray provides a good discussion of how allied reforms were altered over time. Miyagi provides some excellent specific examples drawn from a study of middle school to high school transition. See Henry Wray, "Change and Continuity in Modern Japanese Educational History: Allied Occupational Reforms Forty Years Later," *Comparative Education Review* 35, 3 (1991): 447–75. Yuukazu Miyagi, "Chūgaku ni okeru Kōkō-shingakushidō no Mondaiten" (Problem points in high school guidance in the junior high school), *Gendai Nihon Shakairon*. Chiba: Chiba Daigaku (1988): 29–47.

25. Gerald LeTendre, "Community-Building Activities in Japanese Schools: Alternative Paradigms of the Democratic School," *Comparative Education Review* (August 1999): 283–310.

26. The initial inquiry used in my doctoral research followed the outline suggested in Lincoln and Guba's *Naturalistic Inquiry*. I returned to the schools in Kotani, Japan, where I had been a teacher for three years, with the following set of orienting questions: (1) What incidents do I notice/react to that teachers do not? (2) What incidents do teachers react to? (3) What brought the incident to their attention? (4) What do they say to students? (5) How do students respond? (6) Whom do teachers notify? (7) How is

responsibility distributed? (8) Whom do teachers ask for advice/guidance? (9) What is the time frame? (10) Is there a "resolution"? What else occurs? See Yvonna Lincoln and Egon Guba, *Naturalistic Inquiry* (Beverly Hills: Sage Publications, 1985): 259–67, as well as Martin Hammersley and Paul Atkinson, *Ethnography: Principles in Practice* (New York: Routledge, 1983) 112–26.

27. James Spradley, *The Ethnographic Interview* (New York: Holt, Rinehart and Winston, 1979).

28. See Shirley Brice Heath, *Ways with Words* (New York: Cambridge Press, 1983).

29. Abiko, *Yomigaeru Amerika no Chūgakkō*; Rebecca Fukuzawa, "Stratification, Social Control, and Student Culture: An Ethnography of Three Junior High Schools" (Ph.D. diss., Northwestern University, 1989); Hiroyoshi Shimizu and Kozo Tokuda, *Yomigaere: Kōritsu Chūgakkō (Nanchu: An ethnography)* (Tokyo: Kobunsha, 1991); Everhart, *Reading, Writing, and Resistance*; Janet Schofield, *Black and White in School* (New York: Teachers College Press, 1989); John Singleton, *Nichu: A Japanese School* (New York: Holt, Rinehart, and Winston, 1967).

30. Many Western and Japanese psychologists adamantly argue that such an interpersonal sense of self or identity cannot exist: that our selves cannot be partially located outside our self. Nonetheless, there are prominent scholars in Japan and East Asia who argue that this is the case, such as Eshun Hamaguchi. Forms of psychological or emotional therapy developed in Japan also suggest that there are widespread beliefs in a permeable, interpersonal sense of self. David Reynolds, *The Quiet Therapies* (Honolulu: University of Hawai'i Press, 1980); Davis also describes the beliefs in spirits and spiritual possession which are still found in Japan, particularly among rural and poor Japanese: Winston Davis, *Dojo: Magic and Exorcism in Modern Japan* (Stanford: Stanford University Press, 1980).

### Chapter 2. Oak Grove and Kotani

1. The majority of the quotes, observations, and excerpts from documents used in this book come from these schools. I visited and conducted research in a range of other middle schools in both countries, including fieldwork in California, Georgia, Pennsylvania, and North Carolina schools as well as in Nagoya, Kanagawa, and Tokyo schools. Appendix I is a list of the teachers and administrators who were involved in the primary study.

2. The strength of ethnographic research lies in generating complex data (Geertz's "thick description") about a given local culture. These data can be used to identify dominant cultural beliefs and cultural conflict or to generate further hypotheses. The ability to gain the trust of the research participants is paramount. It was thus more important for my research to work with schools in which I had established a strong relationship with teachers than to find schools that were more comparable in terms of demographics but in which no working relationship existed. See Clifford Geertz, *The Interpretation of Cultures: Selected Essays* (New York: Basic Books, 1973); James Spradley, *The Ethnographic Interview* (New York: Holt, Rinehart and Winston, 1979); Judith Preissle Goetz and Margaret LeCompte, *Ethnography and Qualitative Design In Educational Research* (Orlando: Academic Press, 1992); Martin Hammersley and Paul Atkinson, *Ethnography: Principles in Practice* (New York: Routledge, 1983).

3. In addition to my experience in a range of middle schools throughout Japan, I had numerous occasions to talk with visiting teachers and scholars about their impressions of Kotani schools. Visiting teachers from larger cities noted that there was more emotional connection between teachers and students in Kotani than in schools in large urban areas, but that basic practices and attitudes did not appear significantly different.

4. For details of how these categories are used and constructed, see the major study of young adolescent lifestyles and time use conducted by researchers at Kyoto University. Kyōiku Ningengaku Kenkyūshitsu, *Chūgakusei no Seikatsujikan to Nichijyōseikatsu* (Department of Education, Kyoto University, 1990).

5. Ishida provides an excellent critique of the application of Western theoretical social class constructs and proposes a powerful alternative. For other attempts to operationalize measures of social background in educational research, see also work by Sato. Hiroshi Ishida, *Social Mobility in Contemporary Japan* (London: MacMillan, 1993); Nancy Sato, "Ethnography of Japanese Elementary Schools: Quest for Equality" (Ph.D. diss., Stanford Univesity, 1991).

6. Several scholars offer a detailed analysis and critique of the Japanese academic selection process. See Gerald LeTendre, "Constructed Aspirations: Decision-Making Processes in Japanese Educational Selection," *Sociology of Education* 69 (1996): 193–216; Thomas Rohlen, *Japan's High Schools* (Berkeley: University of California Press, 1983); David Stevenson and David Baker, "Shadow Education and Allocation in Formal Schooling: Transition to University in Japan," *American Journal of Sociology* 97, 6 (1992): 1639–57.

7. The major minority groups in this part of Japan. War-displaced Japanese refers to Japanese children isolated and reared in China after the end of World War II. Some of their children were entering the Kotani schools during my fieldwork. Brazilian Japanese refers to students whose parents or grandparents emigrated to Brazil and have now returned to Japan to work. For both groups, Japanese is usually a second language.

8. A school's image or reputation, however, can be an ephemeral thing. After a tumultuous first two years, Emily had gotten Wade "turned around" and its reputation was on the rise. The speed with which staff and even neighborhood demographics change means that in any ethnographic study of a school the representation of the school's character must be carefully contextualized. Part of the great difficulty in doing the ethnography of schooling in the United States is the tremendous organizational instability that affects so many U.S. schools. For more discussion of this issue, see Everhart, *Reading, Writing and Resistance;* Reba Page, *Lower-Track Classrooms: A Curricular and Cultural Perspective* (New York: Teachers College Press, 1991).

9. The effect of systematic miscommunication between majority teachers and minority teachers has been well studied. See Shirley Heath, *Ways with Words* (New York: Cambridge University Press, 1983); Hugh Mehan, "Language and Schooling," *Sociology of Education* 57 (1984): 174–83.

10. Some of these classrooms have been in constant use for more than five years.

11. Donald Eichhorn provides one of the earliest synopses of the goals and functions of the middle school; the most recent version of these goals can be found in the National Middle School's Mission statement. For a more critical examination of what actually goes on in middle grades schools, see John Loundsbury and Donald Clark. For other compara-

tive studies of U.S. and Japanese middle schools, see Yang and LeTendre. Donald Eich-horn, *The Middle School* (New York: Center for Applied Research in Education, 1966); John Loundsbury and Donald Clark, *Inside Grade Eight: From Apathy to Excitement* (Reston, Va.: National Association of Secondary School Principals, 1990); Hua Yang, "A Comparison of U.S. and Japanese Middle School Teachers" (Ph.D. diss., Stanford University, 1993); Gerald LeTendre, "Willpower and Willfulness: Adolescence in the U.S. and Japan" (Ph.D. diss., Stanford University, 1994).

12. Office of Educational Research and Improvement, *The Educational System in Japan: Case Study Findings* (Washington, D.C.: U.S. Department of Education, 1998).

13. Hua Yang's study of six U.S. and six Japanese middle schools demonstrates that there are statistically significant differences in how the teachers' work week is allocated in Japan and in the United States, Japanese teachers spending more time on administrative tasks. See Hua Yang, "Work Roles and Norms for Teachers in Japan and the United States" in Gerald LeTendre, ed., *Competitor or Ally: The Uses and Abuses of Japanese Educational Data in the U.S.* (New York: Falmer Press, 1999.)

14. Again, see Hua Yang's work as well as James Stigler, Clea Fernandez, and Makoto Yoshida, "Cultures of Mathematics Instruction in Japanese and American Elementary Classrooms," in Thomas Rohlen and Gerald LeTendre, eds., *Teaching and Learning in Japan* (New York: Cambridge University Press, 1996), 213–47.

15. See Gerald LeTendre, "Constructed Aspirations: Decision-Making Processes in Japanese Educational Selection," *Sociology of Education* 69 (1996): 193–216.

16. Douglas MacIver and Joyce Epstein, "Responsive Practices in the Middle Grades: Teacher Teams, Advisory Groups, Remedial Instruction and School Transition Programs," *American Journal of Education* 99 (1991): 591

17. Ibid., 592.

18. National Middle School Association, *This We Believe* (Columbus: National Middle School Association, 1995), 41.

19. Carnegie Council on Adolescent Development, *Turning Points: Preparing American Youth for the 21st Century* (New York: Carnegie Council on Adolescent Development, 1989); Carnegie Council on Adolescent Development, *Great Transitions: Preparing Adolescents for a New Century* (New York: Carnegie Council on Adolescent Development, 1995); Superintendent's Middle Grade Task Force, *Caught in the Middle* (Sacramento: California Department of Education, 1987).

20. See MacIver and Epstein, "Responsive Practices."

21. Henry Becker, "Curriculum and Instruction in Middle-Grade Schools," *Phi Delta Kappan* (February 1990): 454.

22. For two exemplary pieces that analyze the emotional problems young adolescents face in school, see Roberta Simmons and Dale Blythe, *Moving into Adolescence* (New York: Aldine de Gruyter, 1987); David Kinney, "From Nerds to Normals: The Recovery of Identity among Adolescents from Middle to High School," *Sociology of Education* 66 (1993): 21–40. For recent work on the impact of puberty on academic achievement, see Judith Dubas, Julia Graber, and Anne Petersen, "The Effects of Pubertal Development on Achievement during Adolescence," *American Journal of Education* 99 (1991): 444–59.

23. Jacquelynne Eccles, Sarah Lord, and Carol Midgley, "What Are We Doing to Early

Adolescents? The Impact of Educational Contexts on Early Adolescents," *American Journal of Education* 99 (1991): 521–42.

24. Two widely read works have led to the conclusion that girls are somehow particularly at risk, academically and emotionally, in U.S. middle grades schools: Mary Pipher, *Reviving Ophelia* (New York: Ballantine, 1994); Myra Sadker and David Sadker, *Failing at Fairness: How America's Schools Cheat Girls* (New York: Macmillan, 1994). The best work on the topic, however, suggests that while gender is a key factor, the results are mixed. "Whether one or the other gender was at a disadvantage in adolescence was a key question guiding this analysis. In terms of the *self-image,* girls clearly appeared at a disadvantage throughout the age period. However girls did not score more unfavorably than boys on a depressive affect or happiness scale, and girls indicated fewer school behavior problems." Simmons and Blythe, *Moving into Adolescence,* 96.

25. Roberta Simmons, Ann Black, and Yingzhi Zhou, "African-American versus White Children and the Transition into Junior High School," *American Journal of Education* 99 (1991): 481.

26. Clarissa Scott, Danette Arthur, Maria Panizo, Roger Owen, "Menarche: The Black American Experience," *Journal of Adolescent Health Care* 10 (1989): 363–68.

27. Jomills Braddock, "Tracking the Middle Grades: National Patterns of Grouping for Instruction," *Phi Delta Kappan* (February 1990): 456.

28. For studies of the impact of tracking, see Sally Kilgore, "The Organizational Context of Tracking in Schools," *American Sociological Review* 56 (1991): 189–203; Jeannie Oakes, *Keeping Track: How Schools Structure Inequality* (New Haven: Yale University Press, 1985); Maureen Hallinan, "The Organization of Students for Instruction in the Middle School," *Sociology of Education* 65 (1992): 114–27. Awareness of social class distinctions among adolescents in school and the impact of social class on peer formation have long been documented in American schools. See Robert Lynd, *Middletown: A Study in American Culture* (New York: Harcourt Brace, 1959); August Hollingshead, *Elmtown's Youth and Elmtown Revisited* (New York: John Wiley and Sons, 1975); Adam Gamoran and Mark Berends, "The Effects of Stratification in Secondary Schools," *Review of Educational Research* 57 (1987): 415–35.

29. Linda Burton, "Conceptual Issues in the Study of Development Among Disadvantaged Inner-City African American Teens," Paper presented at the Conference on Ethnographic Approaches to the Study of Human Development, Oakland, Calif., 1993, 8.

30. In addition to the ethnographic work discussed in previous notes, see Carl Grant and Christine Sleeter, *After the School Bell Rings* (London: Falmer Press, 1996).

31. Compare Grant and Sleeter's work with that of Everhart or Schofield. These qualitative studies demonstrate the wide variety of institutional forms that exist in the United States and how few curricular goals are shared by schools which educate young adolescents. Grant and Sleeter, *After the School Bell Rings*; Janet Schofield, *Black and White in School* (New York: Teachers College Press, 1989).

32. Witness recent critiques of mathematics instruction in U.S. middle schools. Edward Silver, "Improving Mathematics in Middle School: Lessons from TIMSS and Related Research," Report to the U.S. Dept. of Education, 1998; Joan Lipsitz, Anthony Jackson, and Leah Austin, "What Works in Middle-Grades School Reform," *Phi Delta Kappan*

78, 7 (1997): 517–56. Gilbert A. Valverde and William H. Schmidt, "Refocusing U.S. Math and Science Education," *Issues in Science and Technology* (Winter 1997–98).

33. Other authors have noted that the diversity of organizational forms and lack of a clear goal for U.S. middle grades schools leads to a chaotic and disruptive transition process between the middle grades and high school. Jennifer Rice, "The Disruptive Transition from Middle to High School: Opportunities for Linking Policy and Practice," *Journal of Education Policy* 12 (1997): 403–17.

34. This is the gist of the arguments given by many analysts using the recent TIMSS data, such as Valverde and Schmidt, "Refocusing U.S. Math and Science." However, my colleagues and I have conducted our own analysis of the data that shows that U.S. math and science begins to slump in the upper elementary grades and that middle schools in the TIMSS sample tended to have significantly higher math and science scores than most other types of middle grades schools. See David Baker, Gerald LeTendre, Martin Benavides, and Zhang Yu, "First in the World or Falling Behind? National Patterns of U.S. Math and Science Achievement from an International Perspective," Paper presented at the American Sociological Association Meeting, San Francisco, August 21–25, 1998.

35. Robert Felner and his colleagues conducted a study that shows significant effects of level of implementation of middle school reforms on academic achievement. See Robert Felner, Anthony Jackson, Deborah Kasak, Peter Mulhall, Steven Brand and Nancy Flowers, "The Impact of School Reform for the Middle Years," *Phi Delta Kappan* 78 (1997): 528.

### Chapter 3. The Common Problem of Responsibility

1. *Shūban* means roughly "weekly supervisor" or "in-charge," to borrow a British phrase. In Japanese middle schools, both teachers and students take on added responsibilities for overseeing the general management of the school. Some of these assignments are weekly, others rotate by the day. *Tōban,* used in the next sentence, refers to a daily post. Japanese middle schools vary in how they use these weekly and daily supervisory positions for teachers and students.

2. Japanese middle school students routinely report colds, the flu, and other ailments to the student-in-charge of health, even though the problem is not serious enough to prevent them from attending class. In Kotani, the school nurse recorded these reports each day and could provide information to the homeroom teacher about any given student. This information was sent to the prefectural office on a regular basis. This is evidence that Japanese believe that schools have some responsibility for the physical health of the adolescent.

3. Under California law, minors cannot be left alone in a classroom without an adult present. However, I did observe teachers leaving students unsupervised in classrooms, usually when the class was the teacher's homeroom or when it was a higher ability group class. In some U.S. homerooms, I found almost the same sense of student community one frequently finds in Japanese homerooms. Homeroom teachers in California middle schools do have regular daily contact with their students, and many homerooms at Wade and Pleasant Meadows develop a sense of community.

4. I interviewed teachers and conducted observations in two schools with substantial

minority populations. One was a large, urban middle school where many students were of *burakumin* descent, the other was a medium-sized, urban middle school where many Vietnamese refugee children were in attendance. In both schools, teachers would leave students unattended once specific classroom routines were under way.

5. I and other scholars of Japanese education have documented this deemphasis of individual responsibility and emphasis of group responsibility in Japanese classrooms. See Nancy Sato, "Honoring the Individual," in *Teaching and Learning in Japan,* ed. T. Rohlen and G. LeTendre (New York: Cambridge University Press, 1996), 119–53. This deemphasis of the individual is consistent with Japanese beliefs in the fluidity or permeability of the self. Japanese psychologists and social theorists like Hidetada Shimizu and Eshun Hamaguchi argue that Japanese folk construals of self are context oriented (see chap. 1, nn. 1, 2). These beliefs have specific consequences for school organization. For a discussion of how democratic processes, for example, are carried out in Japanese middle schools see references to LeTendre, "Community-Building Processes."

6. Although individual teachers that I worked with, particularly Gretchen Jondervag, did indeed explicitly state such expectations. There was considerably more variation among teacher expectations in the United States than in Japan with regard to group responsibility. In a related observation, among my student teachers those who were raised in military families and those who had extensive experience on sports teams were more likely than other students to believe that groups should be responsible for the conduct of their members.

7. One critical difference was that in Oak Grove students with low grades could not participate in many extracurricular activities whereas in Kotani students with poor academic skills were often encouraged to participate in such activities. This is consistent with the American belief that the individual should take responsibility for his or her actions, and the Japanese belief that everyone must have some place in an organization like the school. Americans also see extracurricular activities as a privilege, whereas Japanese tend to see them as an essential part of the curriculum. The very term "extracurricular activity," then, like "adolescence," is difficult to translate simply and requires an extended explanation.

8. But this does not mean that Japanese students are incapable of creative, individual expression. In my article on democracy in Japanese classrooms I describe how at one cultural festival, students were allowed to perform their own events without extensive teacher management beforehand (LeTendre, "Community-Building Processes"). The result was a show similar to Oak Grove's talent show in terms of the kinds of performances and the range of quality of the performance. This suggests that it is a high degree of management by teachers, rather than authoritarian imposition of rules, that tends to decrease student creativity. For more on this topic see chapter 8.

9. My initial fieldwork at Wade was conducted during a time when organizational instability coincided with heightened media coverage of gang violence and school violence. The organization of the festival reflected concerns about an inexperienced staff and community/social influences on adolescent behavior. The fact that the organization has changed over a matter of a few years in one school highlights the degree to which school practices, classroom routines, and even some teacher beliefs change quickly in the United States, whereas in Japan change occurs more slowly.

10. See example of peer-counselors in chapter 6. Teachers believed these students to be highly mature for their age, thus making them candidates for increased responsibility.

11. I document Japanese teachers' belief in the important role that clubs play in supporting the social curriculum. See Gerald LeTendre, "Guiding Them On: Teaching, Hierarchy and Social Organization in Japanese Middle Schools," *Journal of Japanese Studies* 20 (1): 37–59.

12. The following incident is condensed from LeTendre, "Guiding Them On."

13. Murata apparently offered the older boys "loans" ranging from five thousand to ten thousand yen. The teachers believed he was trying to ingratiate himself with the senior club members. This behavior was very close to certain forms of extortion and bullying which occur in Japanese middle schools in which larger students or groups of students bully others into providing them with loans of money.

14. See Catherine Lewis's chapter "Resilient Myths" for a discussion of the role of reflection (*hansei*) in Japanese education, in Gerald LeTendre, ed., *Competitor or Ally?* (New York: Falmer Press, 141–48).

15. Students sitting in these chairs or benches are generally recognized by others as being in trouble. Students who pass through the office occasionally query the sitters on why they were sent to the office. At Wade, one student remarked to another, "What are you down for?"

16. For more details, see my article on guidance in Japanese middle schools. Gerald LeTendre, "Disruption and Reconnection: Counseling Young Adolescents in Japanese Schools," *Educational Policy* 9, 2 (1994): 169–84.

17. Most of these were not discipline referrals. The majority were students needing late-to-class passes, students needing to use a telephone, and students who did not feel well.

18. Many of the vice-principals I have worked with in Pennsylvania and Georgia report that handling discipline duty is a major cause of administrator "burnout." They describe the task as stressful and demoralizing, as they rarely have time to adequately counsel students in the way they would like.

19. I have records of this regarding broken windows, an incident with a Frisbee on a field trip, as well as poor student behavior during class time. See Fukuzawa, "Stratification, Social Control, and Student Culture," for her description of the tribunal set up to review distribution of chewing gum on campus.

20. I observed at least one fight at which the police were called and the students turned over to the police. Ritualized fights between juvenile males (which appear to have been common in U.S. middle and high schools in previous decades) are now more likely to be handled by outside authorities, especially if any injury occurs. This trend appears to be driven by a fear of parents suing schools for negligence, fear for teacher safety if they try to intervene, fear of increasingly violent behavior among students. Compare with the school life described in Everhart, *Reading, Writing and Resistance.*

21. Some Bay Area cities have recently enacted legislation requiring minors to wear helmets when riding bicycles. Schools in the Oak Grove district issue warnings on the need for bicycle safety, but in no way are the teachers regarded as responsible for the accidents, and parents are less likely to hold the school responsible for providing inadequate safety instruction, as they would be at Furukawa or Aratamachi.

22. Japanese middle school teachers spend a significant part of their time planning and executing activities designed to clarify students' goals, increase information, and motivate students to study in order to reach these goals.

23. Merry White describes this phenomenon as "mutual envy." See Merry White, "Introduction," in *Competitor or Ally*, ed. Gerald LeTendre (New York: Falmer Press, 1999), i–xv. Both Americans and Japanese tend to project onto the other their idealized images and stereotypes. Many Americans see Japanese as orderly, obedient, and hardworking but ultimately servile and uncreative. Japanese see Americans as creative and self-confident but ultimately as selfish and lazy. For an excellent comparative elicitation of educator opinions, see Mariko Fujita and Toshiyuki Sano, "Children in American and Japanese Day-Care Centers: Ethnography and Reflective Cross-Cultural Interviewing," in *School and Society: Learning through Culture*, ed. Henry Trueba and Concha Delgado-Gaitan (New York: Praeger, 1988), 73–97.

### Chapter 4. Puberty and Sexuality

1. Rebecca Fukuzawa has argued that in the Tokyo middle schools she worked in teachers assumed that the vast majority of adolescents were basically energetic (*genki*) and had a positive (*akarui*) disposition. She documents how these traits have been institutionalized into norms for behavior and adopted by students as categories for distinguishing peer groups. Thus students identify themselves as *akarui* when they are in friendship groups in which peers emphasize academics and club participation. Students who feel incapable of being successful in academics or who feel ostracized will choose alternative categories such as obstreperous (*urusai*). Similar self-categorization can be found in work on older adolescents by Shimizu. See Hidetada Shimizu, "Individuality, Learning, and Achievement: Japanese Perspectives," in *Competitor or Ally*, ed. G. LeTendre (New York: Falmer Press, 1999).

2. See Marianne Whatley, "Raging Hormones and Powerful Cars: The Construction of Men's Sexuality in School Sex Education and Popular Adolescent Films," *Journal of Education* 170 (1988): 100–21; Margaret Finders, "Raging Hormones: Stories of Adolescence and Implications for Teacher Preparation," *Journal of Adolescent and Adult Literacy* 42 (1998–99): 252–63.

3. Brooks-Gunn and Petersen lay out the difficulties of studying the pubertal process in Jeanne Brooks-Gunn and Anne Petersen, "Problems in Studying and Defining Pubertal Events," *Journal of Youth and Adolescence* 13, 3 (1984): 181–96.

4. J. M. Tanner, "Sequence, Tempo and Individual Variation in Growth and Development of Boys and Girls Aged Twelve to Sixteen," in Jerome Kagan and Robert Coles, eds., *12 to 16: Early Adolescence* (New York: Norton, 1972).

5. Even if we restrict ourselves purely to the realm of physiology, pubertal change is difficult to measure. See Jill Rierdan, Elissa Koff, and Margaret Stubbs, "Timing of Menarche, Preparation, and Initial Menstrual Experience: Replication and Further Analyses in a Prospective Study," *Journal of Youth and Adolescence* 18, 5 (1989): 413–27.

6. See Van Gennep, *Rites of Passage* (Chicago: University of Chicago Press, 1960), 66–68.

7. For two viewpoints on the interaction of culture, environment, and biology, see

Carolyn Zahn-Waxler, "Environment, Biology, and Culture: Implications for Adolescent Development," *Developmental Psychology* 32, 4 (1996): 571–73, and Jeanne Brooks-Gunn, Julia Graber, and Roberta Paikoff, "Studying Links between Hormones and Negative Affect: Models and Measures," *Journal of Research on Adolescence* 4, 4 (1994): 469–86.

8. Most readers will be aware of Derek Freeman's exposé of Margaret Mead's work in Samoa, in which he not only critiques her anthropological work, but basically argues that puberty and adolescence are hard biological facts. Few readers, however, have probably read the work of Holmes, who spent nearly two decades working in Samoa. His basic conclusion is that both Mead and Freeman got some things right and some things wrong about Samoa and that they both selectively ignored data that did not support their grand theses. See Lowell Holmes, *Quest for the Real Samoa: The Mead/Freeman Controversy and Beyond* (South Hadley, Mass.: Bergin and Garvey, 1987).

9. Most of the work in this area centers on pubertal timing, social adjustment, and subsequent effects on academic performance. It is almost impossible to disentangle the physiological impact from the sociocultural impact of pubertal change. See Roberta Simmons and Dale Blythe, *Moving into Adolescence* (New York: Aldine de Gruyter, 1987), and Anne Petersen and Lisa Crockett, "Pubertal Timing and Grade Effects on Adjustment," *Journal of Youth and Adolescence* 14, 3 (1985): 191–206.

10. Rather elaborate studies have looked at the effect of hormonal levels on various aspects of behavior in young adolescents. The effects generally are remarkably small. Even in the most rigorously controlled studies, hormonal fluctuation (even when several distinct hormones are assayed) is weakly correlated (although statistically significant) with behavior. Jeanne Brooks-Gunn and Edward Reiter provide a concise synthesis of the research literature on the physiology and psychology of pubertal change. Rather than linking specific hormones with specific behaviors (i.e., testosterone and aggression) they make the interesting argument that "the production of hormones, but not the development of secondary sexual characteristics, is associated with emotionality, specifically aggressive affect in boys and both depressive and aggressive affect in girls" (44). This suggests that hormonal changes during puberty might increase the propensity for boys to feel anger or girls to feel anger and depression. A close reading of the literature, however, demonstrates that the level of hormones generated by the pubertal process is not the only factor involved in hormone production. They note, for example, that it is not clear if increased hormonal levels result in increased sexual behavior or if engaging in sex increases certain hormone levels. Finally, they add, "situational effects, if added to the equation, may account for more of the variation in sexual behavior than hormonal levels" (44). See Jeanne Brooks-Gunn and Edward O. Reiter, "The Role of Pubertal Processes," in *At the Threshold: The Developing Adolescent*, ed. S. Shirley Feldman and Glen R. Elliott (Cambridge: Harvard University Press, 1990), 16–53. See also Elizabeth Sussman et al., "Hormones, Emotional Dispositions and Aggressive Attributes in Young Adolescents," *Child Development* 59 (1987): 1114–34.

11. The response rate of teachers in the Japanese field sites was higher than in the U.S. sites, partly because teachers in Japan have their desks in one common room, making it easier to contact teachers who had not turned in surveys.

12. Van Gennep cites data that indicate a mean age of 15.6 for a sample of Tokyo

women around the turn of the century. This is consistent with the average age of menarche in 1900 in Denmark, Sweden, the United Kingdom, and Norway. Since then, the average age of menarche has fallen steadily in all industrialized countries. Following trends presented by Tanner (1973), the average age of menarche would now be around 12 years of age for Japan. The age of menarche in the United States seems to occur about half a year earlier than in the European sample, leaving open the question of an earlier puberty in the United States, but this general difference would not account for why American teachers' placement of menarche was, on average, a year earlier than that of the Japanese teachers. See Van Gennep, *Rites of Passage,* 66, and J. M. Tanner, "Growing Up," *Scientific American* 3:34–43, and J. M. Tanner, "Sequence, Tempo, and Individual Variation in Growth and Development of Boys and Girls Aged Twelve to Sixteen," in *12 to 16: Early Adolescence,* ed. Jerome Kagan and Robert Coles (New York: W. W. Norton, 1972).

13. See Madeline Goodman, John Grove, and Fred Gilbert, "Age at Menarche and Year of Birth in Relation to Adult Height and Weight among Caucasian, Japanese, and Chinese Women Living in Hawaii," in Sharon Golub, ed., *Menarche: The Transition from Girl to Woman* (Lexington, Mass.: Lexington Books, 1983). See also data from Korea that suggests there is no difference in average age at menarche compared to Western nations. Sang Hee Park, Young Kyoo Shim, Huyng Seok Kim, Baik Lin Eun, "Age and Seasonal Distribution of Menarche in Korean Girls," *Journal of Adolescent Health* 25 (1999): 97.

14. But remember that with such wide variation in onset, teachers may have experience with menstruating nine year olds. See M. Muscari, J. Faherty, and C. Catalino, "Little Women: Early Menarche in Rural Girls," *Pediatric Nursing* 24 (1998): 1–15.

15. See Kett, *Rites of Passage,* and Chudacoff, *How Old Are You?*

16. "Transescence" is a relatively new term in American educational psychology used to label early adolescents (ages ten to fourteen) who are in a period of change or transition. It is linked to the accelerated growth of adolescence by some authors, and to the lack of brain growth by others. In spite of conflicting theoretical formulations and the lack of solid empirical evidence that links this stage with behavior, some educators have rushed to promote transescence as a useful concept in formulating middle grades educational practices. See, for example, Cheryl Steele, "The Truths of Transescence," *Principal* 65, 2 (1985): 50–52.

17. During both my pilot and main study, only one person in Japan made a spontaneous reference to hormones. This was Eriko Banba, the Furukawa school nurse, who used the term "hormonal imbalance" (*horumon imbaransu*) during an interview on psychological stress. Many Kotani teachers recognized the term *horumon,* although some did not. In one of the more amusing miscommunications, one teacher thought I was talking about a Japanese dish which includes the liver and other internal organs: *horumon yaki.*

18. I observed the same behaviors only infrequently at Pleasant Meadows. There may be some connection between the socioeconomic background of the student body and teachers' tolerance of such expression. I have noticed more hand holding and kissing in both Pennsylvania and Georgia middle schools in low-income districts, but I do not have enough evidence to assert that there are regional differences in the United States in young adolescent public displays of affection.

19. Teachers were not the only ones to make use of the hormonal explanation: another

graduate student (American) who worked in the same schools with me said that she had a videotape of two adolescents which captured the "hormonal attraction between them."

20. Wagatsuma and DeVos describe such a link between interest in pornography and the juvenile delinquents in their study. Hiroshi Wagatsuma and George DeVos, *Heritage of Endurance: Family Patterns and Delinquency Formation in Urban Japan* (Berkeley: University of California Press, 1984).

21. The involvement of middle and high school girls in prostitution rings is not unknown in this area, and a dramatic case of a local prostitution ring that ensnared high school girls was in the news in the late 1980s. In the mid-1980s, when I was teaching with Mrs. Kawaguchi, she spent several evenings looking for a runaway middle school girl because she feared the girl might be lured into a prostitution ring. The girl was located and returned to her home without any serious incident.

22. Kotani teachers linked early sexual intercourse with a breakdown of family structure or family instability much the same way that Oak Grove teachers did. In this regard, teachers exhibited strong beliefs that were not impacted by national boundaries. The stability of family life was a major concern for Japanese and U.S. teachers, and all teachers I interviewed expressed the belief that most serious problems found among young adolescents were linked to family problems.

23. White notes the widespread availability of these pornographic cartoons. Merry White, *The Material Child* (New York: Free Press, 1993), 182–83.

24. Like Fine, I found no official discourse on sexual desire in American schools. I did find frequent informal discourse between teachers about students' sexual desire. The topics of student sexual attraction and sexual activity usually occurred in the context of expressions of fears about pregnancy and sexually transmitted disease. Michelle Fine, "Sexuality, Schooling, and Adolescent Females: The Missing Discourse of Desire," *Harvard Educational Review* 58 (1988): 29–53.

25. In virtually all Japanese schools, students leave their street shoes in a small box at the student entrance and change into slippers, which are worn only inside the school. I often observed high school students placing letters in or retrieving them from the shoeboxes but did not observe middle school students doing this.

26. Japanese terms like "school refusal" (*tōkōkyohi*) and "dropout" (*ochikobore*) are both used to apply to students who may still come to school, but who are absent for a long period of time and evince little interest in school while they are there.

27. In 1988 at a high school awards ceremony, an older male teacher explained to me why it was that the homeroom teachers were yelling at the students, admonishing them to stand at attention. He said that such order presents a "tightly pulled atmosphere" (*pin to hippareta*): an atmosphere that would energize and focus the students' attention. And, indeed, the Japanese students did seem to become more excited and focused on the event after they were lined up. The American and Canadian exchange students in the school did not feel this energy and later expressed their revulsion for such "militaristic" ceremonies.

28. Van Gennep argues that "physiological puberty and 'social puberty' are essentially different and only rarely converge." *Rites of Passage,* 65.

29. The historian Joseph Kett would likely note that this is an age-old American concern — the sexuality of adolescents and its perceived threat to the moral and social orders has been a common theme in public discourse since Puritan times.

30. Everhart, *Reading, Writing and Resistance,* 38, notes, "Thus the majority of teachers saw their job as one of passing out information to students and seeing [that] the organizational procedures of the school were followed."

31. The degree to which teachers assume responsibility for their students' behaviors in Japan is truly remarkable to most Americans, but it would also be seen as bizarre or intrusive in the U.S. context. Gail Benjamin's account of the degree to which teachers feel a right to criticize and advise parents reflects her own resentment as an American mother with children in a Japanese school (Gail Benjamin, *Japanese Lessons* [New York: New York University Press, 1997]). For an even more powerful analysis of the kind of power that teachers in Japan have over parents, see Mariko Fujita, "It's All Mother's Fault: Childcare and the Socialization of Working Mothers in Japan," *Journal of Japanese Studies* 15, 1 (1989): 67–92.

## Chapter 5. Toward Maturity: Self-Control and Academic Goals

1. Robert Bellah, Richard Madsen, William Sullivan, Ann Swidler, Steven Tipton, *Habits of the Heart* (New York: Harper and Row, 1985), 56–57.

2. Takeo Doi, *The Anatomy of Dependence* (Tokyo: Kodansha, 1988), 144–145.

3. Erikson, *Childhood and Society,* and *Identity: Youth and Crisis*

4. Both American and Japanese mainstream cultures project an image of an ideal family that may not typify the majority of families in the nation. In the United States people still idealize the two-parent, never-divorced, middle-class family, although this configuration is becoming less and less common. Similarly, although only about 30 percent of Japanese families contain three generations, the image of a harmonious family composed of grandparents, parents, and children is ubiquitous.

5. The same line of reasoning was used to explain Japanese achievement motivation. Essays in DeVos suggest that achievement motivation is exceptionally strong in Japan. They argue that one factor promoting such motivation is that Japanese are constrained in most areas of social expression except achievement. George DeVos, *Socialization for Achievement* (Berkeley: University of California Press, 1973). I find that there is another reason for the emphasis on achievement. The goal (*mokuhyō/yume*) for Japanese in general and adolescents in particular offers a "way out" or an "escape mechanism" for the self constrained within the interstices of social expectations.

6. Many Japanese middle schools do have cafeterias.

7. Although Japanese teachers in the middle grades do use a range of instructional strategies, including whole class instruction, individual and group recitation, group problem solving, and pair work. The size of Japanese classrooms and the number of students per class (usually more than thirty-five) make it very difficult for teachers to organize group work or learning centers in the regular classrooms.

8. The range of variation in one U.S. school can be truly remarkable. Mathematics classrooms tended to be less heavily decorated than others, yet many teachers hang student projects on the walls or suspend them from the ceiling. Teachers also tended to disagree in terms of how much of the classroom wall and ceiling space should be devoted to student work and how much to charts, graphs, maps, or pictures that provided information (alphabet charts, history time lines, tables of elements, etc.).

9. Some years both schools had competitions in which each class painted a group picture that was part of the school art festival. These pictures were then hung in the back of the classroom. I saw this practice in only one other school in Japan.

10. Harold Stevenson and James Stigler, *The Learning Gap* (New York: Summit Books, 1992).

11. A study by Tsuchida and Lewis shows that these teaching strategies are common nationwide. See Ineko Tsuchida and Catherine Lewis, "Responsibility and Learning: Some Preliminary Hypotheses about Japanese Elementary Classrooms," in *Teaching and Learning in Japan,* ed. Thomas Rohlen and Gerald LeTendre (New York: Cambridge University Press, 1996), 190–212.

12. Ethnographers of U.S. middle grade schools like Everhart find very high levels of disruption and time spent on classroom management. See also Shelley Goldman, "Sorting Out Sorting: An Ethnographic Account of How Stratification Is Managed in a Middle School" (Ph.D. diss., Columbia University, 1982).

13. This emphasis on developing student social skills begins very early on in Japanese schools. Both Lois Peak and Catherine Lewis have documented the large amount of time pre- and elementary school teachers devote to this task. In particular, Japanese teachers spend a good deal of time working on conflict negotiation and group problem solving. These activities appear to give children opportunities to learn how to express their feelings in socially appropriate ways. Lois Peak, *Learning to Go to School in Japan* (Berkeley: University of California Press, 1991).

14. As discussed below, many Oak Grove teachers presented an inconsistent message about how well adolescents are supposed to maintain control over their changing minds and bodies.

15. Both Reba Page and Jeannie Oakes have provided in-depth studies of the tracking phenomenon in the United States. How students are selected into these high school tracks from middle schools is an area that has received insufficient attention. See Oakes, *Keeping Track,* Reba Page, *Lower-track Classrooms: A Curricular and Cultural Perspective* (New York: Teachers College Press, 1991), Tom Loveless, *The Tracking Wars* (Washington: Brookings Institute, 1999). For a study of parent's impact on placement, see Elizabeth Useem, "Middle Schools and Math Groups: Parents' Involvement in Children's Placement," *Sociology of Education* 65 (1992): 263–79.

16. *Hensachi* is a term used to describe the "cut-off line" or normalized distribution of scores of prospective applicants for a given high school or college. Each year, millions of practice tests are given by private companies and cram schools to middle and high school students. These tests allow teachers and students to estimate a student's chance of gaining entry into a given school with a high degree of accuracy. They have been the subject of much debate and reform attempts in Japan. See Gerald LeTendre, "Distribution Tables and Private Tests: The Failure of Middle School Reform in Japan," *International Journal of Educational Reform* 3, 2 (1994): 126–36.

17. Both LeTendre, "Constructed Aspirations," and Kaori Okano, *School to Work Transition in Japan* (Philadelphia: Multilingual Matters, 1993), document how teachers can be powerful advocates of students in the entrance examination process. Unlike the American counselors described by Cicourel and Kitsuse, Japanese teachers occasionally "cool down" students whose scores are higher than their aspirations warrant; yet teach-

ers work to "heat up" aspirations in students whose scores are high. See Aaron Cicoural and John Kitsuse, "The School as a Mechanism of Social Differentiation," in *Power and Ideology in Education,* ed. Jerome Karabel and A. H. Halsey (New York: Oxford University Press, 1977).

18. In addition to Rohlen, *Japan's High Schools,* see Herbert Passin, *Society and Education in Japan* (New York: Teachers College Press, 1965).

19. LeTendre, "Constructed Aspirations."

20. See Jennifer Rice, "The Disruptive Transition from Middle to High School: Opportunities for Linking Policy and Practice," *Journal of Education Policy* 12 (1997): 403–17.

21. Which raises the question of whether or not students from low-income, low-educational level, minority, or non-English speaking homes are consequently tracked into lower-level academic schools. In addition to works by Oakes and Kilgore, see Maureen Hallinan and Aage Sorensen, "The Formation and Stability of Instructional Groups," *American Sociological Review* 48 (1983): 838–51.

22. There is a strong sense in Japan that educational equality in the public schools is based upon everyone being at the same "starting line" at the end of middle school. Parents attempt to buy extra educational support through cram schools or by enrolling their children in private middle schools. Attempts to study whether or not this policy is indeed effective are made difficult by the sensitivity of the Ministry of Education toward any study of family background and educational attainment. See G. LeTendre, T. Rohlen, and K. Zeng, "Merit or Family Background? Problems in Research Policy Initiatives in Japan," *Educational Evaluation and Policy Analysis* 20, 4 (1998): 285–97.

23. As children, Japanese are allowed or even encouraged to *amaeru,* to "indulge oneself in love." The adult (mother) is expected to *amayakasu* — to "defer to the other lovingly in love." See Hisa Kumagai and Arno Kumagai, "The Hidden 'I' in Amae: 'Passive Love' and Japanese Social Perception," *Ethos* 14, 3 (1986): 305–20, 308. As Kumagai and Kumagai point out, some Western scholars of Japan like Ruth Benedict and George DeVos have linked this concept of loving with guilt, shame, and lack of sense of self. Kumagai and Kumagai contend that the sense of self is not absent, but very different.

24. Yang, "The Teacher's Job," and Fukuzawa, "The Path to Adulthood," both found that a substantial part of Japanese teachers' time was spent in guiding clubs, supervising student committees, and organizing special events. Teachers in Japan recognize that these nonacademic tasks constitute a major part of the curriculum. Through working with teachers in a variety of committees and clubs students learn how to act as seniors and juniors (*senpai/kōhai*), and teachers believe that children also acquire essential character traits: *omoiyari, nintai, dōryoku.*

25. Abiko's work in a Florida middle school confirms these assumptions. Teachers in his study saw counseling as neither their job, nor a *primary* responsibility of the school. See Abiko, *Yomigaere Amerika no Chūgakkō,* chap. 2.

26. In addition to Teruhisa Horio's vigorous critique, scholars of Japanese education should look at qualitative studies of Japanese middle schools to understand the rather insidious effect that the complex of practice tests, cut-off lines, cram schools, and placement counseling have on young adolescents. See Tamotsu Sengoku, Haruhiko Kanegae, and Gunei Satou, *Nihon no chūgakusei* (Japan's middle schools) (Tokyo: NHK Books, 1987) and Hiroyoshi Shimizu and Kozo Tokuda *Yomigaere: Kōritsu Chūgakkō* (Re-

vitalizing the public middle school) (Tokyo: Kodansha, 1991). Teruhisa Horio, *Educational Thought and Ideology in Modern Japan* (Tokyo: University of Tokyo Press, 1988).

27. Abiko, *Yomigaeru*, 40–41.

28. For more details of the effect of competitive studying on the curriculum, see the section on adolescent lives in Office of Educational Research and Improvement, *The Educational System in Japan: Case Study Findings*. Horio has been especially critical of the dehumanizing effect of increased competitive consciousness (*kyōso ishiki*). A less polemic, yet thought-provoking look is provided by Kawahara. who suggests that this competition is a major force impeding reform throughout the Japanese educational system. See Takumi Kawahara, *Gakkō ha Naze Kawaranai Ka* (Why don't schools change?) (Tokyo: JICC Publishing, 1991).

29. Young Japanese adolescents do face an identity crisis, but it is one precipitated by the school and managed by the teachers. Here, Erikson would likely have noted how different patterns of child rearing and socialization in the two cultures engender different identity crises. I would point out that, unlike Erikson, few U.S. teachers recognize the role of culture in shaping the process of identity development.

30. Several teachers used cooperative discipline or alternative classroom management strategies. At the third middle school in the Oak Grove district, a schoolwide program of peer conflict mediation had been run for two years. Yet not one of these programs was ever institutionalized at the district level, and when staff members transferred schools or retired, the program disappeared.

31. For a critique, see Kangmin Zeng and Gerald LeTendre, "Adolescent Suicide and Academic Pressure in East Asia," *Comparative Education Review* 42, 4 (1998): 513–28.

## Chapter 6. Managing Crises

1. See the following publications of the Carnegie Council on Adolescence: *Great Transitions* and *Turning Points*.

2. Gang (*yakuza/bōryokudan/bōsōzoku*) involvement in Kotani was considered to be mostly a problem with high school boys and boys who had failed to enter high school, but sometimes older middle school boys may be involved in gangs. In simple terms, Japanese society hosts a range of gang-type affiliations ranging from groups of teens on souped-up motor scooters (*kaminarizoku*) to large crime syndicates (*yakuza*). Kotani teachers use the term *yakuza* to refer to the organized family operations in the area that appear to control the local bars, *pachinko* parlors, and prostitution. *Bōryokudan* referred to violent gangs, sometimes youths affiliated with *yakuza* families. *Bōsōzoku* was used to denote groups of young people, often from outside the area, who stage drag rallies and occasionally engage in street fights. For in-depth studies of Japanese gangs and gang formation, see Hiroshi Wagatsuma, and George DeVos, *Heritage of Endurance: Family Patterns and Delinquency Formation in Urban Japan* (Berkeley: University of California Press, 1984); Ikuya Sato, *Kamikaze Biker* (Chicago: University of Chicago Press, 1991).

3. Middle schools in Japan are now required to have one counselor on staff, but the training of these counselors varies enormously from school to school.

4. Being bullied into crime or having a weak will (*ishi ga yowaii*) is sometimes given as an excuse by parents for their child's behavior. In her confessional novel, the daughter of a

famous Japanese actor links her initial abuse of paint thinner to the influence of bad companions. Yukari Hozumi, *Musume no Tsumiki Kuzushi* (Tokyo: Data House, 1991).

5. Kotani is a small city, so teachers are able to patrol large areas of the city quite effectively. In larger cities like Nagoya and Tokyo, teachers are simply unable to do such monitoring. At two of the urban middle schools I visited, however, parents had organized patrols like the ones described at Furukawa, augmenting the teachers' numbers with volunteers from the PTA. And even in urban middle schools teachers were routinely asked by parents to help find students who were staying out late, had run away, or were otherwise causing their parents to worry.

6. Donald Roden, *Schooldays in Imperial Japan, A Study in the Culture of a Student Elite* (Berkeley, University of California Press: 1980); Mamoru Iga, *The Thorn in the Chrysanthemum* (Berkeley: University of California Press, 1986); Lee Headley, ed., *Suicide in Asia and the Near East* (Berkeley: University of California Press, 1983).

7. While physical punishment (*taibatsu*) is against Japanese law, I sometimes saw students being slapped or hit on the head. The most common form of physical punishment was being forced to sit *seiza* (with one's knees beneath one and the buttocks resting on the heels). Many of the teachers and parents I spoke with drew the line at hitting, however, and did not consider *seiza* a form of physical punishment.

8. LeTendre, "Disruption and Reconnection," 172–73.

9. Again, some details of the circumstances of these deaths have been modified to ensure the anonymity of the families involved.

10. The lack of counseling services in this part of Japan is also a factor. In Kotani, there was no one to play a role equivalent to Debbie's.

11. Michelle Guido, "Prosecutor Turns Fight at School into Felony," *San Jose Mercury News*, 14 July 1993, 1.

12. Aleta Payne, Fernando Quintero, and Dale Rodebaugh, "Why Schools Increasingly Call on Police," *San Jose Mercury News*, 7 June 1993, 1.

13. Rohlen's account of violence at a Japanese high school is remarkable in that although parents stormed the school and virtually held teachers hostage while subjecting them to a variety of physical abuse, the police never intervened. See Thomas Rohlen, "Violence at Yoka High School," *Asian Survey* 16, 7 (1976): 682–99.

14. These incidents were notably different from what I would call semihostile interactions in which verbal threats or taunts were accompanied by smiles or laughter. Such incidents proved too numerous to record, and I gave up trying to note them all in my field notes.

15. "Jumping in" someone is supposed to be an initiation ceremony in which the new member is beaten up by the gang. This and other violent initiation rites have been luridly described in the press. See, for example, Barbara Kantrowitz, "Wild in the Street," *Newsweek*, 2 August 1993, 40–46.

16. There were no weapons incidents in Kotani during the study, but I did witness one event in 1986 in which a boy brought a hatchet handle to Aratamachi. Teachers saw the handle in his bag and made him leave it in the teachers' room until after school, when he was told to take it home.

17. Times have changed. A plea in 1998 by the Japanese minister of education to elementary and middle school students not to bring knives to school suggested that a new

wave of school violence was occurring. However, in the wake of the school shootings of 1999 in the United States, it is difficult to imagine that fear of school violence plays anywhere near the role in Japan that it does in the United States.

18. Asahi Shimbunsha Kaibu, *Gakkyū Hōkai* (Breakdown of the class) (Tokyo: Asahi Shimbun, 1999).

19. Trueba, Spindler, and Spindler, eds., *What Do Anthropologists Have to Say About Dropouts?*

20. The Ministry of Education recently required all middle schools to create a position of full-time counselor, suggesting that many Japanese see their system as needing significant reform.

## Chapter 7. The Disruptive Adolescent

1. For a description of the techniques and theoretical underpinnings of this work, see Elizabeth Cohen "Making Groupwork Work," *American Educator* 12, 3 (1988): 10–17, and Elizabeth Cohen, "Restructuring the Classroom: Conditions for Productive Small Groups," *Review of Educational Research* 64, 1 (1994): 1–35.

2. Several cooperative discipline strategies use physical proximity as a way to redirect individual student behavior without disrupting the flow of the lessons. For example, while telling students about the next day's work, Gretchen Jondervag would walk over to a boy who was tapping his pencil, put her hand on his hand, and stand by him for a few seconds before moving slowly away. For a detailed description of other positive or cooperative discipline practices, see Rudolph Dreikurs, *Children: The Challenge* (New York: Penguin, 1964); Jane Nelsen, *Positive Discipline* (New York: Ballantine, 1981).

3. I witnessed only one incident in which a student verbally defied his teacher during class in Kotani.

4. An interpretation consistent with the analysis of Lois Peak, *Learning to Go to School in Japan* (Berkeley: University of California Press, 1991), and Catherine Lewis, *Educating Hearts and Minds* (New York: Cambridge University Press, 1995).

5. Recent data from the TIMSS study show that eighth grade mathematics teachers in Japan had been teaching an average of 13.7 years, while in the United States it was 14.9. A comparative survey of sixteen hundred U.S. and Japanese middle school teachers conducted in 1986 showed that Japan had more very senior teachers (i.e., 20 years plus) and more novice teachers (fewer than 4 years) than the United States. While years of teaching does impact individual teacher patterns, differences in national mean years of teaching may be less important than the roles that senior teachers take in schools. See TIMSS Data Almanac for population 2 mathematics teachers: *http://wwwcsteep.edu/ TIMSS/Database.html* and Nihon Seishōnen Kenkhyū Shitsu, *Nichibei Chūgakkō Kyōshi Chōsa* (Tokyo: Nihon Seishōnen Kenkhyū Shitsu, 1987).

6. See also Stigler's work identifying "national scripts" for teaching. James Stigler, "Understanding and Improving Classroom Mathematics Instruction," *Phi Delta Kappan* 79, 1 (1997): 14–21.

7. Both Goldman, "Sorting Out," and Everhart, *Reading, Writing and Resistance,* assert that American teachers spend a significant portion of their time disciplining students, redirecting behavior, and otherwise monitoring student behavior. These tasks are

often subsumed under the category of classroom management by teachers — meaning any task not related directly to instruction of the lesson. Among my student teachers in the United States, classroom management has been the topic they expressed the most interest in and the task they were most apprehensive of, with the possible exception of teaching sex education.

8. In their study of elementary schools, Tsuchida and Lewis, "Responsibility and Learning," found that American teachers spent much more time on classroom discipline and managing student behavior.

9. See Tsuchida and Lewis, "Responsibility and Learning," for a good description of the flow of lessons in elementary school classrooms; the lessons they describe are very similar to the one I saw in Kotani. See also Ineko Tsuchida, "The Basics in Japan: The Three C's," *Educational Leadership* 55, 6 (1998): 32–37.

10. The extent to which these conflicts were staged on my behalf is a serious methodological question. Gretchen Jondervag noted that when either I or visitors were in her class, Roy was more likely to try to disrupt the class. I watched Roy out of the corner of my eye one day in class while pretending to follow the lesson. As I sidled closer to him, he began to throw bits of eraser at his desk neighbors with increasing vigor and frequency, and when I moved back to the opposite end of the class, he stopped throwing and put his head on his desk, looking as if he were resting. Janice Leitskov, however, told me that Mary "challenged her authority" as much when I wasn't there as when I was.

11. Use of derogatory language is an automatic suspension according to written school policy.

12. Lee Canter and Marlene Canter, *Assertive Discipline* (Los Angeles: Canter and Associates, 1976).

13. This behavior occurred in Oak Grove as well. Given the work done by Tsuchida and Lewis, it would be interesting if future comparative classroom studies could systematically count the number of times that a teacher ignores students' requests to intervene with or censure another student.

14. See LeTendre, "Disruption and Reconnection."

15. Some veteran teachers who used cooperative management techniques, like Gretchen Jondervag, did not always follow this rule; others, like Tom Brabeck, did. Neither vice-principal appeared to be concerned about those senior teachers who overlooked student swearing. Both men thought that teachers like Gretchen were better able than they to monitor, guide, and, if necessary, punish students, and both told me they wished more teachers would deal with problems inside the classroom.

16. Nevertheless, while teaching in Japanese schools I observed several occasions when students were punished by the homeroom teacher. In two cases I witnessed students receiving physical punishment — slaps on the face, a rap on the head, kneeling on the floor for a period of time.

17. Teachers in elementary school and lower middle school grades tend to use group punishments more frequently than teachers in upper middle school grades. I interpret this as further evidence that teachers expect students to become responsible for their own actions as they pass through puberty.

18. School violence was not unknown in Kotani. A former coworker of mine in a local high school was knocked unconscious in front of his class by an irate student.

19. "L.A. School Bans Baggy Pants," *San Jose Mercury News,* 14 December 1993, 3b.

20. Logan argues that rags are indeed accurate indicators of gang involvement for young adolescents and are the source of potentially violent conflict. It is interesting to note that in his discussion, his respondents linked the use of rags to movies that depicted gang life. See Frank Logan, "Turning Their Lives Around: Cultural Therapy and Mentors in a Program for the Modification of At Risk Behavior" (Ph.D. diss., Stanford University, 1992); Frank Logan "Youths in an Intensive At-Risk Program: A Critical Look at Cultural Therapy," in *Pathways to Cultural Awareness,* ed. George and Louise Spindler (Thousand Oaks, Calif.: Corwin Press, 1994), 285–322. The interaction between the depiction of gangs in popular culture and the actual behavior of gangs in communities and schools is interconnected, but informants like Barbara Lane thought that actual criminal gangs in this area had distinct patterns of dress and interaction from the adolescent groups which existed in the schools.

21. E. A. Torriero, M. A. Ostron, and E. Pope, "Police Try to Keep S.J. Gangs in Check," *San Jose Mercury News,* 6 May 1993, 1; Raoul Mowatt and Renee Koury, "Gang Crackdown," *San Jose Mercury News,* 22 April 1994, 1.

22. Edwin Garcia, "Even Littlest Students Aren't Immune to Gang Influence," *San Jose Mercury News,* 30 April 1994, 1.

23. Mr. Shimoda made the following announcement: "Recently some girls have been wearing bracelets — the rope/string kind. This kind of behavior should not be allowed. Please guide (remonstrate) your students not to do this and make inquiries about those who are wearing the bracelets." There may have been an undertone in his message that boy/girl interactions might be disrupting study patterns. The bracelets seemed to be associated with girls who also had boyfriends, but I am not certain of this.

24. Many of the boys at an industrial high school where I taught wore clothes which are associated with juvenile delinquents (*furyō/hiko shōnen*). Their pants were excessively wide, often tied with a loose belt, their hairline was carefully shaved around the forehead and sides of the neck. Most of the boys smoked, another "delinquent" behavior. A teacher once collected a small bag of cigarette butts in the boys' washroom — setting off a major crackdown on smoking by the teachers.

25. During a teacher-training workshop at Stanford that involved middle school teachers from throughout the Bay area, one participant scribbled a note to her friend, "Why are Hispanics so attracted to gangs?"

26. Jack Fischer and Dale Rodebaugh, "S.J. Boys Arrested in Racial Assault," *San Jose Mercury News,* 29 May 1993, 1; Bill Romano, "Boys Arrested in Beating Case File Suit," *San Jose Mercury News,* 10 May 1994, 4b.

27. See Lewis, *Educating Hearts and Minds.* In Japanese middle and elementary schools there is a common view of the students as being essentially good; that view is not as evident in American schools.

28. Again, these were middle school teachers during the early 1990s. Attitudes of high school teachers or of middle school teachers during the 1950s or other periods of widespread social disruption will differ.

29. Teachers in Japan were afraid of organized crime (mafia — *yakuza*), and women teachers did not wish to patrol the areas of town where mafia members or gangs of hotrodders would hang out. These were, however, adults.

30. At Furukawa and Aratamachi, a missing name badge and a girl wearing gym sweats (rather than a skirt) or a bright blue rather than a dull blue headband were reason enough for a child to receive a scolding, not only by the homeroom teacher but also by the head of the student guidance section.

31. Japanese attitudes about personal appearance diverge sharply from American. Abiko thought that the freedom in dress, makeup, and expression given to American middle school students was the way that schools made American adults out of children. Clothes were, in American culture, *watakushigoto* ("personal affairs"). Dressing in a certain way was not obligatory for participation in school, but rather the "responsibility of the will of the parent or child" See Abiko, *Yomigaeru,* 20–21.

## Chapter 8. Creativity and Self-Expression

1. See the section on reflection in Lewis, *Educating Hearts and Minds,* 170–72.

2. English, formally an elective in the curriculum, was the only exception.

3. One major cultural difference between the United States and Japan which has a dramatic impact on schooling is the degree to which parents comply with school requests for providing students with equipment necessary to carry out school tasks. Lee, Graham, and Stevenson have noted the use of mathematics kits that contain a variety of tools to be used in classroom mathematics activities. Similar preparation goes into school lunches, see Fujita, "It's All Mother's Fault." Calligraphy cases containing brushes, inkstones, ink, and pads are sold by local stores and are remarkably similar nationwide. Shin-ying Lee, Theresa Graham, and Harold Stevenson, "Teachers and Teaching: Elementary Schools in Japan and the United States," in *Teaching and Learning in Japan,* 157–89.

4. See John Singleton, "Japanese Folkcraft Pottery Apprenticeship: Cultural Patterns of an Educational Institution," in *Apprenticeship: From Theory to Method and Back Again,* ed. Michael Coy (Albany: SUNY Press, 1989), 13–30; Tom Hare, "Try, Try Again: Training in Noh Drama," in *Teaching and Learning in Japan,* 345–68.

5. Japanese middle schools still ban dating among young adolescents, and many schools have policies forbidding young adolescents from staying over at a friend's house.

6. Abiko, *Yomigaeru,* 20, 21.

7. The fashion trends that ran through Kotani schools were highly consistent and appeared to be part of larger national trends in clothing. White documents that Japanese magazines and *manga* have developed sophisticated marketing strategies and coordinate their efforts with the producers of clothing, skin care products, and other accouterments. Styles or looks are heavily promoted in the magazines and changed regularly. See White, *Material Child.* Perhaps the single greatest impact on children and young adults was the booming growth of media aimed at young people. Nogaki notes the appearance in 1959 of two magazines devoted exclusively to young readers — *Shōnen Magajin* and *Shōnen Sandei.* He also notes an extreme gap in lifestyle and values between pre- and postwar children. This was the age of the *gendai ko* (modern child), children strong in visual imagery, acclimatized to material wealth, possessing a strong individualism (*jishusei*), and rapidly increasing in size. Nogaki writes that many Japanese blamed the spending boom and growing economy for the problems Japanese children faced. Many fathers were now absent from the household, either working in other cities or putting in long

hours at work and commuting. In their stead, the house now boasted a television and "instant ramen." With the loss of a "natural environment," children grew more and more susceptible to negative influences from the expanding consumer culture. Yoshiyuki Nogaki, *Gendai no Kodomo* (Tokyo: Dai-Ichi Hōki, 1977), vol. 7 in *Nihon no Kodomo no Rekishi.*

8. This situation may be changing. Recently the exchange of "microphotographs" — very small pictures — has become fashionable. My former colleagues in Kotani indicated that students are being allowed more leeway in the display and exchange of these pictures, though it is not clear that boy-girl exchanges are allowed.

9. Different colored hair ribbons, different kinds of haircuts, and more individualized possessions within student knapsacks are now tolerated in Kotani. While Kotani teachers appear to be more conservative than middle school teachers in Japan as a whole, the range of student clothing and adornment tolerated in Japanese schools nationwide is much narrower than in the United States. I have seen more variation in school policies within the state of California than I observed in Japan.

10. The caveat regarding any symbol perceived to be gang or drug related must be kept in mind. Teacher confusion about the crosses students wore is a good example. Teachers and administrators were willing to censure any items that might have dual significance: i.e., a cross that might be related to a gang. It is very likely that if students wore symbols like the marijuana leaf of the National Organization to Reform Marijuana Laws (NORML) or images associated with musicians like Tupac Shakur, then they would face censorship from teachers. The Oak Grove Schools also banned clothes with alcohol or tobacco product logos, which suggests the primary concern was to reduce drug use, not target a specific ethnic or racial group.

## Chapter 9. How Adolescence Gets Institutionalized

1. See Francisco Ramirez, "Reconstituting Children: Extension of Personhood and Citizenship," in *Age Structuring in Comparative Perspective,* ed. David Kertzer and K. Warner Schaie (Hillsdale, N.J.: Lawrence Erlbaum, 1989), 143–66.

2. The policy document of the National Middle School Association was not yet in print during the fieldwork for my dissertation but was widely mentioned by the middle school teachers that I worked with in Georgia. This document appears to be the most cohesive statement of principles set forth by U.S. middle grade educators.

3. I surveyed the following works before selecting the three works I analyzed. Monbusho, *Seito no mondai kōdō kansuru kiso shiryō* (Basic materials regarding student behavior problems) (Tokyo: Government Printing Office, 1979); Monbusho, *Chūgakkō: Omoiyari no kokoro wo sodate shidō* (Middle school guidance for inculcating consideration) (Tokyo: Government Printing Office, 1986); Monbusho, *Chūgakkō: Gakushu Shidō Yōryō* (Points in middle school academic guidance) (Tokyo: Government Printing Office, 1989); Monbusho, *Chūgakkō Shidōsho: Dotokuhen* (Middle school guidance: ethics/morals) (Tokyo: Government Printing Office, 1989).

4. Monbusho, *Mondai kōdō wo Motsu Seito no Shidō* (Guidance for students with problematic behavior) (Tokyo: Government Printing Office, 1977); Monbusho, *Seito shidōjyo no mondai ni tsuite no taisaku: chūggakō/kōtōgakkō hen* (Prevention measures

for problems arising in student guidance) (Tokyo: Government Printing Office: 1980); Monbusho, *Chūgakkō ni okeru kaunseringu no susumekata* (Techniques for furthering counseling in middle school) (Tokyo: Government Printing Office, 1988). The only lengthy descriptions given to adolescent development in the Japanese policy literature at the national level were found in works focused on student problems.

5. I do not challenge the substantial body of research that indicates that young adolescents indeed do have special learning needs. The point I am making is that in the culture of the U.S. schools I worked in, teachers showed a tendency to accept a whole range of characteristics about adolescents without carefully examining which are supported by research and which are not.

6. Quote from *Caught in the Middle,* 145. In the next line, however, the same document notes that young adolescents "lack physical health." The reader is left with an image of a being with a healthy appetite but basically unhealthy.

7. Such as J. Kroger, *Identity in Adolescence: The Balance Between Self and Other* (New York: Routledge, 1989).

8. This is a common rhetorical technique in Japanese writing about juvenile delinquency: authors give general, often vague, theoretical prescriptions and then abruptly switch to discussing concrete examples. M. Kondo and M. Tsukamoto, *Chūgakkō: Hikōtaisaku jireishu.* (A compendium of delinquency prevention examples for the middle school) (Tokyo: Kyōiku Shuppansha, 1988).

9. Monbusho, *Seito shidōjyo,* 103–08.

10. Hall, *Adolescence,* chap. 2.

11. Peter Blos, a prominent psychoanalytic scholar of adolescence, describes the adolescent personality as follows: "Though adolescence cannot be defined with reference to precise age level, it can be described in terms of its characteristic behavior. This behavior is manifested in rapidly shifting and unstable patterns. . . . At eleven or twelve he [the child] ceases, with dismaying suddenness, to be a reasonably responsible and compliant child. He now becomes restless and unstable. . . . Nervous habits, such as nail biting, often reappear at this time. Strange superstitions and rites are quite common." Peter Blos, *The Adolescent Personality* (New York: D. Appleton-Century, 1941), 271.

12. Albert Bandura, "The Stormy Decade: Fact or Fiction," *Psychology in the Schools* 1, 3 (1964): 224–31; James Rosenbaum, "Are Adolescent Problems Caused by School or Society?" *Journal of Research on Adolescence,* 1, 3 (1991): 301–22.

13. Michael Rutter, Philip Graham, O. F. D. Chadwick, W. Yule, "Adolescent Turmoil: Fact of Fiction?" *Journal of Child Psychology and Psychiatry* 17 (1976): 35–56; Sussman et al., "Hormones, Emotional Dispositions and Aggressive Attributes in Young Adolescents"; Judith Dubas, Julia Graber, Anne Petersen, "The Effects of Pubertal Development on Achievement during Adolescence," *American Journal of Education* 99, 4 (1991): 444–59.

14. Jerry Disque, "In Between: The Adolescents' Struggle for Independence" *PDK Fastback* 31 (1973): 7.

15. Jerilyn Pfeifer, "Teenage Suicide: What Can the Schools Do?" *PDK Fastback,* no. 234 (1986).

16. Niki Scott, "Girls Look Beyond the Mirror When You Take Them to Work," *Atlanta Journal/Constitution,* 10 April 1995, E4.

17. Long before multiculturalism became fashionable in educational circles, Erikson devoted an entire chapter ("Hunters across the Prairie") in his work *Childhood and Society* to the impact that cultural differences in child rearing had on development among Native Americans. While Erikson clearly interpreted what he saw in a Freudian framework, his writing conveys a keen insight into the power of culture and the difficulties of creating universal psychological theories.

18. Malcolm Ritter, "It Really Is a Tough Life Out There for Moody Teens," *Peninsula Times Tribune,* 25 January 1993, 1.

19. Cathleen Brown, "Some Incentive for the Adolescent Who's Slacking Off," *San Jose Mercury News,* 10 April 1994, 4H.

20. Lawrence Kurtner, "Parent and Child," *New York Times,* 2 December 1993, B4.

21. As one columnist humorously put it, "Why do humans have a period called adolescence, even though no other species seems to suffer through this?" J. Achenbach, "That's Why," *West Magazine,* 24 May 1992, 5.

22. Carole Rafferty, "Kids and the Static Quo," *San Jose Mercury News,* 11 February 1994, 8G.

23. Kett, *Rites of Passage,* 215.

24. When I talk with Americans about adolescence I find it interesting that they often use strong, even violent, verbs to describe its occurrence. We "suffer" through or "endure" or "hit" puberty and adolescence. The image evoked is one of a trial to be braved.

25. Elizabeth Douvan and Joseph Adelson, *The Adolescent Experience* (New York: Wiley, 1966).

26. *Caught in the Middle,* the document most often mentioned by teachers in the Oak Grove schools, records that *all* middle schoolers are "at-risk."

27. "Erik Erikson describes adolescence as a period of increasing conflict in the quest for self-identity. Middle school teachers can testify best about the transitory nature of early adolescent personalities." Pfeifer, "Teenage Suicide," 18–19.

### Conclusion

1. Like Westney, I argue that schools as institutions are more influenced by other institutions in a given society than by some global idea of school.

2. Abiko, *Yomigaeru,* 37.

3. See Catherine Lewis's article in Rohlen and LeTendre, eds., *Teaching and Learning in Japan.* She notes that Japanese researchers themselves use the terms "wet" and "dry" (*wetto/durai*) to convey a sense of the emotionality and "stickiness" of Japanese relations compared with the logical and distant relations of Americans. Catherine Lewis, "Fostering Social and Intellectual Development: The Roots of Japanese Education Success," in *Teaching and Learning in Japan,* 79–97.

4. The positive associations with rebellion are an old story in the United States: Frederick Marryat, a visitor to the United States in the Jacksonian period, witnessed an incident in which an American child steadfastly refused to obey his parents; his father's reaction was to inform Marryat that the boy was "a sturdy republican," all the while "smiling at the boy's resolute disobedience." Quoted in David Rothman, "Documents in Search of a Historian: Toward a History of Childhood and Youth in America," in *The*

*Family in History,* ed. Theodore Rabb and Robert Rotberg (New York: Harper and Row, 1971), 187.

5. Everhart (*Reading, Writing and Resistance,* 46) estimated that one-third of student time in school was consumed by similar activities.

6. Gerald LeTendre, "Community-Building Activities in Japanese Schools: Alternative Paradigms of the Democratic School," *Comparative Education Review* 43, 3 (Summer 1999): 283–310.

7. "The system projects itself, to outsiders (in particular, to those with a Western background) as what I will refer to as 'paternalistic,' in that the school treats students as 'small children,' deprives them of their independence and autonomy, and controls their decisions by giving over-explicit directions. However, according to those involved in the process (the insiders), the system is in fact what I will call 'maternalistic,' in that students appreciated the 'caring" and 'protecting' aspects of the system more than its elements of 'control.'" Okano, *School to Work,* 141.

8. Horio, *Educational Thought and Ideology,* 297.

9. Kawahara, *Gakkō ha Naze Kawaranai Ka,* and Kitao Norihiko and Kajita Eiichi, *Ochikobore\*Ochikoboshi* (Dropout\*pushout) (Tokyo: Yuhikaku Publishing, 1984).

10. Mochidzuki responds that society is speeding up: "We no longer have the freedom to think or act in a relaxed manner. Therefore, there is no study that is pleasant for children. School has become a place where children compete with their peers on the test. Few have a sense of mastery, and many have complexes about studying. These children wait for the last chime of the day to ring when they at last may escape the school." K. Mochidzuki, *Hankōki: Chūgakusei no shinri* (Rebellion — The psychology of middle schoolers) (Tokyo: Asunaro-shobou, 1990:11–13).

# Index

ability grouping, 21
abstinence, 71
academic achievement, 80–88; and extracurricular activities, 91–93; and social maturity, 79
academic competition, 28, 94–95, 218; negative effects of, 227
academic guidance: and social maturity, 80
academic standards, 26, 80–87, 93, 147–49
achievement motivation, 134, 160, 180–83, 215; and puberty, 65
adolescence, 1–9; American beliefs about, xi–xii; 168–69; and beliefs about development, 93–94; and disruption, 165, 169, 174, 176, 225; history of, xvi; institutionalization of, 6, 179; and intellectual development, 166; and juvenile delinquency, 170; level of institutionalization, 64, 162–77; and life course, 176, 199; and men-tal health, 170; and modern self, 4; in national educational policy 164–65, 171; and physical development, 166–67, 172, 174; psychological theories of, 170, 172–73; research on, 173, 212, 213; and rites of passage, 199; story lines of, *see* story lines; and sui-cide, 173; as time of stress, 165; and turmoil, 16; 172–74
adolescents: adult supervision of, 3, 40–41; assigning responsibility to, 45; and dating, 66; and decision-making, 55–56, 182; and defiance, 13, 70; and fam-ily relationships, 131, 168, 171; inno-cence of, 148; moral nature of, 53; and peer relations, *see* peer relations; sex-ual activity, 66, 67, 72, 73, 75; special learning needs of, 165, 171; and transi-tion to adulthood, 78–79. *See also* students
aesthetics. *See* art, cultural values of
age-graded norms, 63

maturity, 12; and creativity, 148; and
self-control, 87; teacher beliefs about,
84, 87; teachers' role in promoting, 79
menarche, 59; research on, 213; variation in onset, 61
mental health care, 108; and adolescents,
109; and availability of treatment,
115–16, 118
middle schools: and educational reform,
33; goals of, 35; history of, xi; ideal
grade organization of, 35; ideals of and
puberty, 63; and local control, 35; mission, xi, 35; national differences in curriculum, 145; national educational policy, 35; and potential for growth, 79;
rationale for, xi
minority groups: in Japan, 195, 205, 209;
linguistic, 105; percentage in schools,
190–91; and tracking, 217
moral development, 54

National Middle School Association
(NMSA), 10, 28, 163; middle school
goals, 30–31
national testing, 98

organizational theory, 200–01; and linkages, 16; and school boundaries, 117

pair work and group work, 81–82
peer counseling, 106; and school counselor, 105
peer relations, 110, 158; and academic
achievement, 211; clothes as marker,
156; influence on others, 170; negative
effects of, 103; and peer pressure, 56;
and responsibility, 41; and school
rules, 68; teacher control of, 155–58
peer mediation, 97
police: role of, in schools, 24, 41, 42, 52;
and school violence, 112, 210
pornography, 67
pregnancy: of middle school students, 66;
teacher concerns, 66; teenage, 71
principals: role of, 22, 49

profanity: use among students, 37
psychological counseling. *See* counseling
psychology, 15; and psychological theories of adolescence, 172; role in educational policy, 197
PTA, 26
puberty, 32, 58–77; and academic
achievement, 206; and adolescence,
73–74; and adolescent sexual activity,
76; in American culture, 58–60; and
at-risk behavior, 75; contesting images
of, 74; as disruption, 68–70, 74, 165,
170–71; effect on teacher work roles,
73–77; and emotional turmoil, 59; and
energy level, 75; impact on adolescent
behavior, 66; in Japanese culture, 59;
onset and duration of, 61–63; and
physical changes, 60; positive aspects
of, 59–60, 75; in pretechnological
societies, 3; research on, 60–61, 211;
and resistance, 69; role in live course,
75; and school organization, 62; as
self-fulfilling prophecy, 77; and sexuality, 65–68; and teacher beliefs
about, 61–63, 74; and volition, 76

racial diversity. *See* ethnic diversity
racial stereotyping, 114, 132–36, 155–56
rational myths, 6–9; and adolescent story
lines, 201, 202
reading: instruction in, 85
rebellion, 226; and adolescence, 169; and
volition, 184
resource room, 90
responsibility: indicator of social maturity, 43; in U.S. culture, 52–54
routines: and classroom management,
82–85; and creativity, 158; and social
maturity, 86; and student motivation,
97; use of, in schools, 42–43

safe sex, 71
school bells: use of, 39
school counselor, 102, 105, 111; funding
for, 106